Reflective Practice on Doctoral Education

ENHANCING REFLECTIVE TEACHING IN HIGHER EDUCATION

Series Editors:

Paul Ashwin (Lancaster University, UK)

Margaret Blackie (Virginia Polytechnic Institute and State University, USA)

The *Enhancing Teaching in Higher Education* book series is committed to supporting the development of reflective teaching in higher education. Books in this series undertake in-depth explorations of contemporary issues related to the development of reflective educational practices and are informed by the latest research and thinking about teaching in higher education. They are designed around evidence-informed principles for effective educational practices and provide strategies to enhance day-to-day teaching in higher education. In doing so, they build on the foundations provided by *Reflective Teaching in Higher Education*.

Books in this series will explore ways of enhancing reflective teaching in areas such as Doctoral Education and Team-based Learning as well as through strategies such as the Scholarship of Learning and Teaching and Students as Change Makers.

Available in the Series:

GenAI in Higher Education, Sam Illingworth and Rachel Forsyth

Reflective Practice on Doctoral Education

International Perspectives on the Challenges and Complexities of Doctoral Supervision

EDITED BY FIONA HALLETT

BLOOMSBURY ACADEMIC
LONDON • NEW YORK • OXFORD • NEW DELHI • SYDNEY

BLOOMSBURY ACADEMIC
Bloomsbury Publishing Plc, 50 Bedford Square, London, WC1B 3DP, UK
Bloomsbury Publishing Inc, 1359 Broadway, New York, NY 10018, USA
Bloomsbury Publishing Ireland, 29 Earlsfort Terrace, Dublin 2, D02 AY28, Ireland

BLOOMSBURY, BLOOMSBURY ACADEMIC and the Diana logo are
trademarks of Bloomsbury Publishing Plc

First published in Great Britain 2026

Series design by Grace Ridge
Cover image: Ralf Hiemisch via Getty Images

A catalogue record for this book is available from the British Library.

A catalog record for this book is available from the Library of Congress.

ISBN: HB: 978-1-350-49622-4
PB: 978-1-350-49623-1
ePDF: 978-1-350-49625-5
eBook: 978-1-350-49624-8

Series: Enhancing Reflective Teaching in Higher Education

Typeset by Integra Software Services Pvt. Ltd.
Printed and bound in Great Britain

For product safety-related questions contact productsafety@bloomsbury.com.

Contents

Figures

Tables

Contributors

David (Dave) Armstrong is an associate professor, Inclusive and Specialist Education, at La Trobe University, Melbourne, Australia. Dave advocates for children and young people with a disability in education and passionately supports inclusive, high-quality education for all. This drive for greater educational equity is reflected in his career as a specialist teacher, researcher, teacher educator, author and advisor to government. Dave specializes in inclusive Doctoral Supervision of persons with a disability.

Ronald Barnett is Emeritus Professor of Higher Education at University College London, Faculty of Education and Society, where he was a Dean and a Pro-Director. He is currently President Emeritus of the Philosophy and Theory of Higher Education Society.

Ronald has played a major part in developing the philosophy of higher education over the past forty years, with 35+ books and hundreds of papers, and 150 keynote talks in 40+ countries. He has been cited over 30,000 times in the literature.

He has put several ideas and concepts into the higher education literature, including 'criticality', 'supercomplexity' and 'the ecological university'.

He has received many prizes and awards. His very first book (The Idea of Higher Education, 1990) won a major international award, followed by several other book prizes. Other awards include the inaugural annual prize of the European Association for Educational Research for his 'outstanding contribution to Higher Education Research, Policy and Practice'; an earned higher doctorate in education (University of London); and an Honorary Doctorate (Eastern European University). He is a fellow of the Academy of the Social Sciences.

His latest book is 'Realizing the Ecological University: Eight Ecosystems, Their Antagonisms and a Manifesto' (Bloomsbury, September 2024).

Brett Bligh is a Senior Lecturer (Associate Professor) in the Department of Educational Research at Lancaster University and the Director of the PhD Programme in E-Research and Technology Enhanced Learning, which offers a structured approach to gaining a doctorate for in-work professionals who study part-time at a distance. His research interrogates issues of technology and institutional change in post-compulsory education. He prioritizes Activity Theory conceptions of human practice and interventionist methodologies, such as the Change Laboratory, when addressing these issues. Brett has supervised more than twenty PhD students to successful completion.

Susanna Calkins, PhD, is the founding director of the Nexus for Faculty Success and an associate professor in the School of Graduate and Postgraduate Studies at Rosalind Franklin University of Medicine and Science in North Chicago, Illinois (United States). Prior to joining RFUMS in fall 2022, Dr Calkins directed faculty initiatives at the Searle Center for Advancing Learning and Teaching at Northwestern University for eighteen years, focusing on inclusive teaching, curricular and pedagogical innovation, assessment of student learning and programme evaluation. She has co-authored two academic books (*Learning and Teaching in Higher Education: The Reflective Professional* (Sage, 2009) and *Reflective Teaching* (Bloomsbury, 2020, 2024)) and over thirty peer-reviewed articles and book chapters. She's taught courses on the History of Higher Education, Learning and Teaching in Higher Education, world and European history, British history and a professional development course for graduate students. She was a co-PI on an NSF-IUSE grant that created the Inclusive STEM Teaching Project, an open-access course that has served over 11,000 educators across the United States to date. She earned her PhD and MA in History (British history, women and gender studies) from Purdue and an MS in higher education administration from Northwestern University.

Dagrun Astrid Aarø Engen, PhD, is an associate professor in university pedagogy at the Norwegian University of Science and Technology (NTNU) in Trondheim, Norway. Her research interests include theoretical and empirical explorations of knowing and educative processes in higher education and educational practices such as MA and PhD supervision, supervisor training and jazz education. She is currently involved in Reading Time, a British Academy/Leverhulme-funded project that examines reading habits, rhythms and practices among doctoral students in the UK and Norway. Engen recently co-authored an article entitled 'It takes its own time: Reflections on aural learning and higher education' (Philosophy and Theory in Higher Education. 2025, 1). She is an MA and PhD supervisor, a teacher in a supervisor training module and the course coordinator for NTNU's programme for pedagogical basic competence for university teachers.

Carolina Guzmán-Valenzuela is a Serra Húnter Fellow at the Universitat Autònoma de Barcelona, Spain and a Senior Research Fellow at the

Universidad de Tarapacá, Chile. Her research focuses on higher education, equity, marketization, internationalization and knowledge production, with expertise in qualitative research and decolonial perspectives in academia. Trained as a psychologist, she holds a PhD in Education and has developed a critical trajectory in higher education studies, particularly from Latin American and Global South perspectives.

She has led and collaborated on numerous competitively funded research projects and has authored more than forty peer-reviewed articles published in high-impact journals in both English and Spanish. She is also co-editor of the *Bloomsbury Handbook of Student Voice in Higher Education* (2024). Carolina maintains extensive international academic networks in the UK, South Africa, Latin America and continental Europe, which inform her collaborative and comparative approach to research.

Her work seeks to advance a transformative vision of the university, combining rigorous analysis with a critical lens on structural inequalities. She is particularly committed to promoting epistemic justice and supporting alternative ways of knowing within and beyond academia.

Marit Honerød Hoveid is a professor of pedagogy at the Norwegian University of Science and Technology, NTNU, Department of Education and Lifelong Learning. She currently works in the unit for university pedagogy. She is also the current president of the European Educational Research Association (EERA), which organizes the European Conference for Educational Research (ECER) every year. Capacity building for emerging researchers is one of her core interests and work areas. As a pedagogue and philosopher of education, Marit's research has mainly evolved around ways of understanding teaching and learning processes within all levels of formal and informal education. The gendered aspects of education have always been embedded in her teaching and research. For a closer look at her work and publications, see: https://www.ntnu.edu/employees/marit.hoveid

Fiona Hallett is the Associate Dean of the Graduate School at Edge Hill University, where she holds strategic responsibility for doctoral education. Her role involves overseeing policy development and supporting the academic progress of postgraduate researchers and supervisors. She has contributed to PhD summer schools at the Norwegian University of Science and Technology and the University of Hamburg. In 2025, Fiona edited *Debates in Doctoral Education: Challenges and Opportunities* (Routledge), a volume that examines current issues in doctoral study and supervision. She is a Fellow of the Higher Education Academy and a Fellow of the Royal Society for the Encouragement of Arts, Manufactures and Commerce (RSA). Her work reflects a consistent focus on improving doctoral education and contributing to discussions around postgraduate research policy and practice.

Chris Hughes is an associate professor in the Researcher Development Academy at Deakin University. Chris is also a research fellow in the Centre for Research in Assessment and Digital Learning (CRADLE) at Deakin where he is exploring conceptual questions concerning generative AI and doctoral education and assessment. At Deakin, Chris hosts a programme of supervisor development activities to promote progressive models of doctoral supervision that use genuine team-based approaches and mutual responsibility and autonomy. With an interest in philosophical matters concerning learning and thinking, generative AI, in the doctoral research context, raises a series of conceptual questions that require clarity of thought and rational deliberation. It is these questions around notions of idea generation, concept acquisition, thought, writing, communication and feedback that are fundamental to doctoral education and supervision, but which might require delicate treatment in the genAI context.

Barbara M. Kehm was a professor of higher education research and management since 2003, first in Kassel (Germany) and later in Glasgow (UK) and Hannover (Germany). Originally, she studied German literature, history and philosophy. Since 2022 she is retired. During her career she produced almost 500 publications and gave invited talks in workshops and conferences in more than fifty countries around the world. She held guest professorships in Syria, China, Australia, Argentina, Chile and Hong Kong. Her fields of specialization are changes in doctoral education, the Bologna Reform Process, internationalization in and of higher education and higher education governance and professionalization processes in higher education administration. She was a founding member of the German Higher Education Research Society and a longstanding member of EAIR (including Board membership) and CHER (General Secretary). She has also been involved in programme evaluations in several European countries and was a Board member for large-scale research activities and the UK Centre for Global Higher Education. Currently, she is still a member of the Board of Governors of a German University and chairperson of the sociological discipline committee of the Czech national research funding agency. Since 2021 she has been a member of the Academia Europaea.

Peihua Li is a lecturer in the International Business College at South China Normal University. During her PhD studies at Lingnan University in Hong Kong, she conducted a significant research project exploring doctoral students' identity and well-being. Her research interests encompass a diverse array of topics centred on the interplay of teaching and learning, including language, identity and education; teacher and student agency; teacher professional development; and intercultural competence. Through her work, she investigates how these domains shape effective pedagogical practices and foster meaningful educational outcomes.

Gregory Light is a professor (retired) in the School of Education and Social Policy at Northwestern University. He is also a fellow of the Searle Center for Advancing Learning and Teaching, which he directed from 2001 to 2015. He is currently a member of the OISE Professional Advisory Committee at the University of Toronto. He was a lecturer at the Institute of Education, University College London and head of the Lifelong Learning Group from 1998 to 2000. His teaching and research focus on the theory and practice of learning and teaching in higher and professional education. He has written over 75 papers and chapters in national and international peer-reviewed publications and has given 100-plus keynotes, invited talks and workshops in North & South America, Europe, Africa and Asia. His academic books include *Learning and Teaching in Higher Education: The Reflective Professional* (Sage, 2001, 2009); *Making Scientists: Six Principles for Effective College Teaching* (Harvard University Press, 2013); and *Reflective Teaching* (Bloomsbury, 2020, 2025). He earned his PhD in student learning in higher education from the Institute of Education, London.

Jan McArthur is a professor in Higher Education and Social Justice and Head of Department in the Department of Educational Research, Lancaster University, UK. Her research focuses on the nature and purposes of higher education and how these relate to practices of teaching, learning and assessment. She has a particular interest in critical theory and in her published work explores the ideas of Theodor Adorno, Max Horkheimer and Axel Honneth, applying these to higher education. In *Rethinking Knowledge in Higher Education* (Bloomsbury), she explores how Adorno's critical theory can inform our understanding of, and engagement with, knowledge in higher education for the purposes of greater social justice. Her second book, *Assessment for Social Justice* (Bloomsbury), uses Honneth's conceptualization of mutual recognition to rethink the nature of assessment in higher education, where one is committed to greater social justice. She has published a wide range of journal articles on assessment, critical theory and social justice, and most recently rethinking authentic assessment. Jan is the deputy director of the Centre for Global Higher Education (CGHE).

Clive Palmer is a National Teaching Fellow and Principal Fellow of the Higher Education Academy, recognized for the 'reach, value and impact' of his work to promote Doctoral Education on the national stage and at his home institution of the University of Central Lancashire, Preston. He became a UKCGE Recognised Research Supervisor in 2020 and was shortlisted for Times Higher Education's 'Outstanding Research Supervisor of the Year' in 2021. In 2022 he won FindAPhD.com's 'PhD Supervisor of the Year' award, being celebrated for his innovative approaches to support doctoral students over the successive lockdowns of the Covid-19 pandemic. Clive is an advocate for 'learning through doctoral research'; alongside his Editorial Leadership of the *Journal of Qualitative Research in Sports Studies*, which showcases and disseminates doctoral research, he is also the architect and institutional lead for an innovative new PhD pathway at UCLan called PhD by Portfolio.

Aubrey Penney is the Academic Program Coordinator for the School of Graduate and Postgraduate Studies at Rosalind Franklin University of Medicine and Science in North Chicago, Illinois (United States). Since 2018, Aubrey has served as the primary contact point for graduate students in every stage of their academic journey from matriculation through lab placement, candidacy exams and the final dissertation defence. Aubrey works closely with students and research mentors to cultivate a welcoming and inclusive research environment for all, and that work has inspired a love for inclusive teaching with a focus on holistic student success and wellness. Prior to joining the graduate research programme, Aubrey served as the administrative assistant in the Dean's Office of the Chicago Medical School. She has a Bachelor of Arts in English Language and Literature from Wheaton College, IL.

Fiona Philippi leads the Researcher Development team in the Institute for Academic Development at the University of Edinburgh. The team provides tailored training and development for researchers at all levels of their careers (postgraduate researchers, research supervisors, research staff and principal investigators (PIs)) and oversees the implementation of several University-wide initiatives and action plans to improve research culture and environment. These include the Concordat for the Career Development of Researchers, the University Research Cultures Action Plan, support for the Doctoral College and the Research Staff Hub. Fiona has a particular interest in doctoral education and support for supervision and has international experience in workshop facilitation and on external advisory panels. She is also currently a peer reviewer for the UK process of the HR Excellence in Research Award and is an accredited coach.

Ingrid Rewitzky is a professor of Mathematics at Stellenbosch University, South Africa. Her recent research interests focus on mathematics learning and teaching in higher education. She is involved in educational leadership through her roles as Executive Head of the Department of Mathematical Sciences and Vice-Dean (Learning and Teaching) of the Faculty of Science. As Vice-Dean, she has been instrumental in facilitating and supporting a scholarly approach to teaching and learning in science, as well as introducing a differentiated student support approach. In December 2018, she was honoured with the Stellenbosch University Chancellor's Award in recognition of sustained excellence throughout her career. Her personal growth and satisfaction as an academic and educational leader are integrally linked to understanding and establishing connections between a diversity of perspectives.

Baohua Yu is an associate professor in the Department of English at the City University of Hong Kong. She holds a PhD in cross-cultural psychology and applied linguistics from the University of Hong Kong. Her major fields of research are intercultural communication, second language acquisition, self-regulated learning, AI/technology-enhanced teaching and learning and the cross-cultural psychology of international students. She has published in leading international journals such as *Language Teaching, ReCall, System, Higher Education, Studies in Higher Education, International Journal of Intercultural Relations,* and *Journal of Multilingual and Multicultural Development.*

Series Editors' Foreword

The *Enhancing Reflective Teaching in Higher Education* book series is committed to supporting the development of reflective teaching in higher education. Books in this series undertake in-depth explorations of contemporary issues related to the development of reflective educational practices and are informed by the latest research and thinking about teaching in higher education. They are designed around evidence-informed principles for effective educational practices and provide strategies to enhance day-to-day teaching in higher education. In doing so, they build on the foundations provided by *Reflective Teaching in Higher Education*.

Doctoral education is evolving. There are increasing pathways to doctoral education and diversification of what comprises a doctorate. *Reflective Practice on Doctoral Education* is a timely and important contribution to higher education. The purpose of the book is to draw the gaze beyond the supervisor-student relationship to the meta-level of assumptions, ideologies and socio-political contexts that shape doctoral education. The book is practice-oriented and draws on case studies, research findings and reflective activities underpinned by ten principles for reflective teaching. These ten principles have been adapted for application to this book from the principles provided in *Reflective Teaching in Higher Education*. This collection thus provides a well-structured platform from which current practices at any one institution can be interrogated and critiqued.

Introduction: What Do We Mean by Reflective Practice on Doctoral Education?

The choice of the title Reflective Practice *on* Doctoral Education rather than the more conventional Reflective Practice *in* Doctoral Education signifies a purposeful conceptual shift. This distinction is not merely semantic but marks a fundamental change in the positioning of reflective practice within the field of doctoral education. Rather than limiting reflection to the immediate context of supervisory relationships or day-to-day pedagogical practices, this book proposes a broader, meta-level approach. It frames doctoral education itself, not solely the individuals or practices within it, as the subject of sustained, critical reflection.

It is hoped that this approach encourages supervisors, educators and academic leaders to adopt a critical perspective that critiques the structures, norms and institutional logics that underpin doctoral education. Instead of focusing exclusively on reflective strategies that enhance supervisory practices, the contributors to this book challenge readers to interrogate the assumptions, ideologies and socio-political contexts that shape doctoral education as a field.

The timing of this reflection is especially significant in light of the evolving nature of doctoral education in the twenty-first century. The increasing incorporation of taught components within professional doctorate programmes signifies a major shift in doctoral education worldwide. These structured elements, often comprising advanced coursework, research training and professional skill development, aim to complement traditional research components and better prepare candidates for diverse career pathways. This evolution reflects global trends, including the diversification of doctoral models, a growing emphasis on employability and transferable skills, the rise of interdisciplinary and practice-based research, and the influence of contemporary higher education policies. Together, these developments encourage a re-examination of long-standing assumptions, pedagogical practices, and values, fostering innovation and adaptability within doctoral education.

The strength of this book lies in its collective authorship, which brings together a diversity of voices, disciplinary perspectives and institutional experiences. This pluralism enriches the reflective process, ensuring that critiques of doctoral education are both grounded and complex. Many contributors reflect on their own positionalities as supervisors and scholars, modelling the critical reflexivity they advocate. By doing so, the book becomes not just a theoretical exploration but also a pedagogical tool, demonstrating how reflection can drive transformation at individual, institutional and systemic levels.

Pedagogical features and structural framing of the book

This book adopts a varied, practice-oriented structure, designed to facilitate engagement with the diverse dimensions of doctoral education. Recognizing the complexity of supervisory practices and the systemic forces that shape them, the chapters incorporate a range of pedagogical features, including Case Studies, Reflective Activities and Research Briefings. These elements are strategically distributed throughout the book, with individual chapters highlighting different approaches depending on their thematic and methodological focus. This diversity ensures the book engages a broad audience, including both novice and experienced supervisors, academic developers and institutional leaders.

Several chapters foreground Case Studies as a means of illustrating the situated nature of doctoral education. These extended narratives provide detailed, context-rich accounts of real-life supervisory dilemmas, institutional challenges and programme innovations. The use of case studies is not simply illustrative but analytical; each case invites critical engagement and serves as a springboard for broader discussions on policy, practice and pedagogy. In particular, these chapters demonstrate how reflective practice can be embedded in complex, ethically charged situations, highlighting the relational, emotional and intellectual dimensions of supervision.

Other chapters foreground Reflective Activities as tools for encouraging deeper self-inquiry and professional development. These activities are often integrated at key points within each chapter, offering structured opportunities for readers to pause, reflect and apply the content to their own contexts. By incorporating prompts, questions and exercises, these chapters foster a reflective orientation towards supervisory interactions and broader questions of power, equity and purpose in doctoral education.

Several chapters also include Research Briefings, providing concise summaries of relevant empirical studies, policy reports or theoretical frameworks. These briefings serve multiple purposes: they ground the chapter's discussions in current scholarly work, offer accessible entry points to complex debates and support evidence-based decision-making. In doing so, they enhance the academic rigour of the book while ensuring its practical relevance. The briefings also model scholarly synthesis that readers can incorporate into their own supervisory and institutional practices.

Importantly, the inclusion of these features is not uniform across all chapters but is tailored to align with each author's positionality, topic and intended learning outcomes. This flexible approach reflects the book's commitment to reflective practice as an adaptive and context-sensitive endeavour. The book is thus not prescriptive but invitational, encouraging readers to explore, critique and engage with doctoral education from a variety of perspectives.

Using this book

For individual readers, each chapter can be approached as a self-contained unit, allowing for focused engagement with specific themes such as supervisory relationships, equity in doctoral education or interdisciplinary practices. The Reflective Activities encourage readers to examine their own assumptions, experiences and institutional contexts, fostering ongoing personal development through practices such as reflective journaling.

For facilitators of academic development programmes, the book serves as both a core and supplementary text within structured training sessions. Case studies can be employed to stimulate group discussion, enabling participants to explore multiple interpretations, identify challenges and propose context-sensitive solutions. These case studies are particularly suited to scenario-based learning and can be adapted for problem-solving exercises.

Research briefings offer facilitators a way to integrate evidence-based content into workshops without requiring extensive preparatory reading. They can form the basis for further reading or serve as starting points for group critique, encouraging participants to assess how empirical findings apply to their institutional contexts.

Ultimately, the book is intended to be adaptive and dialogic. Whether used in formal training or informal reading groups, it functions both as a resource and a provocation, supporting supervisors not only in refining their individual practices but also in contributing to broader conversations about the future of doctoral education.

Designing ten principles for doctoral education

Doctoral education demands a careful balance of academic rigour, personal growth and strong institutional support. To help navigate this complex process, we propose ten guiding principles designed to support supervisors, institutions and doctoral candidates alike. Rather than being tied to specific chapters or sections, these principles encourage broad thinking about the many dimensions of doctoral education.

Building on the original Teaching, Learning and Research Principles (James and Pollard, 2011) and their adaptation by Ashwin et al. (2020) for *Reflective Teaching in Higher Education,* these principles have been further refined to highlight the need for reflection and self-evaluation in doctoral supervision. When applied in practice, it is hoped that they will enable supervisors to effectively manage the academic, ethical and social challenges of the doctoral journey, creating environments where students can flourish intellectually and professionally.

Principle 1: Preparing for academic and professional life
Doctoral education should equip students with a broad range of competencies that prepare them not only for academic careers but also for diverse professional roles beyond the university.

Principle 2: Engagement with advanced and discipline-specific knowledge
Students must develop a deep understanding of theoretical foundations as well as practical research applications specific to their disciplines.

Principle 3: Building on prior experience
Recognizing and valuing students' previous academic and professional backgrounds enriches learning and encourages critical inquiry.

Principle 4: Scaffolded learning and skill development
A structured, scaffolded approach to learning supports students in progressively building their research skills and autonomy.

Principle 5: Aligned and meaningful assessment
Assessment methods should be coherent with learning goals, providing clear and constructive feedback on students' progress.

Principle 6: Active student engagement
Doctoral education fosters students' active participation, encouraging self-directed research, critical thinking and problem-solving.

Principle 7: Balancing individual and collaborative growth
Supervision should support both independent scholarship and collaborative interactions, such as peer learning and teamwork.

Principle 8: Valuing informal learning opportunities
Mentorship, peer discussions and academic networking are vital informal learning experiences that contribute significantly to doctoral development.

Principle 9: Continuous professional development for supervisors
Supervisors and support staff must engage in ongoing learning to maintain up-to-date supervisory practices.

Principle 10: Institutional support and policy alignment
Consistent institutional frameworks and policies are essential to prioritize and sustain the learning and development needs of doctoral candidates throughout their academic journey.

Together, these principles provide a comprehensive roadmap for enhancing doctoral education in ways that are thoughtful, inclusive and adaptable. They remind us that doctoral supervision is not just about guiding research but also about fostering growth, resilience and professional readiness. By embedding these principles into everyday practice, supervisors and institutions can create environments where doctoral candidates feel supported, challenged and empowered to achieve their full potential.

The structure of the book

The first four chapters of this book offer an examination of the challenges and opportunities embedded within doctoral education. They lay the groundwork for focused reflection on the nature and framework of doctoral education explored more deeply in later sections. By engaging with concepts such as assemblage, the hidden curriculum, process, product and the various types of doctorates, these chapters invite readers to consider not only the structural dimensions of doctoral education but also the underlying influences that shape it. In doing so, they challenge supervisors, academic leaders and institutions to evaluate their roles in either reinforcing or disrupting these dynamics, fostering a more comprehensive engagement with the field.

The second section of this book explores the evolving role of doctoral supervisors, emphasizing the importance of establishing and nurturing strong supervisor-student relationships. This section includes discussions on the dynamics of co-supervision and collaboration, offers models of effective supervisory practice and addresses the challenges and strategies for online supervision of distance doctoral researchers. Together, these chapters provide insights for developing supportive and productive supervisory partnerships.

The third section focuses on creating academic spaces that recognize and support the diversity of doctoral candidates. Topics include supervising a diverse student body, fostering inclusion and support within doctoral education, and understanding how identity and well-being influence the doctoral experience. These discussions highlight the role of the supervisor in promoting equity and nurturing a positive and inclusive academic environment.

Section 4 highlights key supervisory responsibilities related to doctoral progression and completion. It covers giving constructive feedback on research progress and outputs, supporting candidates throughout their doctoral journey and guiding the examination process. These chapters offer a range of perspectives on how supervisors can effectively facilitate academic development and help students successfully achieve their doctorate.

A collective and international approach

Professor Fiona Hallett authored the *Introduction* and *Conclusion* of this volume, led Chapter 9, *Supervising a Diverse Doctoral Student Body*, and Chapter 14, *Examining Doctoral Research*. She also contributed to several other chapters throughout the book.

Professor Ronald Barnett and Professor Carolina Guzmán-Valenzuela jointly led Chapter 1, *Reimagining Reflective Practice in Doctoral Education: Assemblage, Ecology and Wisdom*, and contributed to Chapter 4, *Different Types of Doctorates*.

Professor Ingrid Rewitzky led Chapter 2, *The Hidden Curriculum of Doctoral Education*, and contributed to Chapter 5, *Building Good Doctoral Supervisory Relationships*.

Professor Marit Honerød Hoveid and Dr Dagrun Astrid Aarø Engen jointly led Chapter 3, *Process and Product*, and contributed to Chapter 2, *The Hidden Curriculum of Doctoral Education*.

Professor Barbara Kehm led Chapter 4, *Different Types of Doctorates*, and contributed to Chapter 3, *Process and Product*.

Professor Jan McArthur led Chapter 5, *Building Good Doctoral Supervisory Relationships*, and contributed to Chapter 8, *Online Supervision of Distance Doctoral Researchers*.

Dr Fiona Philippi led Chapter 6, *Co-supervision and Other Models of Collaborative Supervision*, and contributed to Chapter 9, *Supervising a Diverse Doctoral Student Body*.

Dr Chris Hughes led Chapter 7, *Modelling Doctoral Supervision*, in collaboration with Dr Clive Palmer. He also contributed to Chapter 1, *Reimagining Reflective Practice in Doctoral Education: Assemblage, Ecology and Wisdom*.

Dr Brett Bligh led Chapter 8, *Online Supervision of Distance Doctoral Researchers*, and contributed to Chapter 14, *Examining Doctoral Research*.

Dr Susanna Calkins and Aubrey Penney jointly led Chapter 10, *Fostering Inclusion and Support in Doctoral Education*, and both contributed to Chapter 12, *Giving Constructive Feedback on Research Progress and Outputs*.

Dr Lucy Baohua Lu and Peihua Li co-led Chapter 11, *Understanding and Nurturing Identity and Well-being*, and both contributed to Chapter 13, *Supporting Progress through the Doctoral Journey*.

Professor Gregory Light led Chapter 12, *Giving Constructive Feedback on Research Progress and Outputs*, and contributed to Chapter 10, *Fostering Inclusion and Support in Doctoral Education*.

Dr David Armstrong led Chapter 13, *Supporting Progress through the Doctoral Journey*, and contributed to Chapter 11, *Understanding and Nurturing Identity and Well-being*.

References

Ashwin, P., Boud, D., Calkins, S., Coate, K., Hallett, F., Light, G., Luckett, K., MacLaren, I., Mårtensson, K., McArthur, J., McCune, V., McClean, M. & Tooher, M. (2020) *Reflective teaching in higher education*. London and New York: Bloomsbury.

James, M. & Pollard, A. (2011) 'TLRP's ten principles for effective pedagogy: Rationale, development, evidence, argument and impact', *Research Papers in Education*, 26(3), pp. 275–328. doi:10.1080/02671522.2011.590007

PART ONE

Doctoral Education: An Overview

1

Reimagining Reflective Practice in Doctoral Education: Assemblage, Ecology and Wisdom

Ronald Barnett and Carolina Guzmán-Valenzuela

Introduction – the argument summarized

The doctorate has been swept up into mass higher education and moreover, especially over the last three or four decades, has come to play its part in the formation of what has come to be known as cognitive capitalism. This is a form of capitalism in which knowledge is not merely a resource to be drawn upon but in which knowledge has itself come to constitute a form of capital. In the process, the doctorate has shifted its position from being marginal in higher education to being a major component in this re-alignment of the academic world and the economy.

In turn, the doctorate no longer possesses its inward and enclosed character as the epitome of academic culture but instead has been broken open to form an assemblage of multiple elements. At the same time, in becoming an assemblage, the doctorate also comes to be a part of a huge knowledge ecosystem, as well as having interconnections with the ecosystems of the polity and the economy. These structural movements hold disconcerting implications but also educational potential for the doctorate as a space of reflection.

A short history of the doctorate

The modern PhD is a relatively modern development. The PhD originated in medieval Europe. Initially focused on advanced scholarship rather than original research, these degrees required a period of residence and examinations, but not a dissertation (Ruano-Borbalan, 2022). This model persisted until the early nineteenth century, when Prussian Enlightenment thinkers advocated a new kind of university focused on the creation of original knowledge, reflected in Wilhelm von Humboldt's educational reforms at the University of Berlin, which placed inquiry and teaching in close juxtaposition. The University of Berlin became the first explicitly research-led institution and introduced the Doctor of Philosophy (PhD) to recognize a significant contribution to knowledge and understanding. It was out of these developments that the research university subsequently developed (Ostling, 2018), so leading the way to the modern doctoral model.

This German model influenced higher education worldwide (Ruano-Borbalan, op. cit.; Taylor, 2023), particularly in Europe and the United States, where Yale University awarded the first American doctorates in 1861 (Rosenberg, 1961; Ruano-Borbalan, 2022; Taylor, 2023). By the early twentieth century, Germany and the United States dominated the landscape of doctoral education (Taylor, 2023). The UK adopted the PhD after the First World War, and by the mid-twentieth century, it had spread to other countries with similar higher education systems. The PhD model was further exported globally in the post-Second World War era, driven by the emergence of the knowledge society and a recognition of the importance of research for economic growth and defence capabilities. It was in this context that the PhD gained traction worldwide, a process enhanced by the association between the PhD and elite higher education (McCulloch & Thomas, 2013).

In the late twentieth and early twenty-first centuries, several overt changes have characterized the expansion of the modern doctorate. According to Taylor (2023), these changes include formalization (e.g. clear guidelines for supervision and increased accountability); growth and diversification of the candidate population; diversification of modes of study to include part-time, online and profession-based doctorates; a wider use of technology; a broader student base; and diversification of purposes, from a focus on academic careers to the production of skilled professionals for various sectors, with an emphasis on practice-oriented research. Concomitantly, doctoral programmes have become standardized and efficient, with a focus on quantifiable metrics such as publications and citations to measure output. This shift has led to a more regimented and less personalized educational experience, aligning doctoral education with broader market demands and management principles. However, the question then arises as to how we might account for these changes and that question calls for a deeper analytical framework.

Reflections on a metamorphosis

In the early European model, it was assumed that the student would work by him- or herself (Taylor, 2023) and produce a significant text that engaged with the luminaries in the field (from whom might be drawn the candidate's examiners). The oral examination (the viva) was a space in which the candidate was expected to demonstrate that they were worthy of entering the academic profession, competent to pass muster in the company of the established authorities. The dissertation was expected to constitute a major work, boldly stating and advancing a large thesis, and ideally carrying forward a key set of debates. If the viva met with success, an academic career was virtually assured, with the doctorate being published in book form and academic reputation already starting to form. Under such conditions, the presentation of the thesis and the viva could be a high-risk affair, not least since one of the examiners could be a target in the thesis itself.

That model has been overtaken as the doctorate has been subsumed into mass higher education. However, a reference to massification here can be only a shorthand for a complex of factors. As stated, the growth of the doctorate has to be understood in the context of the emergence of cognitive capitalism (Boutang, 2011), that form of capitalism in which knowledge is not simply drawn upon in the world of work but becomes a force of production – and so has capital – in its own right. The doctorate is key to this form of capitalism in two senses. It becomes a space for the acquisition of high-level cognitive skills (of which more below), and it becomes directly a means of knowledge production as the doctorate, especially in the STEM disciplines but now also even in the social sciences, becomes an integral part of science projects leading to papers in the literature and even on occasions producing significant discoveries.

The traditional doctorate was a substantial offering in its own right; but, more importantly, it foretold of much more to come. In its ambition and its daring, it set out an agenda for a future research programme. It was a *doctorate-before-the-event*. In contrast, the modern doctorate is a *doctorate-after-the-event*. The thesis is now of little importance in itself. What is important is that it signifies both the production of texts and the acquisition of certain skills that possess academic capital, such that there may have already been a kind of profit in the publication of academic papers en route to the doctorate.

To put this reflection more formally, we may say that the ontology of the doctorate has fundamentally changed. From a process and a text that was in-itself and for-itself, the doctorate has become a process and a text that is in and for-the-world, and for a world of action at that.

Assemblages

No longer understood as a process of academic enclosure leading to a unitary text offering a definite and large (and even revolutionary) thesis, the doctorate has been disassembled. Now, the doctorate has become a process with the task of engaging in discrete tasks and in producing a dissertation that – despite its superficial appearance as a single text – is actually an *assemblage* of different units. Its summary ('abstract'), its literature review, its statement of its methodology, its collocation of the data and the analysis thereof, and its concluding reflections are separate entities, jostling with each other. Several observations may be made about this dissertation-as-an-assemblage:

i That there are separate parts to the dissertation reflects that the doctoral journey has become a process of acquiring *separate* skills. These skills include those of (i) forming or identifying a problem (a 'research question'); (ii) being able to conduct an inquiry into the relevant material in the literature that bears upon the problem situation, to ferret out that material, organize it cogently and display capacities for interrogating it and making judgements about it; (iii) having competence in relation to research methodology, which calls for an understanding of a range of possible approaches to research and demonstrating the capacity to choose an appropriate method (which may be a carefully selected mix of approaches); (iv) actually orchestrating a research project, putting the chosen methodology into effect, generating data and analysing it; (v) producing findings; (vi) concluding with a reflective section that articulates how the study could have been conducted with even greater effect and/or how the study opens to future work. This is a wide range of skills, and key is that they are separable.

ii The separability of these skills is reflected in the very character of the dissertation, with its chapters and sections given over to displaying in turn each of these skills. The titles of the chapters reflect this division into its component parts ('literature review', 'methodology', 'data analysis' and so forth).

iii The separateness of the components of the research study makes it possible with relative ease to their having an additional life as multiple papers in the literature and being picked up subsequently for disparate purposes.

iv Because the inquiry in question and the ensuing dissertation have been broken into discrete parts, its unity is at best severely diminished, if not entirely negated.

v The dissertation is characteristically *devoid* of a large and compelling thesis that seeks to inject a new framework or a critique of a dominant framework or a new perspective. The near-concluding section of reflections is often perfunctory, even in terms of its (short) length. The abstract typically contains no bold and large thesis or summary argument but describes the path taken in the study and is replete with verbs such as (this thesis) 'explores' or 'discusses' or 'considers'. Accordingly, the submitted text *becomes a thesis without a thesis.*

REFLECTIVE ACTIVITY 1.1: THE DOCTORAL THESIS AS AN ASSEMBLAGE

Frankenstein's monster (as conceived by Mary Shelley, 2012) is an assemblage of all the required components for sentient human life, and at times it looks and sounds, well at least remotely, much like a human being. The novel shows a monster that lacks not the capacity to love, to think, to reflect and act. What the creature lacks, however, are the things that society is unwilling to afford it. Is the current assembled doctorate thesis, the one we see described above, one lacking in theses, claims, outlook and intellect not, in a sense, our own mangled creation?

Activity: Consider the analogy between Frankenstein's monster and the doctorate thesis. What does it mean to view the thesis as an assemblage?

How does its reception influence its perceived value?

Reflect on whether a thesis should be assessed primarily on its content or on the intellectual qualities of the candidate.

Think about how the viva voce examination moves beyond the written document into broader discussions about knowledge and expertise.

This evolution of the doctoral dissertation – a process from which the social sciences have not been immune – can be described through the lens of assemblage theory, as articulated by Manuel DeLanda (2013) (drawing on the work of Deleuze and Guattari). Historically, the doctorate was characterized by 'relations of interiority', with an integrated internal unity. The dissertation was deeply embedded in academic disciplines, engaged with existing theories and debates, and its parts were tightly interwoven to advance a strong central thesis. This internal coherence meant that no part of the dissertation could be easily separated from the whole without losing its integrity and meaning.

In contrast, the contemporary doctoral dissertation functions more as an assemblage characterized by 'relations of exteriority'. In *this* relationality, parts of the dissertation can be detached and used in different contexts and for different purposes, not only to serve as discrete papers in academic journals but also to symbolize skills for the labour market. Internal links within the dissertation are weaker, leading to a structure where the literature review and other sections may be at best loosely coupled, resulting in less cohesive narratives and arguments through the text. These changes reflect wider trends in academia towards flexibility and applicability in external settings.

The doctorate and the political economy

An explanatory framework – in comprehending the evolution of the doctorate sketched here – lies in a coupling of two sets of theories, those of political economy and of cognitive capitalism. These two overlap but they have distinctive centres of gravity. Although the theory of political economy is by far the longer-standing of the two, it is that of cognitive capitalism that has had a more immediate bearing on higher education studies.

'Cognitive capitalism' – which we have touched on – is actually a shorthand for a penumbra of terms and ideas, which include those of knowledge economy, knowledge society, knowledge capitalism, capitalocene, algorithmic capitalism, information capitalism, cybernetic capitalism and globalizing knowledge. Key scholars in this bailiwick are Boutang (2011), Peters (2013), Roggero (2011), Stehr (2022) and Kennedy (2015). This set of ideas has developed and spread conceptually and theoretically over the past twenty years, but it contains in its contemporary formation the central idea that the relationship of knowledge and capitalism in the twenty-first century is not merely a strong relationship but takes a particular form. Knowledge is not merely a resource on which society draws in enhancing capital in society but is itself a form of capital. Knowledge can be put to work not just in support of other mechanisms and processes but has become a direct form of capital and, thereby, of power.

This theoretical literature and its many debates contain varying degrees of a critical tinge and have been supplemented in four ways. *First,* Bernard Stiegler mounted (2015) a 'stupidity' thesis: twenty-first-century society is heavily structured by knowledge but, especially through its increasing reliance on technological systems ('technics'), that knowledge is accompanied by a weak or absent reflexivity (not a term that Stiegler used but it is fair to his arguments). *Second,* the 'Mode 2' theory of Michael Gibbons and associates (Nowotny, 2001) not only pointed to the emergence of ephemeral, problem-focused, team-processed and interdisciplinary modes of knowledge production in the world of work but also implied that universities had to emulate the new mode if they were to retain their epistemic value. *Third,* an interest in science and technology has been elevated into a global discourse of 'STEM', the acronym having taken on a holy status and treated as immutable, despite the fast-changing formations in question (and the expansion of the acronym into 'STEMM' (Cohen, 2021)).

Fourth, and most pertinently for our purposes, Krystian Szadkowski (2023) has recently developed an ambitious critical theory of higher education by depicting the sector through the perspective of (Marxist) political economy. *Capital in Higher Education* is a major work that systematically unravels both the political economy of higher education and ways in which higher education is embedded in the wider political economy. At the centre of these structures lie the generation and value placed upon knowledge and, thereby, the work of academics (in 'academic labour'). The book explicitly goes beyond the 'cognitive capitalism' thesis by depicting knowledge as a structure of value – knowledge takes on value and can thus produce surplus value. Key here, therefore, is the processes of academic labour and also their measurement (to which we alluded earlier).

The doctorate as capital

The conversion of the doctorate under conditions of cognitive capitalism permits the production of two kinds of capital, epistemic and ontological. Epistemic capital is produced insofar as the doctoral student produces papers for the literature and/or contributes to work being undertaken by her/his supervisor(s) that leads to academic papers and/or whose doctorate thesis can quickly provide the basis for papers soon after the successful completion of the study. (Naturally, there are variants of these possibilities). This is epistemic academic labour being deployed *directly* to produce academic capital both of direct financial profit and, via reputational capital, *indirectly* to additional academic capital.

Academic capital takes on a heightened form with the formation of global science as an ecosystem, elements of which are global academic publishing, the internet, university rankings and individuals' performance ratings (in citation indices and H-scores). This ecosystem makes possible vast data banks of information derived from measurements, which have come to be a driver of the academic world, and into which the doctorate has become embedded. These phenomena are possible only because the doctorate has become an assemblage, the parts of which directly or indirectly can generate academic capital.

However, the doctorate is a source of academic capital more indirectly in supplying capital ontologically, through the formation of new kinds of academic *being*. In being broken into a series of discrete parts, the doctoral journey lends itself – as noted – to the acquisition of a number of discrete skills. Again, there are direct and indirect forms of capital to be observed here. Directly, the various skills – searching, collating and reviewing existing literature; discerning a problem worthy of investigation; determining and selecting an appropriate range of methods by which to investigate the problem; generating first-hand data that informs the problem; interrogating the data; and coming to conclusions – are each of value in the wider labour market.

We may note that not only is the doctorate process an assemblage through which such discrete skills may be acquired from its components but that the individual is accentuated as an assemblage her/himself. The individual acquires value in the labour market in her/himself being an assemblage of *skills-as-components of the self*. The student, as successful 'Doctor', has enhanced value precisely as an assemblage that can bend with the exigencies presented by the labour market. It is precisely not because she/he has an incisive, critical and self-critical, and well-formed singular position honed in argument with the major intellectual figures of the day. Rather, it is that she/he can bring skills and combinations of skills to bear on problem situations as they emerge (and so frames her/his CV in that way, to delineate *separately* her/his skills). In this situation, reflection takes on a meagre, flimsy and superficial character, constraining thought largely within given frameworks.

These ontological facets of the doctorate in the political economy have a more subtle and indirect aspect. The phrase 'soft skills' has emerged (and there are concomitant references to communication skills, team-player skills, complexity skills, leadership skills and so forth). The ugliness and thinness of this language only hint at the substantial changes in the *being* of the doctoral candidate that the doctorate-as-assemblage is expected to bring about and how that contrasts with the older doctorate-as-unity model.

Whereas the doctorate-as-unity model was associated with the formation of (an) intellectual being, steeped in an academic culture, able and willing to trade arguments, perspectives and frameworks in defence of a definite intellectual position (the doctor as intellectual), the doctorate-as-assemblage model positions the candidate as nomadic between the academic world and the world of work and able to respond and to adapt to exigencies as they present (the doctor as agent in the world). This adaptability is associated with the dispositions and qualities of a supple, pliant-but-inquisitive-and-problem-formation-and-problem-solver, who is able to add (cognitive) value to an organization.

An ecosystem reading

We may say that the doctorate is now emmeshed in a number of mega-ecosystems. Its unity was a phenomenon of a previous age, of academic autonomy, separateness from the world and self-enclosure. Now, the doctorate has been broken open into discrete parts forming an assemblage and those parts are hooked onto wider ecosystems of the world. Principally, the ecosystems most implicated here are *three world ecosystems* of knowledge, the economy and the polity. Alongside the transformation of the doctorate in the interests of cognitive capitalism, and of its knowledge systems and labour markets, stands the polity, and not just nationally but cross-nationally (for the doctorate has acquired geopolitical aspects). Especially in STEM disciplines, but increasingly in the social sciences, the state bears the greater portion of the funding burden along with private corporations.

However, other ecosystems are present too – albeit in the shadows – in processes of mutual implication with the doctorate, including the ecosystems of society (especially in its social institutions, such as its communicative processes), of learning (as an ecosystem of the world) and of persons (especially of the doctorate student, with his/her own ecology). To these (now) six ecosystems, we might also more even dimly glimpse the further two ecosystems of culture and of Nature. There are, therefore, at least eight mega-ecosystems with which the doctorate is now entangled, albeit to differing degrees, with their corresponding differing relationships, agency, subservience, dependence and domination.

Spaces of wisdom

The narrative unfolded here may seem largely pessimistic. Wrenched out of the clutches of the academic world, the doctorate is now a creature of the wider world, serving multiple interests implicit in dominant global ecosystems. Moreover, having been transformed into the assemblage associated with this multiplicity that the doctorate has become, the Enlightenment ideals of spacious and critical reason have been vitiated. No longer a space for large intellectual horizons and forensic argument, the being-possible of the doctorate candidate has severely altered to horizons of action and pay-off.

Yet, this is not the end of the doctorate. 'End' here is nicely ambiguous. Its use here points to the doctorate evolving over time, and its present state need not be its final stage. But 'end' here also alludes to the larger purposes towards which the doctorate might be intended. We may briefly pursue both senses of 'end' together.

Originally, undertaking a doctorate was to be part of an elite within an elite. Even so, the doctorate was understood to enable those who followed its path to gain a largeness of view, a panoramic perspective and an authority from which positions could be taken up in engaging with the foremost understandings of the day. It was a vehicle through which a form of wisdom might be attained, with large intellectual horizons. With the coming of the doctorate-as-assemblage, that kind of formation of self has dwindled. However, a new kind of doctorate-of-and-for-wisdom may be at hand.

The argument here has been that the doctorate has become intermeshed with mega-ecosystems of the world. However, *that* relationality – the doctorate having interrelationships with ecosystems – is unbalanced, since the ecosystems of knowledge, the economy and the state are especially powerful in the modern shaping of the doctorate. Other ecosystems – of persons, culture, learning, society and Nature – are downplayed. Nevertheless, in an interconnected world, those other ecosystems are present. A doctorate has connections with each of those five other ecosystems which may be subtle, subdued, depressed or neglected but they are still present. A doctorate has an *ecosystem hinterland* in which each of those other five ecosystems – of persons, learning, society, culture and Nature – are present, alongside the three dominant ecosystems of knowledge-as-action, the state and the economy.

It follows that a new kind of wisdom is potentially in reach of the doctorate. In principle, and without too much difficulty in practice, the doctorate could be reshaped so that – even while it focuses on a local problem area and even while it seeks to develop discrete skills – it could require that candidates spend a little time identifying and working through some ecosystem possibilities that their dissertation opens. Each doctorate has its own ecosystem hinterland – that complex of networks that lie to hand – offering learning and inquiry *potential*. Given that consideration, what we have in mind is a substantial concluding section to a thesis where the text looks outward to the wider world and seeks to identify connections with a number of ecosystems that do lie at hand, given the complex that forms the dissertation in question – perhaps in society, or in the formation of persons, or the development of

REFLECTIVE ACTIVITY 1.2: REIMAGINING DOCTORAL EDUCATION

The kind of 'ecosystem hinterland' that is envisaged really does 'lie to hand', but it will be what we as educators do, and the freedoms afforded by supervisors, who themselves need to be ecosystem-minded, that do the nudging, cajoling and 'offering learning and inquiry potential'. Realizing the reimagined doctoral thesis will, in all likelihood, require a philosophical/conceptual reorientation to learning, skill, imagination, inquiry and supervision. It could well be that the doctoral thesis as assemblage is perhaps a remnant of, or feature of, a contemporary shortsightedness which often confuses teaching with learning, satisfaction with attainment, volume with insight, knowledge with understanding.

Putting thoughts about ecosystems and wisdom aside for a second, whatever the doctoral thesis of the future might in fact look like (assemblage or otherwise), it would be terribly unwise to intentionally lose sight of that serious higher-level education, an education in questions, concepts, logic, language, knowledge, reason and argument, that difficult and disruptive kind of education.

A sensible returning to these concepts might be the only way to credibly turn to those ecosystems, understand them, preserve them, change them or, even, save them. One thing is for sure, the doctorate, much like Frankenstein's monster, is dispensable. Those ecosystems, very much in the same vein as logic, morality, sense and wisdom, should not be going anywhere anytime soon.

Activity

How might supervisors and examiners shape the future of doctoral research to balance tradition with innovation?

Consider whether the future of doctoral education should involve a return to foundational intellectual values or embrace new, evolving academic ecosystems.

learning systems, or the growth of public understanding of knowledge or in Nature or some mix of such insights.

Numerous advantages would flow from implementing such a proposal. The doctoral student, while still focusing their study on a particular research question, would be obliged to leave its safety and extend *themselves* in identifying connections to the ecosystems of the wider world. The doctorate, thereby, would gain *reflective potential*. Tracing some of these

REFLECTIVE ACTIVITY 1.3: REIMAGINING THE DOCTORAL THESIS

Take a moment to reflect on the evolving nature of the doctoral thesis and its place within academic and intellectual traditions. Consider the following questions and prompts as a means of engaging with this transformation:

Shifting traditions in writing:

What do you think has become of traditional academic writing forms such as essays and dissertations?

How have other forms of intellectual expression – such as poetry, letters and philosophical treatises – changed over time?

In what ways have the style and substance of academic articles evolved?

The doctoral thesis in transition:

Given the increase in publications and changes in scholarly discourse, how do you perceive the role of argument, reasoning and intellectual outlook in today's doctoral research?

Do you believe a thesis should still embody these elements as fundamentally as it once did? Why or why not?

Wisdom and the doctorate:

What does wisdom mean in the context of doctoral research?

How might the thesis be reframed to integrate wisdom alongside traditional scholarly rigour?

Consider the concept of the eight eco-systems – how could this framework enrich a doctorate thesis?

The nature of examination:

When assessing a doctoral candidate, are we examining the thesis, the individual or both?

Reflect on the viva voce examination. Have you experienced or witnessed one that moved beyond the written text into broader intellectual inquiry? How did that shift shape the experience?

Looking ahead:

Imagine a future where the doctorate continues to evolve. What elements should remain integral? What aspects could be reimagined?

networks – from the assemblage of the doctorate – out into, say, two or three of the ecosystems would impart a broad cognitive perspective: a kind of wisdom. The student would be required to bring original and creative thought to the matters at hand (and would not be able to rely on, e.g., large language models). In turn, the doctorate would come to acquire *worldly* value, in helping to ameliorate the impairments of the eco-environment. The contemporary doctorate-in-the-world could proceed to a further stage of its evolution, that of a doctorate-of-the-world and *for*-the-world.

Reflections – or lack of reflections – on AI

In any attempt to enhance the reflexive moments in doctorate education, there is a fly in the ointment. Right at the start of the student's work on their thesis – on say receiving a few pages sketching a draft part of a literature review – dare a supervisor directly ask the student if they have used AI technologies to assist in generating the text in question? The university may have set out at some length guidance to its students in their use of AI for the purposes of the formal submission of theses some three years away, but there is likely to be no ethical guidance for supervisors on the part of the university. The student is not obliged to declare themselves as they submit draft chapters and the supervisory shrinks from enquiring of the student. As a result, the supervisory relationship – from its outset – lacks reflexivity on a crucial matter.

It is, however, not just that there is a lack of resources to hand to prompt that reflexivity. Rather, the total assemblage that constitutes the current supervisory relationship contains resistance to reflexivity. The companies that have built the large language models decline to be open both about the structures of these technologies and about the data that they have mined, journal publishers decline to require transparency in the authors of the papers that they publish, book publishers fail to require any kind of statement from their authors about their uses of AI and universities – knowing that it is impossible to determine the use of AI with any accuracy – also resist requiring any declaration on the part of students in the inside cover of their theses. In turn, the academic world is slipping into a situation of hybridized texts, and this is tacitly known and understood, but it is never admitted or declared.

The result is that the supervisory relationship is freighted with opaqueness: the student does not declare to their supervisors that they are using AI, and the supervisors dare not ask. Of course, in some – even many – situations the student's use of AI may be entirely open and transparent, and may be vital (e.g. to the manipulation of large datasets). But the point is that the total AI assemblage is shot through with opacity. Indeed, there is a conspiracy of opacity for it is in no one's immediate interests that this assemblage be made transparent. The publishers are keen to publish books, the journals and their editors are keen to generate papers and universities are wanting to see their students 'progress' through their programmes of study as quickly and as effortlessly as possible. The parties in this assemblage are encouraged in these behaviours, with the total audit, rankings and financial regimes exerting their pressures.

We have, then, in the research supervision-student-AI relationship, a significant part of higher education that is structurally opaque and whose potential reflexivity is limited. This is a fly in the ointment of reflexivity that is not easily removed.

Conclusion

In becoming an assemblage, the doctorate is no longer characterized by relations of interiority but by relations of exteriority. This remarkable – but largely unnoticed – inversion of the doctorate has come about since the doctorate has been incorporated into the contemporary forms of capitalism (named alternatively as cognitive, cybernetic, knowledge and algorithmic capitalism).

This is a serious matter. The doctorate was a vehicle through which the candidate would undergo a process of personal transformation in acquiring an intellectual habitus and composure to mount a critique of a current understanding of the world and even strike out with a revolutionary framework (to lay the basis for a professorial position and career), and now that insertion into a deep disciplinary habitus is no more. In turn, the doctorate has passed from a space of contemplation to a space of action in the world. Where the doctorate offered a path to wisdom of a kind, now it offers a path to the acquisition of numerous skills with potential pay-off in the world. In turn, the doctorate as a space of serious reflection and critique is now substantially diminished, if not extinguished.

However, a third stage may lie within grasp. Precisely on account of its becoming an assemblage and connecting with manifold ecosystems of the world, the potential arises for the doctorate candidate explicitly to pursue the latent links that lie to hand with at least some of those ecosystems. By at least glimpsing worldly ecosystem implications that arise from the study in question, the doctorate candidate may yet form an outlook *on* the world. In this way, it may be possible to do new justice to the idea of the thesis as a bold integrated set of truth-claims about the world and one that has some general import. It may be just possible, too, to recover the idea that the thesis (as text) should actually contain a thesis (as a claim or argument). This would be a kind of wisdom, and it would grant the doctorate a space as a new kind of reflective practice.

References

Boutang, Y.-M. (2011) *Cognitive capitalism*. Cambridge: Polity.

Cohen, E. (2021) *The University and its boundaries: Thriving or surviving in the 21st century*. London: Routledge.

DeLanda, M. (2013) *A new philosophy of society: Assemblage theory and social complexity*. London: Bloomsbury.

Kennedy, M.D. (2015) *Globalizing knowledge: Intellectuals, universities and publics in transformation*. Stanford, CA: Stanford University Press.

McCulloch, A. & Thomas, L. (2013) 'Widening participation to doctoral education and research degrees: A research agenda for an emerging policy issue', *Higher Education Research & Development*, 32(2), pp. 214–27.

Nowotny, H., Scott, P. & Gibbons, M. (2001) *Re-thinking science: Knowledge and the public in an age of uncertainty*. Cambridge: Polity.

Ostling, J. (2018) *Humboldt and the modern German university: An intellectual history*. Lund: Lund University.

Peters, M.A. (2013) *Education, science and knowledge capitalism: Creativity and the promise of openness*. New York: Peter Lang.

Roggero, G. (2011) *The production of living knowledge: The crisis of the university and the transformation of labour in Europe and North America*. Philadelphia, PA: Temple University Press.

Rosenberg, R.P. (1961) 'The first American Doctor of Philosophy degree: A centennial salute to Yale, 1861–1961', *The Journal of Higher Education*, 32(7), pp. 387–94.

Ruano-Borbalan, J.C. (2022) 'Doctoral education from its medieval foundations to today's globalisation and standardisation', *European Journal of Education*, 57(3), pp. 367–80.

Shelley, M. (2012) *Frankenstein*. London: Penguin Classics.

Stehr, N. (2022) *Knowledge capitalism*. London: Routledge.

Stiegler, B. (2015) *States of shock: Stupidity and knowledge in the 21st century*. Cambridge: Polity.

Szadkowski, K. (2023) *Capital in higher education: A critique of the political economy of the sector*. Cham: Palgrave Macmillan.

Taylor, S. (2023) 'The changing landscape of doctoral education: A framework for analysis and introduction to the special issue', *Innovations in Education and Teaching International*, 60(5), pp. 606–22.

2

The Hidden Curriculum of Doctoral Education

Ingrid Rewitzky

Introduction

When embarking on their doctoral education journey the doctoral researcher may envisage a structured path characterized by well-defined research phases, planned learning mechanisms, rules and regulations for progression and support opportunities to reach their doctoral qualification. However, it has been widely acknowledged that the doctoral education journey is non-linear in nature (Elliot, 2022) and is developing and adapting with scholarly and personal learning continually emerging in accordance with the formal and hidden curriculum of doctoral education (Elliot et al., 2020a).

In the first inquiry (Snyder, 1971) of the hidden curriculum in higher education it was highlighted that the formal curriculum of a course or programme emphasizes the formal aims and learning outcomes in terms of, for example, Bloom's taxonomy (Bloom, 1969) in the present, while teaching and learning happens, practices will always evolve, some that support the formal curriculum, others are not that apparent suggesting there is a hidden curriculum that at times can be counterproductive. The term 'hidden curriculum' has been defined as 'what is implicit and embedded in educational experiences in contrast with the formal statements about curricula and the surface features of educational interaction' (Sambell et al., 2006, pp. 391–2). The term hidden curriculum came from the United States in the 1970s and soon spread into European pedagogical thinking. According to Broady (1981) the hidden curriculum cannot be done away with; it will accompany any teaching and learning processes. It can be made less hidden, if one works on uncovering the mechanisms that creates it. The hidden curriculum has been expanded to include all the informal mechanisms of learning that take place to maintain a healthy study-life-family balance and sustain sound health and well-being (Elliot, 2022). But, one also needs to remember that a hidden curriculum 'exists of values, norms, and beliefs, amongst others, that are not documented or part of the official teaching, but that students are exposed to' (Rossouw & Frick, 2023, p. 2); they are not necessarily conducive to good teaching and learning.

The hidden curriculum in doctoral education refers to the learning experiences that are not explicitly taught and from which knowledge and skills emerge for the successful completion of the doctoral studies and for post-doctoral work. For the doctoral student to thrive along their doctoral journey knowledge and skills beyond the formal curriculum of doctoral education include motivation, academic identity, self-efficacy, self-discipline, self-awareness, sense of belonging, work–life balance and financial security. As a more concrete example, when given the task of writing a literature review the doctoral student will through feedback and conversation with their supervisor realize that the literature review is more than a summary of the literature. From the experience of writing a literature review the doctoral student will gain the skills of reflective thinking and of making an argument about what is known about their research topic and what are open questions.

Since our doctoral education journey is about fostering emergence of creativity, analytical, reflective and critical thinking (Elliot, 2022), as well as developing research independence, transforming the students' interaction with the world and acquiring transferable skills, we propose in this chapter that the doctoral education journey is envisioned as a complex adaptive system where learning is understood as a dynamic elaborative process (Davis & Sumara, 2008, p. 13; Piaget, 1968). Although there is no universally accepted definition of a complex adaptive system (Carmichael & Hadzikadic, 2019; Holland, 2006), an integrative approach for understanding a complex adaptive system is complexity theory (Cilliers, 1998).

There is a wide range of case studies proposing complexity theory as an approach for addressing different challenges in higher education (Morrison, 2006), for challenging cause-and-effect and linear models of education (Radford, 2008), for providing a descriptive and unified theory of established approaches (Kuhn, 2008; Morrison, 2010) as well as for expanding our perspective of 'to educate and to be educated' (Davis & Phelps, 2004). It has been shown that 'new properties and behaviours emerge not only from the elements that constitute a system but from the myriad connections between them' (Mason, 2008) and that 'the emergence of learning, of creativity, of imaginative and critical perspectives' (Mason, 2008) is fostered.

RESEARCH BRIEFING 2.1: COMPLEXITY THEORY

The complexity theory approach to addressing challenges in education was pioneered by Davis and Sumara (2008) who characterized a complex adaptive system as a system which displays behaviours of complex self-organization and emergence, adapts of its own accord due to agent behaviours, rather than because of the influence of central authorities, and exhibits 'capacities that can exceed the possibilities of the same group of agents if they were made to work independently' (Davis & Sumara, 2008, pp. 14–15, 81). Also, 'education ... conceived in terms of expanding the space of the possible ... must be principally concerned with ensuring the conditions for the emergence of the as-yet unimagined' (Davis & Sumara, 2008, p. 135). Six necessary but not sufficient characteristics of a complex adaptive system have been identified (Davis & Sumara, 2008, pp. 129–52) for such emergence:

1. *Agents* or 'neighbours that must interact with one another are ideas, hunches, queries, and other manners of representation' but are 'not physical bodies or social groupings' (Davis & Sumara, 2008, p. 142).
2. Internal *diversity* of the agents is defined as 'the range and contours of possible responses' (Davis & Sumara, 2008, p. 138).
3. Internal *redundancy* refers to 'the deep commonalities of its agents' and 'enables interactions among agents' and 'when necessary, ... makes it possible for agents to compensate for others' failings' (Davis & Sumara, 2008, p. 139).
4. *Decentralized control* refers to 'emergent conceptual possibilities' and 'interpretive possibilities' (Davis & Sumara, 2008, p. 144).
5. Sources of *disruption* or randomness 'compel the collective to constantly adjust and adapt' (Davis & Sumara, 2008, p. 147).
6. Sources of *coherence* 'allow a collective to maintain a focus of purpose/identity' (Davis & Sumara, 2008, p. 147).

In a complex adaptive system, all the agents participate collectively, each with their unique contribution, and enabling constraints 'maintain a delicate balance (or equilibrium) between sufficient coherence to orient agents' actions and sufficient disruption to allow for flexible and varied response' (Davis & Sumara, 2008, pp. 143, 147, 148).

A powerful metaphor and conceptual tool for viewing and understanding the long-term dynamics of learning in complex adaptive systems is the adaptive cycle (Gunderson & Holling, 2002). In three-dimensional space the adaptive cycle is shaped by three properties of a complex adaptive system: the inherent potential of the system that is available for change, the connectedness or controllability (in terms of the relation with the context) that may impact the change, and the adaptive capacity of the system. A two-dimensional representation of the complex adaptive cycle is a lemniscate illustrated in Figure 2.1, which is adapted (Rewitzky, 2023) from that of Gunderson and Holling to include the sources of disruption and coherence of a complex adaptive system for emergence.

It has been explained (Rewitzky, 2023) that the potential of a complex adaptive system describes the capacity for change in terms of the internal diversity and internal redundancy available. Too much diversity will limit the potential for meaningful interactions between agents and too much redundancy will inhibit the potential for creativity (Davis & Sumara, 2008). The potential ranges from certain to uncertain about what are possible future responses to a source of disruption. The connectedness of a complex adaptive

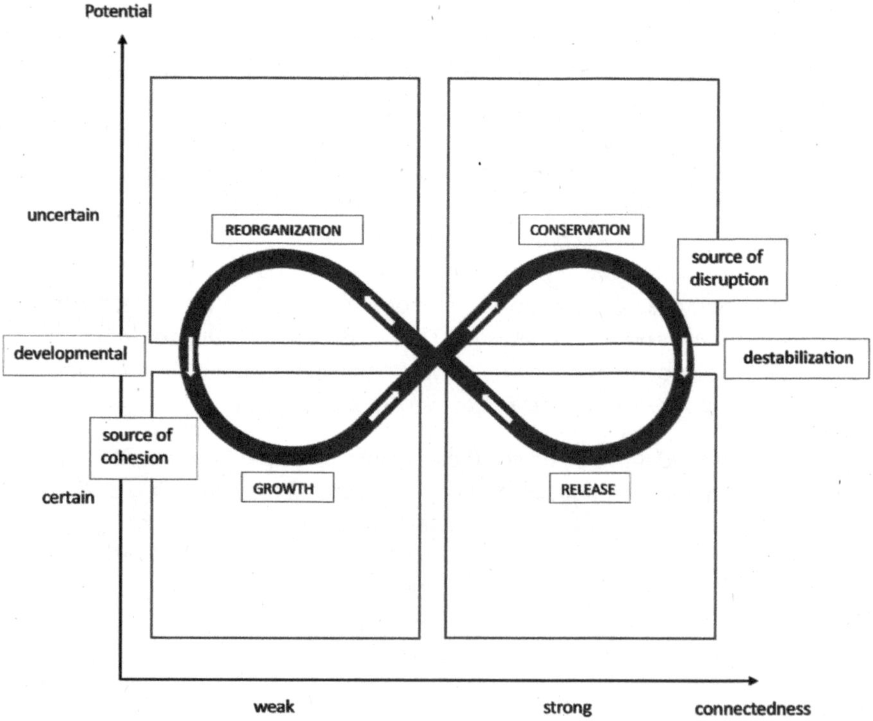

Figure 2.1 *Adaptive cycle.*

system describes how well a system adapts using internal connectedness of agents as opposed to centralized controlled by the context (which is not conceptually distinct from the system). It ranges from weak centralized control (and strong interconnectedness of agents) to strong centralized control (and weaker interconnectedness of agents).

The adaptive cycle of learning is shaped by two complementary phases: a destabilization phase and a developmental phase. This may be described in relation to the hidden curriculum of doctoral education as follows. The destabilization phase will be triggered by a source of disruption that may leave the doctoral researcher feeling unmotivated, lacking focus, uncertain, negative and/or having low esteem. As the openness to embrace the disruption increases (or potential increases) and the decentralized control increases the system will move to the reorganization phase, depicted as the back loop of the cycle. This will involve the doctoral researcher transitioning from withdrawing, questioning or doubting a source of disruption to (re-)building connections, (re-)introducing healthy study-life boundaries, (re-)investing in self-care as well as interpreting and exploring the source of disruption from different perspectives. As a balance between internal diversity and internal redundancy is restored, the doctoral student will enter the developmental phase having built a stronger foundation of self-awareness and emotional intelligence. There will be a decrease in potential while the decentralized control will remain unchanged. The foreloop is the slow, incremental phase of growth with renewed energy. There will be acceptance of the source of disruption and the consequences. As the system moves from the growth phase to the conservation phase, the doctoral researcher will focus on their endurance to successfully complete their doctoral journey. Then there is an increase in potential for change, making the system open to a new source of disruption.

In relation to the hidden curriculum, the adaptive cycle model for understanding learning gives the doctoral student reassurance that, if open to it, growth opportunities arise from sources of disruption such as stepping out of their comfort zone and/or from unproductive periods along their doctoral journey.

The adaptive cycle with release, reorganization, growth and conservation phases aligns with Wallas' (1926) cyclical model of the creative process of preparation, incubation, illumination and verification. Preparation involves preparatory work on a problem that focuses the individual's mind on the problem and explores the problem's dimensions. During the incubation phase the problem is internalized into the unconscious minds. Then there is a phase of feeling the solution is eminent until that moment of insight when the idea bursts forth during the illumination phased. This is followed by consciously elaborating on the idea and application thereof during the verification phase.

There have been several models of the hidden curriculum in doctoral education, including the doctoral learning ecological model (Elliot et al., 2020b), the conceptual framework of the hidden curriculum of doctoral education in terms of the intersection of graduate competencies, student learning experiences and relevance (Rossouw & Frick, 2023) and the four-stage competence development framework (Elliot, 2022).

Doctoral education journey as a complex adaptive system

A doctoral education journey may be viewed as a complex adaptive system in the sense of Davis and Sumara (2008) since it is self-organizing through connections within and beyond; it is continually adapting existing knowledge, understanding, experiences to incorporate new concepts, ideas or insights which may be isolated or connected; there is a balance between individual and collaborative work as well as between challenges and development opportunities; and there is emergence of learning beyond the formal curriculum through inductive reasoning, experimenting, going astray, making choices, narrative changing and building resilience.

REFLECTIVE ACTIVITY 2.1: CONDITIONS FOR THE EMERGENCE OF LEARNING FROM THE HIDDEN CURRICULUM

We now identify and discuss the six conditions for emergence of learning from the hidden curriculum along our doctoral education journey – agents, internal diversity and internal redundancy, decentralization of control, sources of disruption and sources of coherence.

1 **Agents**

Before embarking on their doctoral journey, the doctoral researcher will have prior personal, educational, professional work experiences and/or roles. Each of these may inform the insights, views and understandings of the doctoral researcher which in turn give rise to agents in the complex adaptive system.

Along their doctoral education journey the doctoral researcher will build a network of research collaborators, peers, academic colleagues and professional academic support colleagues. Each may offer guidance or support at some stage of the doctoral journey. Each will be represented in the complex adaptive system in terms of agents corresponding to their ideas, insights and skills.

The identity of the doctoral researcher may be influenced by the discipline(s) within which the research is being conducted, their research supervisor(s), the institutional research culture (including developmental, collaborative or competitive) as well as their preferred research paradigm(s) and work style. The associated representations would be agents in the complex adaptive system.

Each discipline has a particular knowledge structure (Bernstein, 2000) and this may influence how knowledge is understood, created and valued. For example, mathematics may be described as having what Bernstein termed a 'horizontal knowledge structure' with 'strong grammars' – that is, 'a series of specialized languages with specialized modes of interrogation and criteria for the construction and circulation of texts' (Bernstein, 2000). Each of these knowledge structures and their representations would be an agent in the complex adaptive system.

Central to doctoral research are different levels of abstraction, thinking and reasoning. The associated representations of each level for each of these would be agents in the complex adaptive system.

From social connections, including personal (family, friends, fellow doctoral researchers), community (clubs, societies) and work-related (internships, volunteering), collective or individual view(s) or perception(s) arise. Each of these would be represented in the complex adaptive system as an agent corresponding to their positive or negative vibes they bring the doctoral research along their doctoral journey.

2 Internal diversity AND internal redundancy

Along a doctoral education journey, the internal redundancy (overlaps) refers to learning experiences that emerge from meaningful interactions and stability. Strong social networks, for example, first-generation doctoral researchers, international doctoral researchers, female doctoral researchers or next generation academics, may impact the social integration, sense of belonging and well-being of the doctoral researcher.

Internal diversity (differences) refers to learning experiences in the hidden curriculum that will inspire creativity, innovation and change according to Davis and Sumara (2008). Diverse experiences and perspectives may be gained through, for example, intentional interaction with international doctoral students either at home institution or through a research exchange programme, collaboration with industry for valuable opportunities to apply their research or to take them out of their comfort zone as well as diverse supervisory approaches such as the cohort model.

3 **Decentralization of control**

Decentralized control in relation to the hidden curriculum refers to the doctoral researcher having space to follow their passion and time to engage with what really interests them. The emerging learning experiences may include an increase in ownership of the research project and self-efficacy.

At the start of their doctoral journey, the doctoral researcher may be part of the research group(s) and research network(s) of their supervisor(s). Over time there may be a shift from the supervisor(s) imposing their structure (their research group) on a social collective (Davis & Sumara, 2008, p. 143) to the doctoral researcher establishing their own research network and contributing to the establishment of a creative collaborative space for connecting ideas, insights and understanding relevant for their research project. The resulting increase in the interaction of ideas, insights and understanding from other researchers results in a decentralization of control of the research context by the supervisor(s). The actual interaction between the parties in a research group varies; some supervisors exert a lot of control, other may be almost laisse-fair.

As the doctoral researcher progresses along their doctoral journey, research independence may be gained if there is decentralized control in the sense that the supervisor(s) relinquish(es) control of the research project and allow(s) the doctoral researcher to discover things for themself while being available as a sounding board for ideas as may be needed.

4 **Sources of disruption**

Along their doctoral education journey the doctoral research may be faced with multiple and potentially overwhelming challenges which will shape their doctoral learning experience. At the start of the doctoral journey, as the doctoral researcher transitions from being a knowledge consumer to a knowledge creator, there may be a source of disruption arising from the tension between 'doing research' and 'being a researcher' as they try and understand what doctoral research entails and what may be acknowledged as research independence (Gower, 2023).

There will be a potential source of disruption in the shift from a rigorous competitive space where individuals are immersed in their discipline in solitude to a creative collaborative space where lecturers and students together explore and discover ideas and reflect on their insights and understanding (Su, 2020).

Poor work-life boundaries, poor time-management, poor writing skills are sources of disruption that may impact productivity of the doctoral research. Limited future career opportunities, little to no sense of control of the direction and focus of the research project, lack of feedback on progress, unclear research goals and milestones, and non-constructive criticism are further sources of disruption that may leave the doctoral research feeling unmotivated to focus on their research.

Through overcoming these sources of disruption, the doctoral researcher grows intellectually and personally, developing emotional resilience and problem-solving skills essential for success along their doctoral education journey and beyond.

5 Sources of coherence

Research conversations with supervisors and research collaborators provide a source of coherence if there is an opportunity for the doctoral researcher to gain insight into the nature, context and impact of research in their discipline or field.

Documents with rules and regulations for doctoral degree admission, progression and graduation as well as guidelines for the code of conduct between the doctoral researcher and their supervisor(s) provide source of coherence for the doctoral learning experience while also acknowledging varied research and supervision approaches or styles.

Postgraduate skills development programmes may be viewed as providing sufficient coherence while allowing each doctoral researcher to make an informed choice about their preferred style and approach. The aim is to supplement the discipline specific tools, skills and strategies with, for example, systems for accountability, solid scientific foundations, workshops on scholarly writing skills, presentations skills as well as strategies for structuring a thesis, time management, project management and stress management.

Supportive family members, guardians or friends are sources of coherence along the doctoral education journey in that they help to re-build self-confidence during setbacks, to keep the study-life-family balance and to celebrate even the smallest of successes.

Sustaining good health and psychological well-being is a crucial source of coherence in relation to the hidden curriculum throughout the doctoral journey.

Questions:

- How do I recognize and respond to the hidden agents (e.g. peers, institutional culture, informal networks) that influence my doctoral students' development beyond the formal curriculum?
- In what ways do I foster both internal diversity and redundancy, encouraging a range of perspectives while reinforcing shared values and practices, in my supervisory approach?
- How do I navigate and leverage disruptions (e.g. academic setbacks, personal crises, disciplinary shifts) and coherence (e.g. shared goals, structured support) to support meaningful learning and growth?

Uncovering the hidden curriculum using the adaptive cycle

We now illustrate in Figure 2.2 how the adaptive cycle may be used to uncover the hidden curriculum of the doctoral education journey.

Before the cycle starts the doctoral researcher would have acquired a level of competence in a particular discipline or field of study that is considered suitable for the purpose of doctoral research, for example, a research masters qualification. The cycle starts with the doctoral researcher reading scientific papers with the goal of uncovering knowledge gaps or open questions in the existing literature for further exploration. There would be an uncertainty in the potential value of exploring some of these. There would be a strong connectedness to the existing research. Based on their previous research experience, the doctoral researcher may feel that their goal and approach for obtaining the doctoral qualification are certain. However, they may not fully appreciate the extent or level of analysis, reflection, critical thinking and reasoning required to identify a research topic, formulate a relevant research question, develop a clear research proposal and decide on the suitable

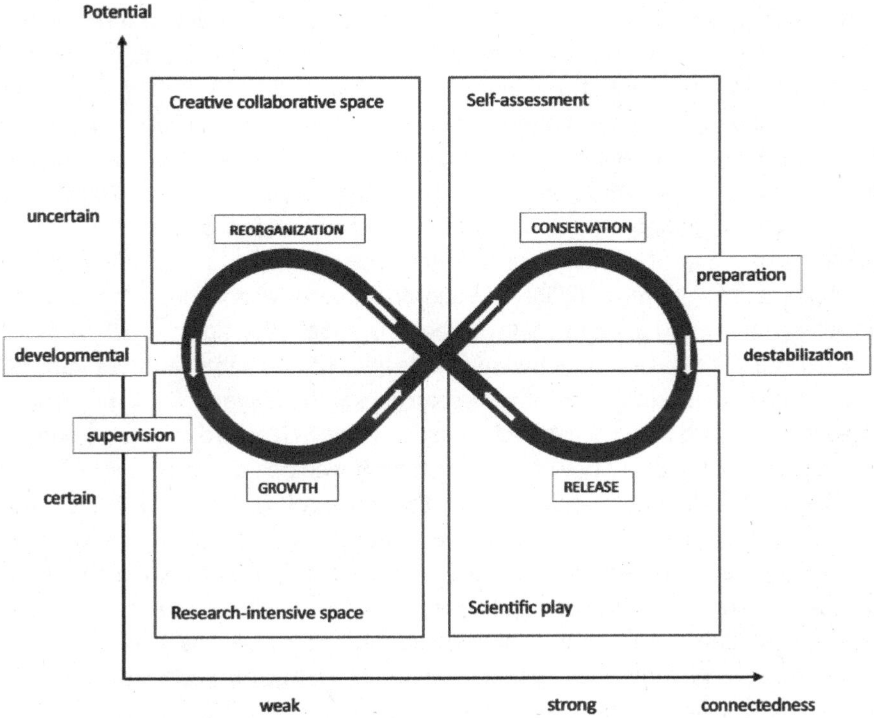

Figure 2.2 *Adaptive cycle of hidden curriculum.*

research methodology. This would be destabilizing in the sense that the research experience may seem unrelated to prior experiences.

At some point the doctoral researcher may be encouraged by their supervisor(s) to step back from the literature review and play with some ideas that are evolving. Focusing on a few potential research topics may bring some certainty of the potential research question. Receiving guidance from the supervisor(s) would maintain some connectedness with successful research strategies. Such scientific play would be a release from expecting a well-defined task and learning to emerge from doing as for undergraduate, honours or masters studies.

There is then a move from the release to the reorganization phase as the doctoral researcher starts acknowledging what knowledge and skills (including level of abstraction, level of reasoning, depth of critical thinking) will be needed to tackle their research question while also realizing they may still need to develop a higher level of research skills proficiency. The back loop of the cycle, from the release phase to the reorganization phase, is meant to be relatively fast, otherwise the doctoral researcher may feel their progress is slow and that they do not have what it takes to undertake doctoral research. This may then 'trigger imposter feelings, burnout and dissatisfaction with the doctoral experience' (Elliot, 2022).

During the reorganization phase, the doctoral researcher will have identified a research topic and will be in a creative collaborative space for formulating their research question(s) and determining their research methodology. This will involve interaction among agents for gaining confidence in what doctoral research entails for their identified research topic (including level of abstraction, level of reasoning, depth of critical thinking) and how to conduct doctoral research (including academic writing, data collection, ethical considerations) on that topic. There will also be interaction of agents (including insights, understandings of the doctoral researcher and other researchers in the research field) for gaining deeper insight and focus of research questions that will make a new contribution to the research topic and how to approach such research questions.

During the developmental phase, the doctoral research will have an increased awareness of their strengths and shortcomings. There will be developmental opportunities for building confidence and research skills proficiency. There will also be opportunity for focused academic reading, deep thinking, academic writing, research presentations (at seminars, workshops, conferences), conversations with established as well as emerging researchers as the doctoral researcher grapples with their research topic.

The doctoral education journey enters the growth phase when there is certainty on the research statement to be investigated, the rationale for conducting the research, the research methodology as well as the research contribution to be made. There will be a strong connection between the various agents (including the insights, ideas, understandings, reasoning approaches) but a weak connection with the institutional and supervisor research context. The doctoral researcher, rather than their supervisor(s), will be in control of the various dimensions of the research project. In this sense the connectedness is weaker.

The front loop of the cycle, from the growth to the conservation phase, is relatively slow and involves many months and years of 'continuous use of the desired skills leading to the conservation phase and a type of proficiency that comes almost naturally and/or with much less effort' (Elliot, 2022). At this stage of the doctoral education journey, the doctoral researcher is developing their research independence and identity as will be conveyed through their research approach, findings, writing and presentations as well as increasing their confidence in self-assessing the strength, integrity and impact of their research.

During each phase there may be unexpected sources of disruption from the hidden curriculum, including navigating intense pressures, balancing research expectations, adhering to tight deadlines, dealing with personal challenges

REFLECTIVE ACTIVITY 2.2: UNCOVERING THE HIDDEN CURRICULUM THROUGH THE ADAPTIVE CYCLE

Step 1: Choose a student experience

Select one doctoral student you have supervised (or are currently supervising). Try to recall their journey in a holistic way, from initial stages to more advanced points in their programme.

Step 2: Guided reflection using the adaptive cycle

Use the questions below to reflect on the student's experiences in each phase.

Growth phase

When did the student show signs of excitement, ambition or intellectual curiosity?

How did informal influences (e.g. peer groups, culture, institutional messaging) shape their early approach to doctoral work?

What implicit expectations may have been communicated at this stage (by you, by others or by the institution)?

Conservation phase

At what point did the student settle into established routines, academic norms or project direction?

What elements of the hidden curriculum were being reinforced (e.g. publishing pressure, competitiveness, perfectionism)?

Did these norms serve the student's learning, or constrain it?

Release phase

Has the student experienced disruption or crisis (e.g. personal difficulties, research failure, confidence loss)?

How was this period handled (by the student, by you and by the broader environment)?

What unspoken rules or expectations may have contributed to this breakdown?

Reorganization phase

How did the student adapt or rebuild after the disruption?

Were there signs of new identity formation, critical reflection or changed direction?

What hidden curriculum elements were challenged or transformed in this phase?

Step 3: Visual mapping

Sketch the adaptive cycle on a blank page (a simple loop with four labelled quadrants).

Place short descriptions of your student's experiences or quotes from supervision meetings in the relevant phases. Use arrows to show how they moved through the cycle.

This visual tool can help you see:

Where students tend to get stuck

When the hidden curriculum is most active

How transitions are supported, or not

Step 4: Synthesis and reflection

After completing the questions, take time to reflect on the following:

What patterns did you notice across the cycle?

Are certain phases more vulnerable to the hidden curriculum than others?

How did your supervisory practices influence what was learned, formally and informally?

Were there moments when your intentions diverged from the student's interpretations?

What might you change in your practice to better support student learning and identity development across all phases of the cycle?

Consider language, expectations, mentoring style or how you respond to disruption and reorganization.

or strained relationship between supervisors and the doctoral researcher and their supervisor(s). These could trigger destabilization and another linked adaptive cycle which will need to be navigated before proceeding with the phase in which the disruption occurred.

Conclusion

In this chapter we have described how our doctoral education journey may be viewed as a complex adaptive system with three complementary characteristics which need to be balanced for enriched learning experiences to emerge from the hidden curriculum. Firstly, there needs to be a balance between development phases, with sources of coherence providing orientation, development and focus, and destablization phases, with sources of disruption bringing challenges, stress, pressure and distractions. Secondly, there needs to be a balance between the internal diversity and internal redundancy of ideas, insights, understandings, experiences, approaches and beliefs. Thirdly, there needs to be a balance between interconnectedness of agents and decentralized control allowing the doctoral researcher freedom to balance collaborative and individual work while creating knowledge and developing their own research identity.

Through navigating the adaptive cycles along our doctoral education journey there will be progression through the formal curriculum while being enriched from the learning experiences emerging from the hidden curriculum. For this emergence there needs to be openness to embrace a disruption, reflection to appreciate the value of addressing the disruption, passion and connection to develop the skills for responding to the disruption as well as inspiration and support to grow and adapt in response to the disruption.

Working with the hidden curriculum in doctoral education is important for the transformative growth of doctoral students, for increasing awareness of the different stages of the doctoral education cycle and the emotional toil doctoral students may experience during some of these stages, for providing self-management strategies through sources of disruption and a welcoming space as a source of cohesion. The hidden curriculum also uncovers the unspoken rules of engagement and expectations to succeed in a particular academic environment. It is important to have open spaces in academic department for informal interactions between all the role players in the department, including professors, early career researchers, postgraduate students as well professional academic support staff.

References

Barnett, R. (2018) *The ecological university: A feasible utopia*. London and New York: Routledge.

Bernstein, B. (2000) *Pedagogy, symbolic control and identity: Theory, research, critique*. Lanham, MD: Rowman and Littlefield.

Bloom, B.S. (1969) *Taxonomy of educational objectives: The classification of educational goals: Handbook I, cognitive domain*. New York: McKay.

Broady, D. (1981) *Den dolda läroplanen. (The hidden curriculum.) KRUT artiklar 1977–1980*. Stockholm: Symposion, p. 315.

Carmichael, T. & Hadzikadic, M. (2019) 'The fundamentals of complex adaptive systems'. In: Carmichael, T., Collins, A. & Hadžikadić, M. (eds) *Complex*

adaptive systems. Understanding complex systems: Views from the physical, natural, and social sciences. Switzerland: Springer Nature, pp. 1–16.
Cilliers, P. (1998) *Complexity and postmodernism: Understanding complex systems*. London and New York: Routledge.
Davis, B. & Phelps, R. (2004) 'Complicity: An introduction and a welcome', *Complicity: An International Journal of Complexity and Education*, 1(1), pp. 1–7.
Davis, B. & Sumara, D. (2008) *Complexity and education: Inquiries into learning, teaching, and research*. New York: Routledge.
Elliot, D.L. (2021) 'A "doctoral compass": Strategic reflection, self-assessment and recalibration for navigating the "twin" doctoral journey', *Studies in Higher Education*, 47(8), pp. 1652–65.
Elliot, D. L. (2022) 'A "doctoral compass": strategic reflection, self-assessment and recalibration for navigating the 'twin' doctoral journey', *Studies in Higher Education*, 47(8), pp. 1652–65. https://doi.org/10.1080/03075079.2021.1946033
Elliot, D.L., Bengtsen, S.S.E., Guccione, K. & Kobayashi, S. (2020a) *The hidden curriculum in doctoral education*. Switzerland: Palgrave Pivot, Springer Nature.
Elliot, D.L., Bengtsen, S.S.E., Guccione, K. & Kobayashi, S. (2020b) 'A "doctoral learning ecology model"'. In: Elliot, D.L., Bengtsen, S.S.E. & Guccione, K. (eds) *The hidden curriculum in doctoral education*. Switzerland: Palgrave Pivot, Springer Nature, pp. 3–16.
Gower, O. (2023) 'The hidden meanings of "independent research(er)"'. In: Elliot, D.L., Bengtsen, S.S.E. & Guccione, K. (eds) *Developing researcher independence through the hidden curriculum*. Switzerland: Palgrave Pivot, Springer Nature, pp. 235–40.
Gunderson, C.S. & Holling, L.H. (2002) 'Resilience and adaptive cycles'. In: Gunderson, C.S. & Holling, L.H. (eds) *Panarchy: Understanding transformation in human and natural systems*. Washington, DC: Island Press.
Holland, J. (2006) 'Studying complex adaptive systems', *Journal of Systems Science and Complexity*, 19(1), pp. 1–8.
Kuhn, L. (2008) 'Complexity and educational research'. In: Mason, M. (ed.) *Complexity and the philosophy of education*. Chichester: Wiley-Blackwell, pp. 169–80.
Mason, M. (2008) 'What is complexity theory and what are its implications for educational change?' *Educational Philosophy and Theory*, 40(1), pp. 35–49.
Morrison, K. (2006) Complexity Theory and Education. *Paper presented at the Asia-Pacific Educational Research Association*, Hong Kong Institute of Education, November.
Morrison, K. (2010) 'Complexity theory, school leadership and management: Questions for theory and practice', *Educational Management Administration and Leadership*, 38(3), pp. 374–93.
Piaget, J. (1968) 'Piaget's point of view', *International Journal of Psychology*, 3(4), pp. 281–99.
Radford, M. (2008) 'Prediction, control and the challenge to complexity', *Oxford Review of Education*, 34(5), pp. 505–20.
Rewitzky, I.M. (2023) 'Re-envisioning our journey of learning in mathematics', *International Journal of Mathematical Education in Science and Technology*, 54(9), pp. 1928–43.

Rossouw, N. & Frick, L. (2023) 'A conceptual framework for uncovering the hidden curriculum in private higher education', *Cogent Education*, 10(1), p. 2191409. doi:10.1080/2331186X.2023.2191409

Sambell, K. & McDowell, L. (1998) 'The construction of the hidden curriculum: Messages and meanings in the assessment of student learning', *Assessment & Evaluation in Higher Education*, 23(4), pp. 391–402.

Sambell, K., McDowell, L. & Sambell, A. (2006) 'Supporting diverse students: Developing learner Autonomy via Assessment'. In: Bryan, C. & Clegg, K. (eds) *Innovative assessment in higher education*. London: Routledge, pp. 158–68.

Snyder, Benson R. (1971) *The hidden curriculum*. New York: Alfred A. Knopf.

Su, F. (2020) *Mathematics for human flourishing*. New Haven, CT: Yale University Press.

Wallas, G. (1926) *The art of thought*. New York: Harcourt, Brace.

3

Process and Product

Marit Honerød Hoveid and Dagrun Astrid Aarø Engen

Introduction

Embarking on a PhD project is often a 'game changer' in a person's life. Developing a research project that has the potential of bringing new and vital knowledge into the world is a responsibility that most early career researchers find daunting. *How's 'little' me going to be able to accomplish this* is not an uncommon experience. In the end, everyone is destined to 'produce' a thesis and defend their work, usually in front of a committee of reviewers or opponents. However, doing doctoral research and going through doctoral education represent a variety of practices across the globe. In most academic settings today, doing a PhD is defined as the highest degree you can achieve academically – meaning doing a PhD is also defined as an educational process. We believe this is an important aspect of PhD work – sometimes overlooked. Often it is required of the candidates that they can demonstrate independent research work, as if they have the knowledge, skills and competencies without the education needed.

Across disciplines and fields of research, as well as national contexts, the trajectory that is followed will vary immensely. Therefore, saying something generic about how *process and product*, and the *purpose* of how a PhD project is lived and practised is challenging. Even so, we believe there are some traits that are common, and there are fundamental questions and common concerns that can be brought to life in a reflexive supervision practice in doctoral education.

We, the authors, are situated in social science and humanities research, more specifically in the field of university pedagogy and higher education research. Also, our context is the Norwegian higher education system, where doctoral researchers as a rule are employed in a three- or four-year type scholarship, defined as a temporary position to conduct a research project and to complete their doctoral education. All scholarships are advertised, and a selection committee will choose the candidate they find best qualified and suited for the given PhD position.

In this chapter our intention is to point to some of the aspects that we have found are crucial for the process an early career researcher is embarking on with a doctoral project. The backdrop for our discussion is that the university has become increasingly production-oriented in a specific manner where the notion of product as deliverable outputs and process as time-spent-o n-completing-production is dominating. This has become the dominant logic. As a result the emphasis is put on pushing timelines for activities within a doctoral project. By exerting more control over accomplishments of activities, an increased focus is put on monitoring that all the deliverables of the project are accomplished on time. We see this in various websites like https://www.finishontime.org/ and books with titles like *Shorten the Time to Doctorate: A Guide to Managing Your Ph.D. as a Project*. In this output-driven approach, the emphasis on the final product is more on completion than on content. The content and ambition of the product will then need to be adjusted to make it feasible and probable without doubt that the candidate is able to deliver on time. To question this logic is common in academia; at the same time it is taken for granted as the way things are.

Our point of departure is different. Anyone who have embarked on a PhD project know that before you get to the final product – a thesis and all it entails in terms of insight, understanding and knowledge – so many things can happen, unpredictable occurrences that will delay your project, and prevent you from following your *plan*. On top of that, much of what you are doing in a research project requires time – the *process is both slow and fast,* it has a complex or even a multitude of rhythms (Dakka, 2024). As pedagogues, we think that the *educational* processes of self-formation as well as the cultivation of the academic field that is actualized through working on and towards the product(s) has the potential of changing one's own life, the field of research and hopefully also have an impact on society in some way.

Our aim with this chapter is to give PhD candidates confidence in their own project and encourage them to take charge of it so that they feel they own it. As supervisors, we have experienced that better research can be conducted on time if we give leeway in how a candidate accomplishes a PhD project, combined with a little less stress related to reporting *on time.*

Instead, we underscore that curiosity and exploration need foregrounding in doing research. In other words, we argue for less prescription and more individuality, collectivity and acknowledgement of different temporal rhythms in doing academic work. Simultaneously knowing that a PhD project has time constraints, but within the time given there are many ways of reaching the end of the process.

Our take on the PhD project is that the interconnectedness between the *process* and the *product* is fundamental. For analytical reasons, though, we are directing our attention to *process* and *product* separately in the first part of this chapter. In the last part of the chapter, we will draw some conclusions based on what we suggest in the two separate parts.

PROCESS: A research process – an educational process

We want to give an example of reflecting on practice and use our own context at the Norwegian University of Science and Technology (NTNU) as a case. Our outset is in the concrete practices and the core actions that are involved in a PhD, which involves doctoral *research* and doctoral *education*. We will start with analysing how the process is formalized by the institution and operationalized in regulations or advice for the everyday practices that are involved in 'doing' a PhD.

In the Norwegian HE system, *doctoral education* is formalized by a certain amount of ECTS points to be earned (produced) through specific *PhD courses* or types of courses. The *thesis* (article based or a monograph) and a *defense* (viva) are the formal products of *doctoral research*. Also, there is an idea of doctoral research and education as integral parts of the completion of the doctoral graduation programme as a trajectory, and as integral aspects of the ideal formative processes of a PhD. However, between different disciplines and professions there are various views on whether the emphasis should be on education or on research. This is one of the issues that are negotiated on national and institutional policy level. At our university, PhD's are organized in programmes through regulations and policy treated primarily as education, but still 'the most important component of a PhD degree is the research project and the PhD thesis' (NTNU PhD Handbook), and it is noteworthy that a PhD is placed under the university's research administration.

A PhD at NTNU is regulated by national and institutional law and advised in NTNU's *PhD Handbook*. In the handbook the institutional view of the PhD process is evident. The common standard that all PhD education at NTNU must follow is operationalized as follows: (1) admission and start-up; (2) implementation; (3) completion and submission of the doctoral work. This expresses the overall idea of the process in an administrative and legal sense. It has a formalized start, and after an agreed time it has a formalized end. During the agreed period certain actions should take place and certain products should be produced. To these actions and products, the standard includes specific duties and responsibilities of the involved parties, which are the PhD candidate, the supervisor(s), the department/research group, the PhD programme and the faculty (i.e. school, college). The handbook also includes a 'Guide to the PhD process', which gives non-compulsory standards. In the guide, two more aspects of the process are operationalized as (4) termination before the agreed time and (5) the doctoral examination (public defence/viva).

In the first phase – admission and start-up – the PhD candidate's responsibility is predominantly *to produce* plans and proper applications. The main products are an application for admission to a PhD programme; a complete project description; a plan for the required coursework; an application for necessary permission for the use of research data and ethics compliance. In the implementation phase the PhD candidate should, in addition to conducting research, participate actively in the academic community, international conferences and research communities, keep supervisors and department/faculty continuously informed about relevant changes, publish research output and submit annual progress reports and evaluations. In the completion phase, the PhD candidate should produce the doctoral work within the agreed time limit and produce documentation that the required coursework is passed and an application for admission to the doctoral examination. Then in the examination phase, the PhD candidate must plan and perform the public defence (disputation/viva).

The first point we draw from our case is that the process in this formalized language is operationalized as a linear production process. Certain products are to be produced at certain (pre-set) times, and the fulfilment of these productive actions counts as tokens of a successful process. When speaking and thinking of the process in a PhD, we are confronted with a choice of metaphors. It makes a difference for our understanding of purposes and practices of a PhD if we see the process as a journey or a trajectory, as building a brick-and-block construction or as leaping from stepping stone to stepping stone on a pathway. In our case, the NTNU PhD handbook, the chosen metaphors are the journey and *the pathway*. The journey along the pathway is to be *planned* and the plan should include setting *milestones* – that is products along the way, operationalizing the process and allowing for instances of control. The supervisors' most important role is 'to *pave the way* for good individual PhD *progression*' (NTNU PhD Handbook, our emphasis). In administrative language the notion of quality in the PhD process is closely linked to process assurance and planning for control. This is evident in the guidelines for supervisors: 'It is especially important to define the content of the project in detail, to define the required scope, and to agree on milestones' (NTNU PhD Handbook).

The second point we draw from this example is that the explicit practices that are involved in this production line are mainly production of text, writing and presentation. The need to read and reflect in an educational process is only implied and hidden in the overall notion of 'coursework' and 'research'.

REFLECTIVE ACTIVITY 3.1: SUPERVISORS' ROLE IN SHAPING THE PhD PROCESS

Vignette: Supervising the PhD process

Dr Larsen has been supervising PhD candidates for over a decade. She prides herself on being a structured and supportive mentor. However, she often finds herself questioning whether her approach provides enough flexibility for candidates to explore their academic interests while still adhering to institutional guidelines. One of her current PhD candidates, Alex, thrives on independence and prefers to work in broad, exploratory ways, while another candidate, Priya, seeks detailed guidance and frequent check-ins. Dr Larsen wonders: How can she adopt a flexible supervisory style to best support both candidates while ensuring they meet their milestones? How much structure is too much, and how much freedom is too little?

Key questions:

As a supervisor, consider your role in guiding PhD candidates through their academic process. Reflect on the following questions:

Which metaphor best describes how you perceive your role in a PhD candidate's process (e.g. a navigator, a coach, an architect, a mentor on a pathway)?

How do your expectations and approaches align with the structured milestone-based model outlined in the NTNU PhD Handbook?

How do you balance process assurance and control with allowing for academic exploration and flexibility?

How do you adapt your supervision style to fit different PhD candidates' needs and working styles?

If you were to redefine your approach to supervision in a way that best supports both academic quality and a reflective approach, what key changes would you make?

We learn from colleagues around the world that this more managerial handling of a PhD as a production process is gaining ground and is becoming more and more prominent for all involved. When using this case as an outset for reflection, relevant questions could be: Is this a common trait across formal PhD descriptions at university level worldwide? What characterizes the formalized process at your university? What happens to the fundamental practices of *thinking, reading, writing* and *communicating* if they are understood and formed by a production logic?

Or we could turn the question towards its own premises and ask: What is missing in this production logic? This is what we will point to: Being oriented towards educational purposes in educational processes, we see that a long process like a PhD could lose some of its potential for creating innovative and 'new' knowledge, if the production process is too dominated by accountability purposes. The discovery aspects like serendipity, curiosity and creativity involved in doing research require trust in operating without pre-set targets. Allowing the process to evolve usually means letting time evolve with exploration, reading, writing and reflection. This can of course be pushed by deadlines, and there may be truth to the saying that academics need deadlines to deliver. However, we believe that when one is immersed in the creative work of research, external deadlines help steer a process, but they do not really interfere with what is going on in the research, and once in a while more time is simply needed. Time to do and to be catches the very essence of academic research work, and points towards processes as movements and change that require flexible time as an enabling medium. For this reason, doing research is incompatible with an understanding of an educational process that solely relies on the notion of chronological time. Duree – experienced, or 'inner' time – is a Bergsonian notion, which the concept of an educational processes relies on.

In many cases a PhD project is part of a larger whole, a national or even an internationally funded project. In other cases, a PhD is more of a singular project developed by the PhD as standalone research. Irrespective of this, the research is always directed towards a specific discipline or transdisciplinary thematic and the basic idea is that the PhD research should help advance the knowledge base of the specific field. This of course then involves looking back, usually undertaking various forms of reviews – meaning having to *read* a lot of literature from the defined field. A shortcut in this work happens when these reviews become descriptive iterations of *who, what, when* – without any deeper conceptual aspirations. Descriptive iterations of who did what at what time can have bibliometric value – digging into what prior research has accomplished and in what way it taps into your research more fundamentally requires a more comprehensive process that involves an interpretative encounter between the doctoral researcher and other researchers communicating in text. Such a process involves reflection and a reflexive research process where you might make discoveries that could change what you are doing – and what then? One scenario is that you must retreat to 'start' to redo the whole outset for the PhD project. With the overall objective of thorough research, a 'restart' is wanted, with the aim of completion on time as principle, this becomes unwanted – a 'worst case scenario'.

This seldom happens, but what we want to warn against is the kind of reviews of former research that are predominantly descriptive without a deeper evaluation of what the reviewed research reflects in terms of your own research. To dig deeper, to see what is there (not only finding 'a gap'), one needs time to read, ponder and reflect to be able to self critically understand and develop in what ways former research plays into your own. This is a much more complex and difficult task to do – and again – it requires time. We argue that the only way for a PhD candidate to discover and develop a professional 'gaze', maybe even an embodied way of seeing and interpreting the knowledge field you are working within, requires a type of slowness in the process. It is not developed by planned milestones or by ticking of tasks as accomplished – what we are talking about here involves the whole person – reflecting what we said earlier that a PhD project can be a life changer. When working with knowledge and contributing to the systematic knowledge of a field, you are engaged in processes that are intertwined with your own life. What we address here is not primarily the fundamental question of some research fields being more distanced and separated from the lived life of the researcher than others. That is also part of the picture, but we are addressing the research process itself as a 'knowing' process. Your life processes will be intertwined with your research as your self-reflection evolves and you discover new understanding. Your understanding is a driver for new understanding in the specific field. Where this will take you in the course of the PhD is unpredictable. In relation to this, *good* supervision is about much more than helping a candidate to complete tasks *on-time* – it is about supporting a deeper understanding that will influence the whole person and the knowledge field.

The educational process of a PhD has to do with learning the handicraft of research. Formally – as we have seen in our case – a candidate will have to fulfil the requirements defined as coursework. The educational processes that are realized through the research come 'on top of' this. Our point is that a PhD project has the potential of changing a person's life. This means that throughout the process you need to continuously work on what it is you want to say – in relation to the questions your research is raising. This part of the process requires critical, reflexive thinking and working. This is not always pleasant or easy to do. This sort of ongoing self-critical work can potentially create an existential crisis and, in that respect, it has the potential of becoming self-destructive. *Good* supervision in this sense involves taking part both in the critique and in the 'self', and it involves a solidaric research environment.

So, what we have pointed to in this part is that the formal requirements of PhD projects tend to underline accountability and managing a project as if it were any regular production process – the 'manufacturing' of a PhD. We are overstating this a bit to point out that managing a PhD project is the easy part – setting up milestones or deadlines for what to do when can help get the PhD done within the given timeframe. However, the process one undertakes in a PhD has an expectation of knowledge contribution to a field. This requires much more, and it entails an engagement in processes that could potentially change your own life. We term these processes *educational* (Engen, 2021; Hoveid & Hoveid, 2019). As we have stated earlier, an educational process is impossible without a product. Let us now turn to the product in a PhD.

PRODUCT: A text – new insight, new knowledge

In the previous part, we drew your attention to the many products to be produced and presented along the way, the milestones, the tasks to be ticked off. We will get back to them but let us first turn to the final product of the PhD. To finalize the work in a PhD is always an accomplishment. Research trajectories usually include various difficulties that require the candidate to find ways of handling resistance, unexpected occurrences, rejections and then to make judgements about what to do. This means most PhD candidates have sometimes during the process had some doubts about whether they would manage and if they would be able to get the project finished. Unfortunately, the hurdles some encounter lead to not completing the project – in some cases better support structures could have prevented this from happening – other times not.

In our case – PhDs at NTNU – the completion and submission of the doctoral work (thesis) and the doctoral examination (public defence) are the last deliverables, or products, of a PhD project. It is not uncommon to have to resubmit a thesis in the Norwegian system, because the first review asks for revisions, minor or major. A thesis, although it takes various forms depending on field and methods of research, usually is a written text, sometimes accompanied by some concrete intervention, model or performance. Getting to this final point of doing a PhD is tightly interconnected with the whole process. In other words, *the product reflects the process and vice versa.*

At NTNU the submitted PhD work should be of 'high quality'. Doctoral work must be an independent academic work of international standard and

REFLECTIVE ACTIVITY 3.2: NAVIGATING THE TENSION BETWEEN ACADEMIC RIGOUR AND PRACTICAL CONSTRAINTS

Supervisors play a vital role in guiding PhD candidates through the complexities of their research process. One of the most challenging scenarios is when a candidate's findings require a fundamental revision of their initial project. While this revision might be beneficial in terms of academic rigour and long-term research quality, it may also present significant challenges in terms of project timeline and the emotional toll on the candidate.

Key questions

Supporting the candidate through emotional and practical challenges
How would you approach the emotional impact on your candidate if their research needs to be redefined or restarted? How would you participate in a collective reflective practice to help the candidate?

How do you recognize when a revision of the research scope is necessary versus when it's due to external pressures such as time constraints? What tools or methods can you use to guide your candidate through this realization?

Balancing rigour with feasibility
What concrete steps can you take to help the candidate recalibrate their project while ensuring it stays within the realistic scope of a PhD programme?

How do you balance the need to push for high-quality research with the awareness of the tight timelines that PhD candidates face? How can you help them set achievable milestones without sacrificing the academic integrity of their work?

Fostering resilience and adaptability
In your experience, how do you help candidates develop the resilience necessary to face setbacks and changes in direction? What kind of emotional and practical support do you offer in these situations?

Reflecting on your role as a mentor, what tools or resources can you provide to your candidates to help them constructively develop new directions in their research?

Past experiences and lessons learned
Think about past candidates who have faced similar situations. How did you handle it, and what were the results? What do you feel you did well, and where could you have done better?

Did the candidates eventually benefit from a 'restart' in their research? What outcomes emerged from this difficult situation? How can you apply these lessons to future candidates facing similar challenges?

Effective communication and setting expectations
How do you invite the candidate into a process where expectations are set at the beginning of the project with the aim of establishing an understanding for a trajectory that may take various directions? How do you revisit these expectations throughout the process? What can you do to maintain an open line of communication so that candidates feel comfortable discussing issues as they arise, rather than waiting until a crisis point?

should be on a level enabling it to be published as part of the academic literature in the discipline. The final product should demonstrate that the candidate is able to do research in line with common criteria inherent to the field, meaning that the work demonstrates the mastery of the handicraft of doing scientific research. Also, the work should comply with an international standard (defined by the specific academic field, more or less formally) and most importantly, the research should demonstrate the independent thinking and reflection of the candidate, and the project should contribute some new knowledge to the field. Apart from this – the way you conduct the research is manifold – the key to 'high quality' is that you must be able to account for what you have *done* and *why* – referred to as transparency (of reliability and validity) in the research process. This might seem like very 'loose' criteria, but the truth is that doing research across academia must be defined as open-ended to allow for creativity and originality in the research process. We believe this is where some of the crux lies. In order to find guidance in the open-endedness, you might be driven to follow a 'script', introducing the risk of a more or less predictable outcome of the research. This is a vital point for asking questions for reflection. What drives you to choose methods for your research? What is given and what is lost in a method or script that provides certain steps to follow?

In our field – the social sciences – we sometimes encounter an understanding of research as equal to following a given method. We hold it as essential to point out that it is not. Following a script has more in common with computing, a machine can do it. It is not until you start analysing and interpreting the data, what you as a human being can do, that the research takes on meaning. This is, we believe, the most strugglesome aspect of a research process. Over a period in academia space and time, the interpretative aspects of PhD research seem to have been downplayed. We see this in the product, in what is produced in research, and what doctoral researchers report as implicit or explicit expectations in their PhD processes. We see that the many products demanded to be presented along the way shape the form and the content of the thesis. And we see that the many milestones sometimes get in the way of finding time to do research that is creative and interpretative and requires 'production-free' time.

We want to stress that there is no opposition between being accountable – on time – and being able to work interpretively with data. All data need interpretation and it is the quality of the interpretation process that will give the PhD research its originality. In higher education, no matter how it is institutionalized in your context, you need to be able to handle two conflicting demands at the same time, being accountable and interpretative/creative. And we raise the question whether the increased control that is exerted in the processes of doing research is connected to candidates wishes for procedures and 'safe' scripts? As a generalization it is a speculative question.

REFLECTIVE ACTIVITY 3.3: THE TRANSFORMATIVE POWER OF PhD RESEARCH

PhD research is more than an academic task; it is a deeply personal process with the potential to transform both the researcher and society. This activity encourages reflection on the profound impact of research, both individually and socially.

Key questions:

Personal transformation
How have you observed PhD candidates change during their research process? What personal development have you experienced through your own research?

Balancing personal investment and objectivity
How do you help candidates maintain objectivity while deeply investing in their work? How can you guide them through emotional highs and lows?

Social impact
How does your research, or that of your candidates, contribute to societal change? How can you support candidates in recognizing the broader relevance of their work?

But as an outset for reflection in and on your own context, it requires you to consider what aspects of procedures and control are evident in your situation.

Calling this a *crux* in the research process means we see this as something candidates struggle with, something they are unevenly equipped to deal with, and where the supervisor can be crucial by helping the candidate to handle all the uncertainties that arise. What we warn against is a strict managerial approach to research where the following of a script is equalled to doing research. In today's academic landscape, where universities push for deliverables, reporting and on-time management – basically to secure/control that a project is finalized within the given timeframe – seem to push candidates towards these kinds of solutions. Holding back and acknowledging the *slowness* of doing research take a type of stamina that one needs to develop to acquire a well thought through and original research work. This needs support from supervisors. We believe it is possible to do both – be on time and to acknowledge the slowness of the process. The challenge is the handling of it in the everyday of doing PhD research. Often reflected in the immense optimism a candidate has at the beginning of a project where there seems to be an abundance of time and the more constrained candidate towards the end where time is about to run out. The process from beginning to end entails a process with its own flow, we argue. Without bringing lived life into the research process, it tends to become stalemate and of less value. In a way the metaphor of mass-production is fitting.

We are of the opinion and value PhD research as a unique contribution. When a candidate invests him/herself into the process and product of research it has a life-changing potential individually and socially.

Concluding remarks

In this chapter we have tried to juggle the control and constraints of doing a PhD with what is important to recognize if research – in this case PhD research – is going to bring new knowledge into the world. In the era of artificial intelligence (calling it intelligence is probably stretching it too far!), the recognition of what PhD research is beyond the mere accountable aspects of reporting, being on time and thus having checked the right deliverables is crucial. To generate new knowledge and insight is a deeply human activity – machines cannot truly interpret the social world of human beings – it can store and systematize large amounts of data. But this is not the same as 'know edging' – an awkward interpretation of the Norwegian word 'kunnskaping'. By making the noun 'knowledge' into a verb, we point to the procedural aspect of creating knowledge. This 'knowledging' is happening on different levels, institutional and personal, in a research process and we argue that neither we must forget its importance. The educational process of PhD work is developed through the kind of experiences a person has with the work done. If the work of a PhD becomes mostly focused on managerial aspects – of reporting, rather than engaging in the messy work of interpretation, analysing and discussing, what ultimately has been learned in the process will differ. We argue for the need to acknowledge slowness and 'production-free' time to accomplish socially relevant research.

In this part we have also highlighted the possibility of bringing oneself into the world, as a world of human interaction. So, beyond all the deadlines and deliverables of a PhD project lie possibilities for self-understanding that also can have societal impact. These possibilities make a PhD journey, if we use that metaphor, an engagement with oneself and others that are unique for research.

References

Dakka, F. (2024) 'Rhythm as form and forms of doctoral education'. In: Cole, D.R., Rafe, M.M. & Yang-Heim, G.Y.A. (eds) *Educational research and the question(s) of time*. Singapore: Springer, pp. 171–88. doi:10.1007/978-981-97-3418-4_10

Engen, D.Aa. (2021) Rom for utdannande prosessar? Ei empirisk og teoretisk utforsking av vegleiingsrommet i masterutdanning (Room for Educational Processes? An empirical and theoretical exploration of the supervision room in master education). PhD thesis. NTNU.

Hoveid, H. & Hoveid, M.H. (2019) *Making education educational*. Berlin: Springer Nature.

NTNU (no date) Handbook on Doctoral Education. Available at: https://i.ntnu.no/wiki/-/wiki/English/PhD+Handbook

4

Different Types of Doctorates

Barbara Kehm

Introduction: Heading towards mass production of doctoral degrees?

Since the year 2000 the goal to increase the number of doctoral degree awards has been high on the policy agenda in many countries around the world. And this policy agenda also called for serious reforms of doctoral education. In Europe, these developments were triggered by the European Commission's agenda to create a European research area – one year after the Bologna reforms to create a European higher education area. The establishment of a European research area basically failed in the end but the presidential conclusions at the initial conference in Lisbon in the year 2000 called on the EU member states to make Europe 'the most competitive and dynamic knowledge economy in the world' (Council of Europe, 2000). Among other things, this entailed increasing the number of doctoral degree awards and reforming doctoral education and training in such a way that the degree holders were fit for the knowledge society and economy. Ever since then, the number of annual degree awards has increased steadily in most European countries. Furthermore, many other countries around the world that aimed to become knowledge economies and societies as well picked up on this issue and began to increase their doctoral degree awards as well. To find doctoral education and training on a policy agenda dominantly geared towards increasing (national and European) economic competitiveness has had several implications for this phase of qualification which will be analysed and described in the following sections. The first implication is a diversification and differentiation of doctoral degree types in the face of growing numbers of awards. The second implication is the role of doctoral degree holders for the knowledge economy and knowledge society and the resulting global competition. The third implication is that doctoral education and training is no longer a purely academic affair serving the reproduction of the professoriate but is expected to contribute to economic innovation in a major way. This means that doctoral students also have to be trained for non-academic labour markets. The conclusions will discuss whether the multiplication of doctoral degree types and the expected role of doctoral degree holders in the knowledge economy and society can be reconciled with the previous functions of doctoral degrees as a first step in an academic career.

Diversification and differentiation of degree types

The growth in the number of doctoral degree awards during the last twenty to twenty-five years has led to similar effects as could be observed during the phases of higher education expansion and the resulting emergence of mass higher education. This development had basically two consequences. First and at an abstract level, massification needs structuring (cf. Palfreyman, Tapper, 2009). Dominant structures in mass higher education are either horizontal diversification (different types of institutions, curricular or programme differentiation) or vertical differentiation (rankings, elite versus non-elite institutions). Second and at a more practical level, institutional, programme and/or degree diversification can cater to the increasing multitude of needs and goals of a highly diverse student body. And this is basically what has happened to doctoral education and training as well. The growing number of doctoral students entailed a multiplication of goals and needs which led to a diversification of degree types. By now most European countries distinguish at least between a research doctorate and a professional doctorate. However, further research has yielded altogether nine different degree types, which will be introduced briefly in the following (Kehm, 2020).

The research doctorate

For the research doctorate, which is the most traditional form of doctoral education and training, the dissertation is central and is expected to be an original contribution to the knowledge base of a discipline or research domain. Independent of the fact whether the degree (or title) is acquired within the framework of a structured programme including coursework or in the framework of a master-apprentice relationship, the research doctorate, as a rule, is a prerequisite for an academic career and typically serve the reproduction of the professoriate. By being responsible for the training, professorial supervisors also have a gatekeeper function. Using the example of six disciplines, Golde and Walker (2006) have characterized the main purpose of doctoral education in the research doctorate as developing students to be 'stewards of the discipline'. The goal of such a training is a scientific or scholarly ideal type characterized as someone 'who can imaginatively generate new knowledge, critically conserve valuable and useful ideas, and responsibly transform those understandings through writing, teaching and application. A steward is someone to whom the rigour, quality, and integrity of the field can be entrusted' (Golde & Walker, 2006, p. 5). This rather normative image contrasts starkly with the image generated by Slaughter and Leslie (2000) of the successful academic as a 'capitalist entrepreneur' who has recognized the demands and challenges of market orientation, competition and globalization in the emerging knowledge societies and knows how to draw advantages from these developments.

The professional doctorate

A number of European countries (e.g. Austria, Belgium, Denmark, France, the Netherlands) have by now picked up the British trend to explicitly distinguish between a research doctorate and a professional doctorate. In Germany, for example, this is not (yet) the case. The professional doctorate is not awarded in all disciplines but restricted to subjects like business administration, medicine and health care, education, engineering, social work, etc., that is to subjects which have a relatively demarcated field of professional practice. In professional doctorates the title usually includes an indication of the professional field (e.g. DBA for Doctor of Business Administration or EdD for Doctor of Education) while research doctorates are typically awarded distinguishing between the sciences (Dr. Sc.) and the humanities (Dr. Phil.). Quite a number of publications have appeared over time on the professional doctorate (Bourner et al., 2001; Green & Powell, 2005; Park, 2005), a systematic overview was provided a few years ago by Hawkes and Yerrabati (2018). Despite the fact that the professional doctorate has been met with more acceptance in recent years, the high number of publications about this doctoral degree type seems to be related to some extent to the fact that in academic circles the professional doctorate is often looked down upon as a second-class doctorate so that pressure for legitimation increased.

The professional doctorate is defined as a programme of advanced studies which – apart from fulfilling university criteria for the award of the degree – is geared towards satisfying a particular demand from a professional group outside the university and towards developing research skills needed within a professional context (Bourner et al., 2001, p. 219). In the United Kingdom, professional doctorates are typically taken up by people who are pursuing a professional career and are employed. Therefore, professional doctorates are frequently offered as part-time programmes and usually require several years of professional experience. Tuition fees are often covered fully or in parts by the employer. The target group wants to gain the degree in order to be eligible for promotion in their professional field. Consequently, the research work carried out for the dissertation is regarded less as a contribution to the knowledge base of a discipline but more as a contribution to the development of a professional domain. The dissertation then focuses on the generation of new but more applied knowledge and the topic is often generated from the respective professional practice. In some areas, for example, in engineering, the dissertation can also have the form of a larger or a series of smaller projects that are carried out within the framework of actual professional practice.

The taught doctorate

By definition, the taught doctorate consists of a substantial proportion of coursework and is offered in the United Kingdom and in Portugal. Other European countries have started to introduce this type as well. Typically, there will be a defined curriculum and learning outcomes will be graded and weighted for the final grade. As in the research doctorate students are supposed to contribute to the generation of new knowledge but they do this in the framework of a research project the results of which are summarized in a project report. The report is presented in the framework of an oral examination and is graded as well. In contrast to the two-phase doctorate in the United States (coursework first, then research and writing of the thesis), the coursework of the taught doctorate is spread over the whole period of degree training. The oral examination and the grade of the research project report are regarded as an equivalent to a dissertation and its defence.

PhD by published work

The model of the PhD by published work is known in Germany since the nineteenth century (where it is called 'cumulative dissertation'). From there it spread to other parts of the world, mainly the United States but also to Belgium, the Netherlands and Sweden. At second glance the British model of the PhD by published work shows that it differs to some extent from the German model of a 'cumulative dissertation'. Both models are basically characterized by combining several articles that have appeared in peer reviewed scholarly or scientific journals into a book and providing them with a coherent framework. But while this option is open for many candidates in Germany, the PhD by published work is awarded in the United Kingdom almost exclusively to members or alumni of the university awarding the degree (Green & Powell, 2005, p. 72).

This model has frequently been criticized for its lack of consistency, for differences in the definition of what constitutes a publication, for its threat to other forms of doctoral education, and for the difficulty to provide adequate supervision. Furthermore, in this type of the doctorate it is predominantly a product which is evaluated and graded and not the process of getting the degree itself. Therefore, most countries which provide this opportunity have regulations in place that determine the character and the content of the dissertation and possibly also the question whether and in which form a programme of additional studies has to be taken (Green & Powell, 2005, p. 71).

REFLECTIVE ACTIVITY 4.1: THE 'PAPERIZATION' OF DOCTORAL TRAINING

The economic reframing of doctoral education has given rise to the phenomenon of 'paperization', prompting critical reflection on its implications. The increasing popularity of the 'doctorate by publication', while offering flexibility to candidates, has also amplified the pressure to publish in high-impact journals. Institutional demands for visibility, accreditation and rankings, coupled with national policies linking doctoral output to performance-based funding, have positioned publishing as a dominant measure of success. This emphasis often comes at the expense of deep, sustained engagement with a specific research topic.

The 'paperization' trend reflects wider systemic challenges in academia, where the prioritization of quantity and public output has created a saturated landscape of publications, many of which lack meaningful impact. This "industry of papers" perpetuates a competitive cycle that values output metrics over substantive contributions to knowledge. Additionally, it marginalizes research addressing critical local or global inequalities, as such work frequently struggles for recognition in high-impact journals dominated by institutions in the Global North.

These issues raise important questions:

To what extent does the emphasis on publishing shape the purpose and experience of doctoral training?

How can doctoral candidates balance the demands of publication with meaningful, reflective engagement in their research?

How might doctoral education better support scholarship that addresses global inequities and fosters impactful, transformative knowledge?

The practice-based doctorate

The practice-based doctorate is a terminological specificity of the British university system, but it is also awarded in Australia. It denotes the award of doctoral degrees in the Arts and in Design. While German universities, for example, award doctoral degrees in musicology or art history, the highest degree in the various arts as such (e.g. painting, sculpting, acting, singing, dancing, playing an instrument) is called '*kuenstlerische Reife*' (which can be translated literally as 'artistic maturity'). No doctoral degree is awarded in these fields.

The practice-based doctorate increased in importance with the integration of colleges of art into the universities in the 1990s in the United Kingdom. The degree is awarded as a result of coursework in the framework of which students are familiarized with theories and research methodologies and the presentation of a work of art or a performance as a substitute for the dissertation. The presentation or performance is accompanied by a text in which the candidate explains how he or she has arrived at the result or product by applying research methods. This is regarded as generating new knowledge through practice. Successful candidates are also expected to demonstrate how their work of art is related to other works of art in the same field (in a theoretical, historical, critical or visual context) and to evaluate possible effects. In the field of composition frequently not just one work is presented but a whole portfolio. In the oral examination the work of art will be presented or performed, and the candidate demonstrates on the basis of the accompanying text that she or he has sufficient knowledge and appropriate skills to independently generate new knowledge.

The practice-based doctorate is contested in the United Kingdom because – compared to all other models of the doctorate – it shows the least proximity to the traditional notion of a dissertation. However, about half of all British universities offer such a doctorate (Green & Powell, 2005, p. 100ff.). In Germany there is a debate going on about creating the possibility of doctoral degree awards in the arts. Currently only one higher education institution, the Film University in Babelsberg near Berlin, has the right to award a doctoral degree in filmmaking.

The 'new route' or integrated doctorate

The model of the 'new route PhD' was developed by ten British universities as a form of brand name in 2001 with the purpose of attracting more international students, especially from Middle Eastern countries. In the meantime, it is offered by more than thirty British universities. It is a four-year degree involving a one-year period of studying for a research Masters degree followed by a three-year period of PhD studies. The programme basically consists of three (integrated) elements: a taught component in the area of research methods and subject specialization, another taught component in the area of transferable skills and the work on a dissertation (disciplinary or interdisciplinary). Admission can be granted right after having completed a Bachelor's degree. The taught components are frequently offered in the framework of related Master's programmes but accompany the whole four years envisaged for getting the degree. For the taught components 240 credit points are awarded (www.newroutephd.ac.uk).

However, in comparison to the research doctorate the taught elements are more important and also prescribed in more detail with respect to the qualifications and competences to be acquired. After having finished all the coursework there is also the possibility to write a master thesis instead of a doctoral dissertation and finish after one year with a Master's degree.

In Germany, this model has become known as 'fast track PhD' and is offered in specific subjects at some universities. As a rule, in Germany the Master's degree is required for admission into doctoral programmes or acceptance as doctoral candidate. The 'fast track PhD' model offers transition into the doctoral phase for particularly talented students right after their Bachelor's degree.

Basically, the new route PhD as well as the fast-track PhD follow the American model of an integrated graduate education in which the master level and the doctoral level are combined in terms of the coursework to be done. However, the American model clearly separates the coursework phase from the phase of writing a thesis which follow each other in sequence and are not integrated. This American two-phase approach results in high drop-out rates after having finished the coursework or (compared to Europe) a rather long time to degree (between six and nine years). Despite the fact that a fast track to the doctoral degree is possible in exceptional cases in many European countries, the European University Association has recommended that the Master degree should constitute the rule for access into doctoral programmes or the doctoral qualification phase (see EUA-CDE website: http://www.eua.be).

Two models of the joint doctorate

The model of the joint doctorate is characteristic for doctoral programmes jointly offered by two or more universities which may be located in the same region, the same country or in different countries. A study carried out by EUA (2005) about changes in doctoral education in Europe included a survey among member institutions. As many as 18 per cent of the responding universities confirmed that they offer joint doctorates. Leading countries in terms of the number of joint doctoral degree programmes are Germany, Spain, France, Italy, the United Kingdom and the Netherlands (EUA, 2005).

In the EUA study (EUA, 2005, p. 28ff.) the joint doctorate is characterized as follows:

- a joint curriculum for the taught components which has been developed in close cooperation among the participating institutions; the doctoral students take courses at several universities;
- an agreement signed by all participating institutions clarifying funding issues and other matters (e.g. mobility, quality assurance, degree award).

Certification of a joint doctorate is regulated in various ways: from award of the degree from the university at which the candidate is enrolled, to a double degree on the basis of joint supervision (i.e. co-tutelle arrangements) and a joint degree.

Joint doctorates are predominantly awarded by universities (or more exactly by faculties and departments) cooperating in transnational networks. The advantages for doctoral students are that in most cases phases of mobility are built into the programme, that they often have more than one supervisor and additionally access to further experts in their field who are members of the network. However, the actual practice differs from this ideal type. Joint doctorates have a higher degree of internationalization and more opportunities for mobility, but they are often not based on a joint curriculum of the participating partner institutions.

A particular variation of the joint doctorate is the 'European doctorate', which does, however, not yet exist in practice. The idea and an informal initiative came up at the beginning of the 1990s during a meeting of the Confederation of European Rectors' Conferences (an organization which has merged with the former CRE to become EUA). The 'Doctor Europaeus', as the planned title was to be, is contested until today, although there is a consensus about promotion and improvement of European cooperation in doctoral education and mobility of doctoral students. Currently another initiative in this direction is undertaken by the European Commission offering funding for joint doctoral programmes emerging from partner universities of an Erasmus Mundus Programme. The difficulty of putting the idea into practice is due to the fact that within Europe there is an increasing competition for best talent among institutions and on the national level a more competitive research policy and innovation strategy. Thus, best talent is not easily 'shared'. Still, the discussion about the 'Doctor Europaeus' has been revived in the context of the Lisbon Strategy to create a European Research and Innovation Area (EUA, 2005) and several Italian universities are offering it by now.

The cooperative doctorate

The cooperative doctorate is a German model in which professors from universities and professors from universities of applied sciences (the latter have, apart from a few exceptions, no right to award doctoral degrees) jointly supervise a doctoral candidate who graduated from a university of applied sciences. Taught elements of such a degree are typically offered in the framework of a university graduate school or doctoral programme while the research topic is often developed between the candidate and his or her professor from the university of applied sciences. The degree is awarded by the university. This model has emerged in the framework of attempts of research-oriented universities of applied sciences to acquire the right to award doctoral degrees. By now a handful of these universities have been granted the right to award doctoral degrees after a thorough evaluation of their research capacity and under very specific conditions. Once Germany officially introduces a distinction between research and professional doctorates, more universities of applied sciences will claim to receive the right to award professional doctorates. Thus, the university monopoly is eroding at the margins. However, the output of successfully completed doctorates at universities of applied sciences is still very low; in fact, official statistics show that only one doctoral has been awarded so far by a university of applied sciences.

The industrial doctorate

The industrial doctorate is mostly awarded in engineering fields and is a rather applied degree which can be found in quite a number of European countries (e.g. Denmark, France, Germany, Italy, the Netherlands, Switzerland). The research work of the candidate is carried out, for example, in the R & D department of a company and is oriented towards the solution of a particular problem or issue. The research work is jointly supervised by a senior engineer of the company and a university professor while taught elements; theory and methodology are supervised by a university professor. Research topics frequently emerge from work in that company during an internship. There is also a European Industrial Doctorate (EID) which is supported in the framework of

Marie S.-Curie Actions. The EID requires that the two organizations involved (a university and a company) must come from two different European countries. This type of doctorate is quite common at technical universities but also has shown to have problems. Very recently a debate has emerged in Germany about the so-called 'cuckoos' egg dissertations'. It seems that a number of private sector companies have established their own doctoral programmes or try to attract young engineering graduates with the promise to offer them an opportunity to get a doctoral degree. All this, without seeking to establish a partnership with a university. Once the dissertation is finished, the companies approach a professor (or a university) with the request to organize the defence and award the degree with the threat that they will stop their research funding for that professor or university if they refuse. This has led to some protest from the side of the universities and official letters to policy makers to stop such kind of initiatives and to companies with the request to observe the sole right of universities to award the degree and seek their cooperation beforehand. Quite frequently there are also issues of confidentiality of results involved while universities continue to insist that results of academic work should be available for open access. However, the industrial doctorate is a particularly interesting model for countries in which doctoral degree holders mostly serve the reproduction of the academic profession (e.g. Portugal, Poland, Spain) and the non-academic labour market is not very open for doctoral degree holders. With the availability of an industrial doctorate private sector companies can experience the added value of research-based knowledge production.

To conclude, in the description of the diversification of doctoral education and training models in Europe one issue stands out. It is related to the fact that a considerable increase in numbers typically leads to a diversification of forms of training as not all doctoral candidates aim for jobs in academia any longer and thus have different purposes and motives to get a doctoral degree. Developing a highly qualified workforce for the non-academic sectors of the economy tends to be a phenomenon of knowledge societies and economies and is by now a relatively well-established phenomenon in Europe. Basically, the growth in the number of doctoral degrees awarded has led to a re-envisioning of the degree itself.

The hidden agenda: Knowledge economies and doctoral degrees

With the increased importance of doctoral degrees for knowledge economies and societies we can also observe an extended policy field. Doctoral education and training is no longer an almost exclusive academic affair but has become an object of institutional management as well as national and supra-national policy making.

I will start my argument by looking at the *supra-national level*: the inclusion, in 2003, of doctoral education as a third cycle of a tiered structure of studies and degrees in the framework of the Bologna Process was, among other things, a consequence of the European Council's and Parliament's strategy in the year 2000 to create a common European Research Area (Lisbon Summit, 2000). As mentioned already, this strategy was supposed to develop Europe into the most dynamic knowledge-based economy of the world in order to be globally competitive. To achieve this, the number of doctoral degree holders was to be increased, and doctoral candidates were supposed to become better prepared for non-academic labour markets (see next section). The descriptors for the doctoral level of the European Qualifications Framework clearly reflect this. And the Lisbon strategy also signifies that Europe is engaged in a global competition concerning its economic competitiveness and capacity for innovation. In particular, doctoral degree holders are expected to make a major contribution to this competition.

At the *national level* we can observe an increasing number of initiatives and support programmes to establish a structure for doctoral education and training (e.g. doctoral programmes, graduate schools and curricula). The number of doctoral degrees awarded has become part of indicator and performance-based funding and budgeting in negotiations between universities and the state about the overall budget as well as in intra-institutional budget allocations. German universities produce about 35 per cent of doctoral degrees in the European Union, that is almost 27,700 in 2022 (Destatis, 2023). The German Excellence Initiative supports the establishment of graduate schools, and the German non-academic labour market is relatively open for job seekers with a doctoral degree. This also implies that the unemployment rate among doctoral degree holders in Germany is the lowest compared to all other levels of education and training. National policy, by and large, is in favour of increasing even further the number of doctoral degree holders because it is believed that a high number of people with high qualifications provide a competitive advantage for the economy on a global scale. And this holds true for all European countries, not just Germany.

At the *institutional level* the policy field has also changed, especially with regard to the performance indicator 'doctoral degrees'. Almost all universities encourage their professors as well as faculties and departments to increase the number of doctoral degrees awarded and to reduce the time-to-degree. The number of doctoral degrees awarded is an important indicator when measuring research output, in the context of establishing a profile and reputation as a research-intensive institution, and in the framework

REFLECTIVE ACTIVITY 4.2: ECONOMIC FRAMING OF DOCTORAL EDUCATION

Doctoral education, once primarily situated within the sphere of academic research, has been reframed as a foundational element of economic competitiveness (Council of Europe, 2000). The Lisbon Strategy, for instance, sought to position Europe as "the most competitive and dynamic knowledge-based economy in the world," with the production of doctoral graduates viewed as integral to achieving this ambition. Yet, this economic framing often eclipses the traditional function of doctoral education as a site for the production of theoretical and practical knowledge.

This reorientation aligns with the notion of cognitive capitalism, where knowledge is commodified and instrumentalized as a key economic resource for market-driven objectives. Consequently, doctoral training increasingly aligns with industrial and economic priorities, emphasizing innovation and labour market preparedness over reflective, critical, exploratory or transformative research.

Such trends invite deeper questions about the purpose of doctoral education:

Should doctoral programmes be reduced to mechanisms for generating knowledge workers?

Could they instead foster the reflexive development of doctoral candidates, equipping them to engage with a complex and evolving world?

Or might they more directly address the pressing global crises of the twenty-first century?

of the general competition for reputation and funds. But there is a further intra-institutional dimension. Within universities competition has also become stronger and departments, research groups or individual professors who have been particularly successful in terms of doctoral education and training can negotiate for extra funds or other material advantages (e.g. additional human resources or better infrastructure). Traditionally a high number of successful doctoral supervisions contributed to the individual reputation of a given professor within the scientific community. This continues to be the case; however, it is complemented by the aspect that this success is also supposed to contribute to the reputation of the institution. Those less successful in the endeavour of doctoral education and training might end up not being allowed to supervise doctoral candidates any longer. In fact, in some European countries (e.g. Spain) it has become a normal procedure to train academic staff in doctoral supervision and require a corresponding certificate before allowing them to carry out doctoral supervision.

As described in the previous section, there have also been changes at the *individual level*. Compared to maybe ten or fifteen years ago, doctoral students nowadays have to acquire a considerably broader set of skills and competences during their education and training. It is no longer sufficient for them to become 'stewards of their discipline' (Golde & Walker, 2006). This tended to be the case as long as doctoral education and training mainly served as an entrance ticket for the academic profession. Today doctoral degree holders in most countries (there are still a few exceptions) are in high demand in the knowledge-intensive sectors of the economy, in public administration, in the media and many other non-academic sectors. And it is expected that they have some international and inter-cultural experience, that they have people skills, network skills, presentation and negotiation skills, leadership capabilities, etc. Having said that, two questions remain that still need further research and debate. The first question is who, within the university, has the knowledge and competence to convey these extended skills set? Certainly not the traditionally trained and educated university professors. The second question is whether academic careers in Europe with their extended periods of uncertainty and even precariousness continue to remain sufficiently attractive to attract the best and the brightest. And these periods of uncertainty have become longer because the opportunities for an academic career as well as the related decision-making processes have now shifted to the post-doc period.

Academic and non-academic labour markets

In most European countries, the doctoral degree has traditionally been the entrance ticket to the academic profession. In particular, the research doctorate mainly served the reproduction of the professoriate, and continues to do so almost exclusively in quite a number of European countries. In contrast to this, the German non-academic labour market has always been quite open for doctoral degree holders. Most of the large companies in the car production sector but also chemical and pharmaceutical companies have their own research and development departments and are keen to hire doctoral degree holders because they have the knowledge of the state of the art in their discipline or field and promise to be innovative. Other sectors of the economy also offer attractive jobs for doctoral degree holders, including law firms and schools. The field with the highest number of doctoral degree holders and doctoral degrees awarded annually is medicine because a doctoral degree is basically part of the education and training of future medical doctors.

There have not been many attempts to explain the fact why the German non-academic labour market is so open for doctoral degree holders. One such attempt has been made early on by Teichler (1991). In his seminal article 'Towards a Highly Educated Society' he argued that research and research findings in the 1970s and 1980s were pre-occupied with concepts like 'over-education' and that there were concerns about appropriate employment of highly qualified (i.e. university educated) graduates. Teichler argued further that higher education expansion should lead to a fundamental change of concepts about graduate employment, including work tasks and division of labour. This was necessary because the (non-academic) labour market was 'no longer determined by scarcity of highly qualified labour but rather by opportunities to make use of a new wealth of potentials' (p. 11). According to Teichler, higher education expansion was leading to a 'push effect' (1991) that was having major effects on the structure of the labour market. I would argue that we are currently seeing a very similar development, including the 'push effect' – at least in some European countries – concerning the employment of doctoral degree holders on the non-academic labour market. One sure sign for such a development is that despite the fact that German universities have a rather high output of doctoral degree holders annually, the unemployment rate among them is the lowest compared to all other university level degrees as well as to all other degrees in general (in all types of education and training). In Germany, only about 10 per cent of all doctoral degree holders eventually end up permanently in academia. The remaining 90 per cent find jobs on the non-academic labour market.

This argument is supported by the results of a research project jointly funded by OECD, UNESCO and Eurostat a few years ago to analyse and systematically measure the careers of doctoral degree holders in the non-academic labour markets. The results were published in 2016 (Gokhberg et al., 2016) and focused mainly on doctoral degree holders in science and technology fields. Despite the fact that the statistical data bases for such analyses are not yet very good (nationally as well as internationally), the researchers came to the conclusion that there are now 'multiple career paths' and a 'labour market premium for doctorates in OECD countries' (Gokhberg et al., 2016, p. 5).

Conclusions: Serving many masters?

To conclude, I'd like to emphasize three main points that have clearly contributed to the fact that doctoral degrees have diversified.

First, during the last twenty to twenty-five years, we can observe a gradual increase in the number of doctoral degrees awarded annually. It is possible to speak of a massification of doctoral degrees similar to the general massification of student numbers in the 1960s and 1970s in Europe (in the United States somewhat earlier, i.e. in the 1950s), which led to a diversification of institutional types and degree programmes. With the growth of graduate students interested in getting a doctoral degree but not necessarily interested in an academic career, doctoral degree types and programmes began to diversify to cater for the broader spectrum of motivations for getting a doctoral degree.

Second, the Council of Europe's call in the year 2000 to make Europe the most competitive knowledge economy in the world has led to a further increase in the number of doctoral degrees awarded, this time, however, as part of an economic and competitive agenda. In addition, global rankings and national excellence initiatives contributed in a major way to the growth in numbers and an increased competition.

Third, with these developments we can also observe an extended policy field concerning doctoral degree production. Doctoral education and training is no longer an almost exclusive academic affair but has become part of policy agendas reaching from the supranational to the national and to the institutional level. Thus, it is possible to say that today the production of doctoral degree holders serves multiple purposes and is no longer restricted to the reproduction of the academic profession itself.

REFLECTIVE ACTIVITY 4.3 REFLECTING ON THE FUTURE OF DOCTORAL TRAINING

The chapter raises important questions about the future of doctoral training. Who within universities is equipped to train students in the diverse skills now required? How can institutions reconcile the traditional functions of doctoral training with the demands of the knowledge economy? Might doctoral programmes be broadened so that students are better equipped to gain understandings – theoretical and practical – of a complex, moving and entangled world? Questions such as these point to the need for a more holistic approach to doctoral education, one that integrates academic, professional and societal goals.

References

Bourner, T., Bowden, R. & Laing, S. (2001) 'Professional doctorates in England', *Studies in Higher Education*, 26(1), pp. 65–83.

Council of Europe (2000) Lisbon Summit: Presidential Conclusions. Available at: http://www.bologna-berlin2003.de/pdf/PRESIDENCY_CONCLUSIONS_Lissabon.pdf

Destatis (Federal Office of Statistics, Germany) (2023) *Prüfungen an Hochschulen 2022 (Examinations at German Higher Education Institutions 2022)*. Wiesbaden: Destatis.

EUA (2005) Doctoral Programmes for the European Knowledge Society. Brussels: EUA. Available at: http://www.eua.be/eua/jsp/en/upload/Doctoral_Programmes_Project_Report.1129278878120.pdf

Gokhberg, L., Shmatko, N. & Auriol, L. (eds) (2016) *The science and technology labor force: The value of doctorate holders and development of professional careers*. Cham: Springer International.

Golde, C.M. & Walker, G.E. (eds) (2006) 'Envisioning the future of doctoral education: preparing stewards of the discipline' *Carnegie essays on the doctorate*. San Francisco, CA: Jossey-Bass.

Green, H. & Powell, S. (2005) *Doctoral education in contemporary higher education*. Maidenhead and New York: SRHE and Open University Press.

Hawkes, D. & Yerrabati, S. (2018) 'A systematic review of research on professional doctorates', *London Review of Education*, 16(1), pp. 10–27.

Kehm, B.M. (2020) 'Reforms of doctoral education in Europe and diversification of types'. In: Cardoso, S., Tavares, O., Sin, C. & Carvalho, T. (eds) *Structural and institutional transformations in doctoral education: Social, political and student expectations*. Cham: Springer Nature and Palgrave Macmillan, pp. 85–104.

Palfreyman, D. & Tapper, T. (eds) (2009) *Structuring mass higher education: The role of elite institutions*. London and New York: Routledge.

Park, C. (2005) 'New variant PhD: The changing nature of the doctorate in the UK', *Journal of Higher Education Policy and Management*, 27(4), pp. 189–207.

Slaughter, S.A. & Leslie, L.L. (2000) *Academic capitalism: Politics, policies and the entrepreneurial university*. Baltimore, MD: Johns Hopkins University Press.

Teichler, U. (1991) 'Towards a highly educated society', *Higher Education Policy*, 4, pp. 11–20.

PART TWO

Becoming and Being a Supervisor

5

Building Good Doctoral Supervisory Relationships

Jan McArthur

Introduction

A good doctoral supervisory relationship has many of the hallmarks of any other good pedagogical relationship, such as mutual respect, kindness, responsibility, commitment to learning and trust. Although far too often, there is an assumption that supervision is just something easy to do and relies on research knowledge alone, rather than pedagogy (Motshoane & McKenna, 2021). Vereijken et al. (2018) reveal the complexity of the supervisory relationship as a place of pedagogy, and also 'a dilemmatic space, a decision-making space indicated by four interrelated questions about regulation, student needs, the supervisor-student relationship and supervisors' professional identity' (p. 534). It is therefore important to understand that this supervisory relationship is a pedagogical one, even though this imagery remains resisted by some academics, particularly in research-intensive universities, where to speak of supervision in terms of teaching and learning seemingly diminishes the role, and themselves (Grant, 2010). Grant herself is ambivalent about the teaching and learning description, worrying that it could signify a neoliberal performativity rather than intellectual nourishment. In this chapter, however, we are clear that for success, this relationship must be understood as a pedagogical one, and yet it also has particular characteristics that differ from other forms of pedagogic relationships.

The supervisory relationship is a sustained partnership in which the student has considerable agency to select their topic of study and approach to that study. There is no set curriculum, and the most important learning outcome of all is to make a significant and original contribution to knowledge in their chosen disciplinary area. The doctoral supervisory relationship is, ideally, a sustained partnership in which the partners share a love of subject and enquiry but otherwise have different roles and responsibilities. This partnership, however, is not simply between two or more individuals, but is a socially situated relationship. There is a growing literature looking at doctoral supervisory relationships in the context of broader policy (e.g. McKenna & van Schalkwyk, 2023) and an understanding of socially situated practices (e.g. Bengtsen & McAlpine, 2022; Mahon, 2023; Trowler, 2022). As Trowler (2022, p. 1745) argues, the problem with a purely individual approach to doctoral supervisory relationships is:

> that attempts to offer recommendations for the enhancement of supervision practices are frequently normative and aspirational without a pathway to achievement other than self-help.

In contrast, a 'social practice perspective sees interpersonal interactions of doctoral candidate and their supervisor as the centre of a nexus of influences':

> Doctoral supervision, therefore, includes multiple activity types. Its components are underpinned by forms of knowledge, symbolic structures, ideologies, discourses, assumptions, values, expectations and subjectivities which are often in tension and are always multiple.
>
> (p. 1745)

Within this broader social sphere, we are better able to understand the power relationship, an institutionally mandated power relationship (Grant, 2010), that must be acknowledged. Such a social perspective is also necessary in order to situate the supervisory relationship in diverse understandings of time, place and knowledge, reflective of the importance for transcultural approaches to supervision in this decolonial age (Manathunga, 2014).

Establishing a supervisory relationship: Expectations and communication

Grant references the importance of the tensions that may exist between university structures and the very private nature of the traditional one-to-one supervision, whereby dialogue can quickly become a situation of the 'listened to' and 'listener'. Once this situation is established, Grant's master and slave trope is hard to escape, and disciplinary knowledge may interrupt the ebb and flow of supervisory conversations.

A successful supervisory relationship therefore requires us to avoid the establishment of this skewed power dynamic from the beginning. A creative and nurturing approach to supervision gains much by an emphasis on partnership rather than power or privilege, and by more open supervisory relationships. Therefore, beginning with a genuine dialogic relationship that recognizes the experience and expertise *both* parties bring to the relationship is essential. The doctoral candidate may lack the particular experience and expertise of their supervisor, but they are the best qualified to articulate

REFLECTIVE ACTIVITY 5.1: EXAMINING POWER DYNAMICS IN DOCTORAL SUPERVISION

Take a moment to reflect on the power dynamics present within your supervisory relationships. As a doctoral supervisor, you hold significant academic and institutional authority, which can influence a candidate's research direction, access to resources and overall progress. Consider how this power is exercised, both consciously and unconsciously, in your interactions.

Ask yourself:

- Do I foster an environment where the student feels comfortable expressing disagreement or proposing alternative perspectives?
- How do I balance providing guidance with encouraging independent thinking?
- Are there ways in which my feedback or expectations may unintentionally reinforce dependency?

Think about how you establish expectations, provide critique and support your candidates' academic development. Reflect on the strategies you use to promote equity in the relationship, such as co-authoring publications, co-developing research agendas or involving candidates in academic networks.

Also consider how broader factors – such as culture, gender, and socio-economic background – may influence the supervisory dynamic.

Use this reflection to identify areas where you might adjust your practice to create a more empowering, collaborative and respectful supervisory environment. The goal is not to eliminate power, but to use it ethically and transparently to support the development of autonomous, confident scholars.

their trajectory into doctoral study, their aspirations and the rich resources they bring with them. Ensuring a mutual understanding of those roles and responsibilities, and thus setting a firm foundation in shared expectations, is vital to the success of this relationship.

In some institutions it is increasingly considered good practice to have a supervisory team, or at least a pair of supervisors. The reasons for this focus on diversity and resilience and a desire to interrupt the damaging forms of relationship captured by Grant's master-slave imagery. Opinion is divided among many experienced supervisors as to whether having a team has this positive impact or simply duplicates work, particularly in times of increased financial constraints. The key message here, however, is that whether a team or a single supervisor, the importance of valuing what each individual brings to the relationship and setting clear expectations remains the same.

A supervisory team may also be a way to help novice supervisors learn the ropes without feeling under pressure. There definitely can be additional challenges for novice supervisors, who may feel they do not have the established gravitas, respect or reputation to carry this important role (Vereijken et al., 2018). The phenomenon of doctoral student 'imposter syndrome' is well-known and well-documented in the research (Nori et al., 2020; Sverdlik et al., 2020). Many doctoral students may be surprised to know that supervisors can feel the same imposter syndrome: acutely aware of the particular institutional responsibilities and epistemological challenges of doctoral level supervision. Clearly students want to feel that their supervisors are confident and able, but this does not mean we cannot share a little vulnerability – perhaps some stories from our own doctoral journey and the inevitable fears and worries we also experienced. A good supervisory relationship ultimately aims to relieve this stress on both parties, but they may initially begin by a kindly acknowledgement of the challenges, and fears, of the other partner.

Manathunga (2019) argues that the time pressures on doctoral supervision are ever increasing, with expectations of publications and the development of so-called generic skills in addition to the core thesis. Such pressures can be overwhelming unless time is spent clarifying individual students' expectations and aspirations early in the supervisory relationship. Increasingly, many doctoral candidates do not wish to forge an academic career, and therefore may not care so much about publishing while they study, but place a great value on broader skills development. The best way to mitigate against these extra pressures is to have a conversation about what the candidate hopes to get out of the overall doctoral experience.

Bogelund (2015) proposes that a supervisor's conceptualization of the nature of knowledge production has a direct impact on their approach to supervision. She outlines three different orientations: the traditional academic, where knowledge production is central and the core role is to contribute to the sum of knowledge in society; the market approach, where the use of knowledge is central, and its purpose is to promote economic growth; and the social transformative approach, where knowledge is important for social transformation and change, in response to global issues. However, in her empirical study, Bogelund found it was common for supervisors to have combinations of these three different orientations.

The lesson we can draw from this, therefore, is not about categorizing yourself as a supervisor under a particular label, but rather a more considered reflection on your assumptions, beliefs and practices regarding the nature of knowledge, and its generation, when approaching supervision. Supervisors will differ, and there is no one right way, but what is essential is the explicit reflection on this issue about the nature of knowledge production when forming a supervisory relationship. How many supervisors explicitly discuss this, including different assumptions and worldviews with their supervisees? We must ensure that the supervisor and supervisee are not talking across each other about the nature of knowledge, which does not mean they have to agree, but rather than assumptions and beliefs need to be surfaced as part of building the supervisory relationship.

Alebaikan et al. (2023) outline the importance of supervisors understanding that something that works OK for one doctoral student may not meet the needs of another. Using the example of feedback on confirmation documents, they demonstrate how students responded differently to the level of feedback, with some feeling it was insufficient, while another student could experience the same approach as overly prescriptive and controlling. While this is true of wider expectations of effective and personalized feedback (McArthur & Huxham, 2013), the problem is so often magnified in the intense but prolonged doctoral relationship.

For students undertaking a traditional PhD, with one long thesis, the experience can be quite isolating, particularly in the social sciences where they are unlikely to work as part of a larger research team (Deem & Brehony, 2000). Here the research culture may feel 'transitory as well as fragmented' (p. 153). This makes the supervisory relationship even more important. This situation can be exacerbated if the student is part-time and on a traditional doctoral programme team (Deem & Brehony, 2000).

A key argument in this chapter is that because the doctoral supervisory relationship is such a long and sustained one, ensuring it 'works' is a matter of regular recalibration and reassessment. Over the course of a thesis supervision, be it the smaller two-year variety or the traditional four-year format, there is an expectation of growing researcher independence on the part of the student, and yet the pedagogical nature of the relationship should not diminish, but it should change. The supervisory relationship must be one of increasing agency for the doctoral student, while maintaining the essence of a proper learning and teaching relationship (Vereijken et al., 2018).

Diversity and inclusion

Given the close and prolonged nature of the supervisory relationship, issues of diversity and inclusion are clearly central. There is also considerable evidence that family background, family responsibilities, work commitments, gender and nationality can shape the supervisory experiences of doctoral students (Deem & Brehony, 2000).

As stressed in the previous section, establishing expectations and mutual understandings is vital. The supervisor's own life course, including major personal events, can also influence the supervisory relationship (Bengtsen & McAlpine, 2022). On the one hand, a supervisor should not feel the need to share too much that is personal with their student. There is considerable debate over practices such as whether or not it is reasonable or necessary to invite doctoral students to the family home for a meal (Deem & Brehony, 2000). On the other hand, unless the two partners understand something of each other's history, identity and life course, how can they sustain a successful partnership? And international students can feel particularly isolated and the supervisory relationship becomes the core connection to the department and wider university (Deem & Brehony, 2000).

Grant (2023) writes about 'dismantling the father's house' of doctoral supervision and explores the implications of gendered aspects of doctoral supervision. Supervisors must be acutely aware that this is a gendered relationship, historically situated in that equally gendered notion of master and slave. Deem and Brehony (2000) report the ways in which male students are more likely to be able to make easy bonds with their supervisors with trips to the pub or the football. They also found that female students with female supervisors often formed very strong bonds, albeit in different ways.

With the increasing internationalization of higher education across most of the world, it is also important to understand the supervisory relationship as often being an intercultural relationship (Pinto & Araújo e Sá, 2020). Language issues can impact on supervisory relationships because they may impair the ability to develop the less formal interactions that are often part of the lengthy supervisory relationship (Alebaikan et al., 2023). While acknowledging the challenges this can bring, Pinto and Araújo e Sá (2020) warn against falling into an easy state of assuming this is a deficit position, in which assumes an 'otherness' on both sides of the relationship. This can be achieved, they argue, by acknowledgement of the differential power positions of those in the supervisory relationship, and one that seeks to harness what all parties bring. As Grant and Manathunga (2011) suggest, supervision across cultures 'becomes a pedagogical site of rich possibility as well as, at times, a place of puzzling and confronting complexity' (p. 351).

RESEARCH BRIEFING 5.1: UNDERSTANDING THE DECOLONIAL IMPERATIVE

Manathunga et al. (2022) emphasize the importance of understanding relationships to place and land for Indigenous doctoral students and their own complex knowledge assemblages: 'First Nations knowledge creation is intergenerational and multidirectional across time and space' (p. 126). Grant (2010) provides insights into the ways in which Māori students may experience supervision differently, ranging from epistemological positions through to suspicions and fears about supervisors' motivations and interests in them and their work. Grant (2016) explores how it is by 'being sensible to the hauntings of colonial history .... In embracing rather than refusing history's ghosts' that productive supervisory relationships can be established between Pākehā and Māori (p. 113). A transcultural approach to doctoral supervision is important to decolonization, which can creatively bring together both Western and Indigenous understandings of time, place and knowledge (Manathunga, 2014; Manathunga et al., 2022).

Getting the thesis written

Many things can potentially go wrong while someone is working on a doctoral project, but nearly all of them can be turned around positively as long as the doctoral student and supervisor have timely and regular contact. There are no or few structured classes or fixed sessions that ensure student and supervisor come into each other's orbit, which is why one of the most common problems in doctoral student is a study who drifts, loses contact and/or struggles on without the necessary guidance. Tales of doctoral students going months, even years, without proper supervision may not be commonplace, but nor are they particularly rare. This is where expectations and responsibilities become so important: who is responsible for ensuring regular supervisory meetings take place? Many academics feel that it is ultimately the doctoral student's responsibility to keep in touch and ensure regular contact, and in one sense this is a reasonable position. We must consider, however, the ways in which we frame a relationship that makes it easier or harder, more or less likely, for the doctoral student to maintain regular meetings. For example, it makes sense to link each supervision meeting to the discussion of a new piece of writing. But what happens if the student doesn't complete the task? They may be embarrassed and avoid the supervisor rather than seek advice. Equally, as Mahon (2023) argues, sometimes a student may want to be left alone for a little while with their ideas, as an important part of developing agency and ownership: supervisors have to know when to hold back.

One of the amazing aspects of doctoral study is surely the size of the canvas on which a doctoral student can think and work. Such an extended and large form of study provides opportunities to explore ideas, literature, concepts and phenomena in considerable depth. An important part of this is simply the space to work with, discuss and debate relevant ideas. This sense of a space for real, insightful thinking is sadly lacking from so many other educational opportunities, run to increasingly strict and often managerialist timetables. It surely goes without saying that an important part of the supervisory relationship is this type spent engaging in the realm of ideas.

Managed badly and/or misunderstood, however, this can also be one of the potentially dangerous aspects of the supervisory relationship. We no longer live in a world where doctorates can take upwards of a decade for completion. And many of us think that is a very good thing for many reasons, not least student well-being. So unromantic as it might sound, a good supervisory relationship relies on keeping one eye on that ticking clock: timely progress.

On the other hand, focusing on nothing but that ticking clock can ruin the real joys of the unique nature of the doctoral experience. It is defined by it being a lengthy and in-depth experience. Moreover, a focus on the ticking clock can lead to a very technocratic and procedural approach: this chapter by x month, the next chapter by x month – relentless efficient churning out of drafts, rather than the building of an intellectual endeavour of depth and richness.

Our notion of balance is useful not only between tasks, but within tasks. Asking for whole chapter drafts from students may seem like it pushes on progress, but can be daunting and unproductive. Sometimes small pieces of writing done regularly are the best way for a particular student to advance, or to enable engagement with particularly difficult topics. It can be a particularly good strategy for part-time doctoral students facing many external demands and time pressures.

A good supervisor understands that the process of writing goes through many iterations in a thesis, and they are not all the same. Sometimes writing is a process of the student working out their own understandings or arguments. They are, in essence, writing for themselves as an intellectual project of engaging with the subject, literature or their findings. Such pieces of writing do not need to take the form of whole chapter drafts, and may indeed be sometimes fairly random bits and pieces, that *may* later contribute to a greater whole. At this stage, the supervisor's role in the relationship is to encourage such writing, to engage with the ideas, but not to necessarily offer detailed feedback or even critique. The ideas may change, the form of writing certainly should evolve, so detailed feedback at this stage is time consuming and may be counter-productive if it leads to the student second guessing this 'free form' writing as they go. Sometimes we just need to write, and an essential part of the supervisory relationship is understanding what this does and does not require.

CASE STUDY 5.1: DEVELOPING A REFLECTIVE PORTFOLIO OF DOCTORAL SUPERVISORY RELATIONSHIPS

Research supervision is mostly considered as a research activity within disciplinary boundaries. By embracing research supervision as a teaching practice, it is possible to nurture critical thinking, foster academic growth and equip students with skills that extend beyond the boundaries of their research projects (Lee & Green, 2009). At most HE institutions, reflective practice is regarded as integral to good teaching practice. So, too should reflective practice be integral to sustained and positive doctoral supervisory relationships. One approach for achieving this, inspired by the Guidelines for Teaching-Learning-Assessment Awards at Stellenbosch University, is through a portfolio of doctoral supervisory relationships that includes

- a philosophy statement and rationale for approach to doctoral supervisions;
- a reflective narrative that describes how doctoral supervisory relationships are built and sustained as well as why the approach is followed;
- evidence supporting the claims made in the reflective narrative.

For the reflective narrative there should be critical reflection on the following four aspects.

- **Reflection on context**
  The context refers to what doctoral supervisory relationships mean in the geographical, historical and social context of your university, your country and your continent. It includes social-situated practices and an understanding of the power relations between doctoral supervisor and student. Some guiding questions include:
  - What is your doctoral supervision context and environment?
  - How does your supervision approach reflect this context?
  - In what ways does your context enable or constrain how you supervise?

- How does your supervision promote a consciousness/awareness of the global context of your research?

- **Reflection on doctoral students**
  This reflection refers to the identity of the doctoral students within a doctoral supervisory relationship. Some guiding questions include:
  - Who are your doctoral students, in terms of their background, community, goals, working style?
  - How do you manage or adjust your supervision style to accommodate diverse needs of your doctoral students (with regard to, for example, feedback)?
  - How do you facilitate increased agency for your doctoral students?
  - What methods do you use to help your doctoral students transition from writing for understanding to writing for sharing understanding?
  - How do you equip students with skills that extend beyond the boundaries of their research projects?
  - What is your strategy for balancing time to completion and time for intellectual engagement with ideas (richness and depth)?
  - How do you maintain a positive supervisory relationship amid personal stresses, worries and problems.

- **Reflection on knowledge**
  This reflection refers to how in the doctoral research different forms of knowledge may be integrated and generated. Some guiding questions include:
  - What are your assumptions, beliefs and practices regarding the nature of knowledge and its generation, when approaching supervision?
  - How do you promote ethical practices (including increasing agency or voice of your doctoral students, fair authorship claims, ethical use of generative AI)?

- **Reflection on growth**
  This reflection includes professional development opportunities for role players in the doctoral supervisory relationship as well as innovative approaches for sustaining a positive and effective doctoral supervisory relationship. Some guiding questions for reflection include:
  - How do you nurture critical thinking and foster academic growth, for yourself and for each doctoral student?
  - How do you and your students use alternative AI research assistants (such as Elicit, Consensus, Scite) to improve literature searches and summaries?
  - What forms of feedback (including student and peer evaluation) do you obtain to enhance your approach to doctoral supervision?
  - In what way is your approach to doctoral supervisory relationships influencing that of others in your institution and beyond?

At some point, or points, the purpose of writing for a doctoral student changes from one focused on their own understanding to one with the intention of how to share this understanding with others – the readers. Supervisors play a crucial role in helping doctoral students to understand this difference between writing for understanding and writing for sharing understanding.

Stress and problems

As Grant (2005) observes, supervision is 'a deeply uncertain practice' (p. 337). Unsurprisingly, therefore, stresses and problems can occur in the relationship. How we deal with these is at the heart of maintaining the positive supervisory relationship.

In most countries students pay huge tuition fees for doctoral education, and even more so if they are classed an international student. The phenomenon of part-time doctoral study is increasing, and often in an online format. Such programmes can be excellent, but they do also mean we have doctoral students with many demands on their time other than their doctoral study. Supervisors also face increasing stress. In many Western countries there is a sense that financial changes in the higher education sector have meant that many academics are taking on more doctoral students, while facing increasing pressure to ensure timely completion and adherence to various quality assurance requirements (Bogelund, 2015).

Sometimes the stress felt by both partners can simply give rise to little niggles. These can be a symptom of other things such as external pressures, such as that imposter syndrome, or just plain tiredness. In such cases a judgement needs to be made as to whether any explicit recognition or intervention may cause more harm than good. It might be a case of one or both partners just giving each other a bit of slack to not always be perfect.

In other cases, however, it can be dangerous to let these things go un-addressed in the hope they will sort themselves out. Difficult as it is, at some point, both parties need to be able to address when the relationship seems to be going wrong. More major relationship problems may require different courses of action. Indeed, most departments will have a policy or protocol for dealing with such situations. This may involve escalating levels of action, designed to help sort out problems earlier when they may hopefully remain more minor.

Even if we think we are being clear to a student about why their work is falling short of expectations, what we think we are saying, and what the student hears, may differ substantially. Remember, most doctoral students are in a position of some stress, or at least worry and concern, about their performance and what may seem the long way off outcome of degree success.

Finally, there are quite a few ways in which unethical practices can become part of supervisory relationships, including over or under supervision, domination of the supervisor's views, unfair authorship claims and collusion in malpractice (Löfström & Pyhältö, 2020). Apart from threats to actual welfare, this is the most serious problem that can occur in a supervisory relationship. As a supervisor we need to employ the same honest, analytic and reflective approach we bring to our own research. Is my offer to co-author an article really in the student's best interest? Is my notion of encouraging independence really just a cover for under-supervision? How intellectually generous am I being in talking about different research approaches? Or do students always seem to do their research just as I do mine? Use my sources? See the world through my eyes?

REFLECTIVE ACTIVITY 5.2: UNDERSTANDING AND MANAGING STRESS IN DOCTORAL SUPERVISION RELATIONSHIPS

Supervisory relationships can be significant sources of stress – for both the supervisor and the doctoral candidate. As a supervisor, it is important to reflect on how stress manifests in your practice and how it may impact your relationship with your student.

Consider the following prompts:

- In what ways might my expectations contribute to a candidate's stress?
- How do I respond when a candidate is struggling with workload, motivation or personal challenges?
- Do I create space for open conversations about well-being and workload?
- How do I manage my own stress, and am I aware of how it might affect my supervision style?

Reflect on specific instances where stress has arisen in your supervisory relationships. What were the contributing factors – tight deadlines, unclear expectations, interpersonal tension or institutional pressures? How was the situation handled, and what might you do differently next time?

Also, think about the support structures you encourage or model. Do you promote a healthy work–life balance, guide students towards support services and model self-care in your own academic life?

Conclusion

There are many aspects to reflective practice in doctoral education, and understanding the supervisory relationship is essential. This is an unusual pedagogical relationship that is sustained over a considerable period of time, and can provide unusual challenges for both student and supervisor. To work well, both partners need to be prepared to move a little beyond their comfort zone and to be supportive of the other partner doing the same.

Establishing clear expectations and communication is essential to the relationship, as is embracing the diverse backgrounds and life stories of both supervisor and student. While the relationship can be a period of joyful exploration, it must also remain focused on timely completion. Stresses and problems will inevitably occur, and we must avoid catastrophizing when things go wrong. Equally, however, doctoral supervision can spiral into unhealthy and unproductive places if major problems are unaddressed. This can be a painful experience for both partners, but manageable if that strong and supportive relationship has already been established.

References

Alebaikan, R., Bain, Y. & Cornelius, S. (2023) 'Experiences of distance doctoral supervision in cross-cultural teams', *Teaching in Higher Education*, 28(1), pp. 17–34. doi:10.1080/13562517.2020.1767057

Bengtsen, S.S. & McAlpine, L. (2022) 'A novel perspective on doctoral supervision: Interaction of time, academic work, institutional policies, and lifecourse', *Learning and Teaching*, 15(1), pp. 21–45. doi:10.3167/latiss.2022.150103

Bøgelund, P. (2015) 'How supervisors perceive PhD supervision – and how they practice it', *International Journal of Doctoral Studies*, 10, pp. 39–55. doi:10.28945/2096

Deem, R. & Brehony, K.J. (2000) 'Doctoral students' access to research cultures – are some more unequal than others?' *Studies in Higher Education*, 25(2), pp. 149–65. doi:10.1080/713696138

Grant, B. & Manathunga, C. (2011) 'Supervision and cultural difference: Rethinking institutional pedagogies', *Innovations in Education and Teaching International*, 48(4), pp. 351–4. https://doi.org/10.1080/14703297.2011.617084

Grant, B.M. (2005) 'Fighting for space in supervision: Fantasies, fairytales, fictions and fallacies', *International Journal of Qualitative Studies in Education*, 18(3), pp. 337–54. doi:10.1080/09518390500082483

Grant, B.M. (2008) 'Agonistic struggle: Master–slave dialogues in humanities supervision', *Arts and Humanities in Higher Education*, 7(1), pp. 9–27. doi:10.1177/1474022207084880

Grant, B.M. (2010) 'The limits of "teaching and learning": Indigenous students and doctoral supervision', *Teaching in Higher Education*, 15(5), pp. 505–17. doi: 10.1080/13562517.2010.491903

Grant, B.M. (2016) 'Living with ghosts: Enabling identities for Pākehā supervisors of Māori doctoral students', *New Zealand Journal of Educational Studies*, 51(1), pp. 113–24. doi:10.1007/s40841-016-0044-1

Grant, B.M. (2023) 'Dismantling the father's house? Women as doctoral supervisors', *Learning and Teaching*, 16(1), pp. 1–30. doi:10.3167/latiss.2023.160102

Lee, A. & Green, B. (2009) 'Supervision as metaphor', *Studies in Higher Education*, 34(6), pp. 615–30. https://doi.org/10.1080/03075070802597168

Löfström, E. & Pyhältö, K. (2020) 'What are ethics in doctoral supervision, and how do they matter? Doctoral students' perspective', *Scandinavian Journal of Educational Research*, 64(4), pp. 535–50. doi:10.1080/00313831.2019.1595711

Mahon, K. (2023) 'Doctoral supervision as and for praxis', *Journal of Praxis in Higher Education*, 5(2), pp. 118–39. doi:10.47989/kpdc318

Manathunga, C. (2014) *Intercultural postgraduate supervision: Reimagining time, place and knowledge*. 1st ed. Abingdon: Taylor & Francis Group.

Manathunga, C. (2019) '"Timescapes" in doctoral education: The politics of temporal equity in higher education', *Higher Education Research and Development*, 38(6), pp. 1227–39. doi:10.1080/07294360.2019.1629880

Manathunga, C., Qi, J., Raciti, M., Stanton, S. & Singh, M. (2022) 'Decolonising Australian doctoral education beyond/within the pandemic: Foregrounding Indigenous knowledges', *SOTL in the South*, 6(1), pp. 112–37. doi:10.36615/sotls.v6i1.203

McArthur, J. & Huxham, M. (2013) 'Feedback unbound: From master to usher'. In: Merry, S., Carless, D., Price, M. & Taras, M. (eds) *Reconceptualising feedback in higher education*. Abingdon: Routledge, pp. 92–102.

McKenna, S. & van Schalkwyk, S. (2023) 'A scoping review of the changing landscape of doctoral education', *Compare*, [online ahead of print], pp. 1–18. doi:10.1080/03057925.2023.2168121

Motshoane, P. & McKenna, S. (2021) 'Crossing the border from candidate to supervisor: The need for appropriate development', *Teaching in Higher Education*, 26(3), pp. 387–403. doi:10.1080/13562517.2021.1900814

Nori, H., Peura, M.H. & Jauhiainen, A. (2020) 'From imposter syndrome to heroic tales: Doctoral students' backgrounds, study aims, and experiences', *International Journal of Doctoral Studies*, 15, pp. 517–39. doi:10.28945/4637

Pinto, S. & Araújo e Sá, M.H. (2020) 'Researching across languages and cultures: A study with doctoral students and supervisors at a Portuguese university', *European Journal of Higher Education*, 10(3), pp. 276–93. doi:10.1080/21568235.2020.1777449

Sverdlik, A., Hall, N.C. & McAlpine, L. (2020) 'PhD imposter syndrome: Exploring antecedents, consequences, and implications for doctoral well-being', *International Journal of Doctoral Studies*, 15, pp. 737–58. doi:10.28945/4670

Trowler, P. (2022) 'Doctoral supervision: Sharpening the focus of the practice lens', *Higher Education Research and Development*, 41(5), pp. 1743–56. doi:10.1080/07294360.2021.1937955

Vereijken, M.W.C., van der Rijst, R.M., van Driel, J.H. & Dekker, F.W. (2018) 'Novice supervisors' practices and dilemmatic space in supervision of student research projects', *Teaching in Higher Education*, 23(4), pp. 522–42. doi:10.1080/13562517.2017.1414791

6

Co-supervision and Other Models of Collaborative Supervision

Fiona Philippi

Introduction

Although traditionally PhD supervision was undertaken by one supervisor, co-supervision is now common practice in many countries and increasingly the need for students to be supervised by at least two co-supervisors has become an expectation, both nationally and institutionally (Taylor et al., 2018). Despite this, there is still relatively little written about being a co-supervisor, what to expect and how to make it work effectively (Navé Wald et al., 2023; Olmos-López & Sunderland, 2017). In this chapter, we start by exploring what is meant by co-supervision and other forms of collaborative supervision, and why this has apparently become standard practice in many countries. In the following section we examine the benefits and challenges associated with co-supervision. The final section considers some of the methods and approaches to making co-supervision work effectively. Central to this chapter is the argument that despite the popularity of co-supervision, the benefits of this approach do not arise solely from putting supervisors together. As in any complex interpersonal relationship, co-supervision requires clear communication and agreement about expectations between supervisors and student. To do this effectively, supervisors should be actively encouraged and supported to reflect on and develop their co-supervisory practice as an integral part of their development as a supervisor. Interestingly, given the importance that some studies have placed on understanding different supervisory styles and approaches and the impact of these on supervisory relationships with students, it is notable that there has been far less attention placed on how these impact relationships between supervisors. This is significant as it is clear that a positive relationship between co-supervisors is fundamental to the success of the supervisory arrangement, and that this has implications for supervisor and student well-being and effectiveness (Hansson & Schmidt, 2023; Pyhältö et al., 2023).

What is co-supervision?

Co-supervision can be defined as supervision by two or more supervisors (one of these supervisors may be from a collaborative arrangement with industry or another higher education institution; Kálmán et al., 2022). The most common arrangement is where there is a principal or main supervisor and one co-supervisor. In such co-supervision arrangements, students usually have a *main* supervisor (also referred to as principal, head or primary supervisor) paired with one or more co-supervisors, sometimes called *second* supervisors (Hansson & Schmidt, 2023). This can be described as a hierarchical co-supervisory relationship, where the main supervisor is more senior than the second supervisor; however, less frequently the relationship can also be horizontal, where co-supervisors are at a similar level of seniority. Although this chapter is primarily concerned with the co-supervisory arrangement, it will also briefly consider other forms of collaborative supervision such as team and group supervision as they are also growing in practice.

Both Olmos López and Sunderland (2017) and Kálmán et al. (2022) present concise but comprehensive summaries of how and why co-supervision has grown to be an expectation of PhD supervision in many countries. In recent decades there has been a rapid expansion of doctoral degrees and numbers of candidates across many countries and with this there has been an increased focus on ensuring quality in the doctoral degree. The nature of research has also changed, with drivers such as interdisciplinarity, innovation and internationalization necessitating greater collaboration and team structures. In terms of their role in strengthening co-supervision through institutional strategies, Kálmán et al. (2022) call these drivers the four 'Is' (Interdisciplinarity, Intersectoral collaboration, Internationalization and Improvement of the quality of doctoral supervision). This is based on the argument that by increasing the number of supervisors working on a project, students are able to access the knowledge and support required to integrate with the greater diversity of disciplines and sectors and that additional supervisors provide a check for the quality of the degree outputs.

Despite the development in co-supervision, there remains a huge variation in expectations and practice. For example, in some countries, such as Sweden, national law determines that all doctoral degrees must be co-supervised (Almlöv & Grubbström, 2023). In other countries, expectations around supervision may be set by individual institutions and may be contained in a Code of Practice or equivalent. The details of what is expected in the co-supervisory arrangement are also imprecise and variable, which means there is lack of consistency around distribution of workload between supervisors and other aspects such as number of supervisees and co-authorship (Amundsen & McAlpine, 2011; Almlöv & Grubbström, 2023; Wald et al., 2023).

CASE STUDY 6.1: ENHANCING DOCTORAL SUPERVISION THROUGH CO-SUPERVISION: INTERDISCIPLINARITY, INTERSECTORAL COLLABORATION, INTERNATIONALIZATION AND QUALITY IMPROVEMENT

CASE CONTEXT

A doctoral programme committed to innovation and research impact introduces a co-supervision model to support a wide range of candidate projects. The programme's emphasis on real-world relevance, international engagement and academic excellence requires supervisors to work collaboratively across disciplinary, institutional and sectoral boundaries.

Interdisciplinarity: Expanding horizons, navigating tensions

A doctoral candidate researching sustainable urban development requires insight from urban planning, environmental science and social policy. To support this interdisciplinary focus, a co-supervisory team is assembled with expertise spanning these fields. The approach allows the candidate to draw from diverse methodological traditions and to build a rich, integrative research framework.

However, this diversity also surfaces tensions. Conflicting epistemologies, differing research priorities and varied expectations regarding evidence and rigour occasionally create uncertainty for the candidate. For instance, while one supervisor emphasizes empirical fieldwork, another advocates for conceptual critique. Co-supervisors meet regularly to clarify roles, coordinate feedback and guide the candidate in navigating these tensions. Participation in interdisciplinary forums is encouraged, helping the candidate gain perspective and confidence.

Ultimately, the co-supervisory model enriches the research but requires sustained dialogue and negotiation to remain coherent and productive.

Intersectoral collaboration: Balancing academic integrity and practical impact

Another candidate undertakes a project on renewable energy technologies in collaboration with a start-up company and a government agency. The co-supervisory team includes an academic, an industry-based mentor and a policy advisor, each offering complementary insights. This model enables the candidate to embed research in practical contexts, enhancing its relevance and applied value.

Yet the collaboration is not without friction. It may be the case that industry stakeholders prioritize speed and market readiness, while academic standards demand critical depth and theoretical grounding. Managing differing timelines, intellectual property concerns and output expectations becomes a recurring challenge. To address this, the team establishes structured monthly meetings to align objectives, clarify ownership of results and ensure academic standards are upheld. When well-coordinated, this model strengthens the candidate's professional readiness and fosters innovation, but it relies heavily on transparent communication and mutual respect among all parties.

Internationalization: Opportunities and cross-cultural complexities

A third candidate pursues research on gender and education through an international comparative lens, with co-supervision shared between the home institution and a university abroad. This arrangement allows the candidate to access diverse datasets, academic perspectives and research cultures, while also building networks across borders. On the surface, the model exemplifies the benefits of global academic collaboration and knowledge exchange.

However, the implementation of international co-supervision reveals underlying tensions and structural asymmetries. Institutional expectations around doctoral progress, authorship norms and examination procedures often diverge, creating misalignment in how success is defined and evaluated. These differences are not merely procedural – they reflect broader disparities in power, resources and epistemic authority between institutions in different geopolitical contexts. For instance, feedback timelines are shaped by academic calendars and workloads that are not synchronized, and communication styles are mediated by cultural assumptions about hierarchy and critique. These tensions can place the burden of navigation disproportionately on the candidate, who must reconcile conflicting guidance and negotiate whose advice to privilege.

Efforts to mitigate these issues – such as joint milestone planning, regular virtual meetings and administrative coordination – can help, but they do not fully resolve deeper systemic imbalances. Additionally, international opportunities often presuppose that candidates have the financial, linguistic and emotional resources to engage fully, thereby reinforcing existing inequities in access and mobility. While international co-supervision can enrich research and professional development, it also risks reproducing global academic hierarchies unless critically examined and actively addressed by institutions and supervisory teams.

Quality improvement: Reflecting on process and practice

Across the programme, co-supervision serves not only to broaden expertise but also to support continuous improvement in doctoral supervision. Supervisory teams engage in ongoing professional development, including workshops and peer mentoring sessions focused on collaborative supervision and candidate well-being.

Tensions occasionally arise when co-supervisors have differing philosophies of supervision or when candidates receive inconsistent guidance. These issues are addressed through structured feedback mechanisms, including candidate evaluations and reflective team reviews. Clear milestone planning and jointly developed supervision agreements promote transparency and shared responsibility. Importantly, co-supervision helps reduce individual bias by offering candidates multiple perspectives, fostering equity in supervisory relationships.

When intentionally structured, co-supervision enhances academic quality, provides a safeguard against supervisory blind spots and supports a more inclusive and responsive doctoral training environment. However, it demands institutional recognition, time and support to function effectively.

Discussion questions

How can institutions best support co-supervision models to ensure clarity in roles, expectations and responsibilities among supervisors?

What strategies can co-supervisory teams employ to navigate tensions arising from interdisciplinary, intersectoral or international differences?

In what ways does co-supervision contribute to equity, inclusion and quality in doctoral education, and what are the potential risks or limitations?

Benefits of co-supervision

The addition of one or more co-supervisors has a range of perceived and potential benefits for the supervisee, the project and the supervisors involved. Olmós-Lopez and Sunderland (2017) sum these up as providing additional 'learning opportunities' over a solo supervisory approach. For the student, this should allow them to access a greater range of intellectual approaches and gain different perspectives on their work. This can be particularly relevant in interdisciplinary projects and projects with international, industrial or other links (Taylor et al., 2018).

The co-supervisory approach hasalso been called a safety-net for students (Kálmán et al., 2022), which could refer to the availability of additional support from another supervisor where there are challenges or in cases of conflict or disagreement between one of the supervisors and the student. Taylor et al. (2018) explain this can also offer continuity for the student and project in cases of supervisory absence or when one supervisor moves institution.

One often cited benefit is the development and learning potential co-supervision provides for new or less experienced supervisors in that the more experienced supervisor can mentor the more junior supervisor and induct them into the supervisory role through observation and sharing of knowledge and experience. In practice, this assumes that there is a hierarchical, rather than horizontal, relationship between the supervisors and that communication between the supervisors is effective (Almlöv & Grubbström, 2023). However, various studies have found that if the co-supervisory relationship is set up effectively, then do appear to be developmental benefits for supervisors. In their study of supervisors in a Finnish institution, Pyhältö et al. (2023) surveyed 651 supervisors to try to better understand supervisors' perspectives of engaging with co-supervision. They found that supervisors who 'engaged in co-supervision were more confident with their supervisory competencies compared to those supervisors who did not have experience in co-supervision'.

A final benefit may be in terms of reduction in workload for the supervisors – this refers to where the supervision is more equally distributed between the supervisors (Kálmán et al., 2022). However, the extent to which this is a benefit can also be questioned and indeed the opposite can be presented as a challenge of co-supervision, particularly in cases where there is disagreement between supervisors or where a more junior colleague feels unable to contest an uneven distribution of the workload (Almlöv & Grubbström, 2023; Wilmot, 2022).

Challenges of co-supervision

Co-supervision is a working relationship and like any interpersonal relationship it requires work and maintenance and can go wrong, and where this happens it can be detrimental for the supervisors, the supervisee and the project. Taylor et al. (2018) and others (Olmós-Lopez & Sunderland, 2017) contend that this potential for things going badly increases when a greater number of disciplines, cultures and work environments are involved. There are a number of possible reasons for this, which include intellectual differences and a lack of mutual understanding about expectations. Conflicts can arise from a lack of communication and mismatch or misunderstanding of expectations. Olmos-López and Sunderland

(2017) build on earlier studies and refer to the supervisory relationship as one which has moral as well as educational aims. They explain that this moral dimension is interpreted and practised in different ways by individual supervisors. For instance, where some supervisors will see their role as supporting a student, 'through thick and thin', others will take a more transactional approach and rely on policy and process when presented with a difficult situation. They add that these differences also exist in student approaches to and understanding of the supervisory relationship. These differing approaches can extend to all the practical aspects of the supervisory relationship. This includes potential disagreements or lack of mutual understanding around how meetings are conducted, workload distribution and how and when feedback is to be given on written work (Kálmán et al., 2022).

One specific challenge relates to the diversity of advice and feedback that supervisees can receive from their supervisors. Of course, it can be expected that supervisors will have different approaches and intellectual perspectives on the work; however, problems arise when they do not reach consensus on the direction that the project should take. In this case, the supervisee is given conflicting advice and is left to navigate and manage this. Given the inherent power relations in the supervisory relationship, assuming this position can be extremely difficult for many supervisees. In their study of PhD candidates in two Australian institutions, Guerin and Green (2013) interviewed a range of students about their experiences of receiving feedback from more than one supervisor. Examples included a student who got completely different advice from two supervisors on structure for a draft chapter, and, then when she followed the advice of one, found that she was heavily criticized at a supervisory team meeting. This meant she lost time and was forced to navigate through the tensions in her supervisory team.

In addition to conflicts and disagreements, there is a delicate power balance in many co-supervisory relationships. In their study of novice co-supervisors across two Swedish institutions, Almlöv and Grubbström (2023) focus on the influence of the supervisor culture which they define as a part of the socially constructed academic culture connected to research education that links people within the departments, the research groups and the supervisory teams. They see this as determining how co-supervisors feel and behave. They found three main themes were highlighted by their research participants: cultures of closedness, dependence and competition. All three of these meant that novice supervisors felt unable to raise issues in supervision with the more senior supervisors for fear of repercussions for their career and work. This corresponds with the findings of Manathunga (2012), who found that the power balance exhibits itself through various examples of self-regulation and peer-regulation when supervisors are both supervising the same project.

REFLECTIVE ACTIVITY 6.1 – ADDRESSING CHALLENGES IN CO-SUPERVISION

Collaborative or co-supervision offers valuable opportunities for both doctoral candidates and supervisors, but it also brings a set of complexities that require careful management and open communication. Use the prompts below to reflect critically on your experiences or expectations of co-supervision. You may draw on specific situations, hypothetical examples or your institutional context.

1 **What is the biggest challenge you have encountered (or anticipate encountering) in co-supervision?**
Consider difficulties such as:
- Conflicting supervisory styles or disciplinary expectations
- Unclear communication or mismatched assumptions
- Unequal power dynamics among supervisors
- Disagreements about intellectual direction, authorship or candidate support

Reflective prompt: Did this issue influence the supervision process or affect the candidate's progress? If so, how?

2 **How did you address (or how might you address) this challenge?**
Think about:
- Practical steps you took or could take to resolve the issue
- Support structures or institutional resources that were helpful
- Lessons learned from the experience

Reflective prompt: If faced with a similar situation again, what would you do differently?

3 **How do you (or could you) respond to differing opinions within a supervisory team?**
Explore strategies such as:
- Setting up regular meetings with structured agendas
- Agreeing in advance on how decisions will be made when viewpoints differ
- Holding open discussions that centre on the candidate's needs

Reflective prompt: How can you ensure respectful dialogue and a shared commitment to the candidate's success when differences arise?

4 **What strategies do you (or could you) use to ensure roles and responsibilities are clearly defined in co-supervision?**
Consider:
- Creating a written agreement early in the process
- Clearly assigning responsibilities related to academic guidance, administration and well-being
- Reviewing and adjusting roles as the research project develops

Reflective prompt: How can greater clarity in supervisory roles prevent misunderstandings or tension later on?

Other forms of collaborative supervision

This chapter is largely focused on co-supervision, defined above, as currently it is the most common model; however as all collaborative models of supervision are concerned with complex, professional relationships much of the argumentation is also applicable. There is also an increased interest across the sector around how these models could aid doctoral education to adapt to future challenges (Clegg, 2024) and as such it would be remiss not to give them some attention here.

Other models of collaborative supervision include team supervision or group supervision. Team supervision is variously defined. Some authors appear not to differentiate between the co-supervision model (two or more supervisors, where often there is a principal and second supervisor) and team supervision (Guerin & Green, 2013; Manathunga, 2012). However, recently there has been a perceivable shift to focus on team supervision as something more, which gives a student access to a multi-supervisory team (Clegg, 2024). In theory this means that different members of the team can offer specific expertise and support. In practice, although many PhD projects do now have a team of supervisors made up of academic and industrial supervisors, these do not tend to be set up any differently from regular co-supervision. In other words, the team aspect could be seen as a consequence of the needs of the project rather than a deliberate intention. Manathunga (2012) defines group supervision as 'where several students work together with one or several supervisors'. Wilmot (2022) elaborates on this to explain that group supervision embraces a 'community approach' to supervision, by gathering a group of students together around a topic or theoretical approach. This assumes a more horizontal approach where peers become important actors.

In many ways the benefits and challenges of co-supervision appear to be amplified for group or team supervision. However, one important additional benefit of group supervision can be to help diffuse the power relationships inherent in the co-supervision model and offer a more social learning ethos to doctoral study. Wilmot (2022) describes two different approaches to group supervision using models of communities of practice. These were undertaken in the South African context and benefits included mitigating some of the negative aspects of doctoral study, such as helping to reduce isolation and a greater emphasis on building confidence in scholarly outputs through articulating and defending ideas to critical peers. Equally a challenge of team supervision is that with more people involved, there is further scope for disagreement and conflict. In the UK, a 2021 review of doctoral education by a major funding council found that where students have multiples of supervisors, perhaps spanning industry and academia, the arrangement is only beneficial where roles are clear and each supervisor is properly engaged. If not, the student is left independently to manage the different supervisory expectations (EPSRC, 2021, p. 40).

CASE STUDY 6.2: MANAGING CONFLICTING FEEDBACK STYLES IN COLLABORATIVE SUPERVISION

In a collaborative doctoral supervision scenario, a team of three supervisors with distinct supervisory approaches are co-supervising a group of graduate students. Each supervisor brings a different method of providing feedback: one tends to give highly structured, detailed critiques; another focuses on the broader, conceptual aspects of development, offering big-picture feedback; while the third adopts a more informal, supportive approach, emphasizing emotional support and nurturing the student's development in a less structured way.

Recently, one student expressed confusion and frustration about receiving mixed feedback. The student felt overwhelmed by the contrasting feedback styles and unsure about how to proceed. This feedback inconsistency not only created challenges for the student but also led to increasing tensions within the supervisory team. One supervisor felt that the more relaxed, informal feedback style was hindering the student's academic progress, while the others argued that the overly rigid feedback from this supervisor stifled creativity and intellectual freedom. The disagreement over supervisory roles and methods started to cause disruptions in team dynamics, making meetings increasingly difficult and leaving both the supervisors and the students frustrated.

Tensions and challenges in collaborative supervision

The central challenge in this case lies in the divergence of feedback styles within the supervisory team. While co-supervision offers the potential for a rich approach to doctoral guidance, it also brings the risk of inconsistent and sometimes contradictory feedback, which can confuse and overwhelm students. This inconsistency often arises from differing expectations about what constitutes appropriate academic support. For example, the supervisor who emphasizes structured, technical feedback may perceive the more informal approach as insufficiently rigorous, while those offering broader feedback may view the technical critiques as overly restrictive. This tension is compounded by differences in personal supervisory philosophies, institutional norms and perhaps even cultural assumptions about academic authority and student autonomy.

The lack of clear communication and coordination among the supervisors can lead to a failure in aligning expectations with the students. When feedback is delivered inconsistently, students may struggle to understand how to integrate it into their work, which can result in feelings of frustration, self-doubt and confusion about how to proceed with their research.

Impact of cultural and supervisory differences

The tensions in this case are also compounded by cultural differences, both within the supervisory team and between the team and the student. Different cultural backgrounds may influence supervisors' perspectives on authority, feedback and academic relationships. In some cultures, direct and structured feedback is expected as a sign of academic rigour, while in others, feedback may be more implicit or delivered in a more supportive, relational manner. For example, one supervisor may be accustomed to a feedback style that emphasizes clear, actionable instructions, while another may prefer a more reflective, less directive approach that prioritizes the student's independence and creativity.

These differences can affect the supervisory experience not only for the student but also for the team. Supervisors may find themselves caught in a cycle of frustration and misalignment, where their feedback is not aligned with one another's, leaving the student with a fragmented understanding of their progress and areas of improvement. The lack of consistency in feedback undermines the coherence of the supervisory process, diminishing its potential for effectively guiding the student.

Reflective questions:

What are the underlying tensions in this case study that arise from differing feedback styles and how might these tensions affect the student's experience?

How might cultural differences within the supervisory team influence feedback styles and expectations?

How can the supervisors balance their differing views on academic authority, creativity and feedback to ensure the student receives cohesive and constructive guidance?

How to make it work

It is generally accepted that effective co-supervision is not automatic and that the relationships between the various actors in the relationship (supervisors and supervisee) must be actively set up, managed and maintained (Taylor et al., 2018; Wald et al., 2023). However, in practice this can prove difficult to initiate and continue unless supervisors take an intentional approach.

One method of addressing this is to place much greater emphasis on expectations setting and management from the start. This could take a number of approaches, but all are based on opening up channels of effective communication. Wald et al. (2023) argue that co-supervisors are unlikely to have such conversations without the aid of a tool or prompt. This builds on previous work by Grossman and Crowther (2015) and Taylor et al. (2018), which advocates for initial and periodic meetings between supervisors to share and discuss expectations and challenges as they arise, using a long list of issues and sub-issues. Wald et al. (2023) support the framework of intentional initial and regular discussion; however, they argue that a long list of potential broad-based issues for co-supervisors to discuss is time-consuming and difficult to manage. Instead, they propose a more focused, research-informed conversation-based tool for co-supervisors which identifies areas for discussion under three headings: co-supervision arrangements, the research project and pedagogies of supervision. The areas were selected based on the importance placed on them during semi-structured interviews and through survey responses of co-supervisors at a University in New Zealand. This discussion tool is reproduced in Table 6.1. The accessibility and simplicity of

Table 6.1 A conversational tool for an early discussion among co-supervisors

Three areas to guide early discussion among co-supervisors		
Co-supervision arrangements	**The research project**	**Pedagogies of supervision**
(a) Areas of expertise	(a) Size, scope and viability	(a) Meetings
(b) Workload allocations	(b) Funding and resourcing	(b) Reading drafts and providing feedback
(c) Roles and responsibilities	(c) Timeframes	(c) Authorship and publication

From Wald et al. (2023)

this tool are particularly attractive as it encourages in-depth discussion on these areas, rather than the more superficial approach of answering a long list of questions. It seems sensible that supervisors and students should also agree on a method to record such discussions so that they can revisit the agreements reached in future discussions.

An example of the type of discussion that could take place under the heading 'reading drafts and providing feedback' is given by Guerin and Green (2015), who argue that at the set-up of the project, a discussion around feedback should take place as an 'explicit pedagogical strategy'. This should create space to openly discuss what the supervisors and supervisee will do when the there are differences of opinion and how feedback on written work should be managed. In this discussion, they include coming to an agreement about who is the final arbiter in a dispute, the role of the student and whether total or partial agreement is necessary between supervisors.

Robertson (2017) argues that engendering and maintaining trust is a central component of these initial discussions which should aim for clarity between supervisors around expectations and roles. However, to build mutual trust between supervisors and between supervisors and students, continued communication is also required. Lack of trust in the supervisory arrangement is detrimental to the people involved and the project and can lead to a dysfunctional team. On the other hand, mutual trust can increase enjoyment of the process and provide support and motivation for the students and supervisors.

Examples are given by Robertson (2017) of experienced supervisors who deliberately create the conditions for building trust in a team setting, by involving all parties in the design and development of the team. This active role of the supervisor in setting up these initial discussions is vital. It can be unrealistic and unfair to expect that the student will be in a position to initiate these discussions, particularly at the start of the degree. Despite this, the potential role of the supervisee in managing and maintaining effective work relationships should also not be overlooked. Guerin and Green (2015) contend that supervisors 'need to consider developing strategies for nurturing the capacity of doctoral students to manage an appropriate level of diversity of opinion on their work' and examples are given of students who have taken a proactive approach to managing the difficult dynamics between their supervisors, to make it work for them and the project.

Another approach to actively managing co-supervision is to formally identify the roles of the supervisors as those of mentor and mentee. An example of this is given in the Australian context where the practice of appointing 'mentor supervisors' has become increasingly popular across institutions (Kiley, 2020).

In exchange for supporting early career supervisors and providing advice and guidance in supervisory practice they hold this title and may be eligible for financial support for professional development. Even where there is not a specific scheme as in the Australian example, supervisors could be routinely offered formal mentoring training and support and be encouraged to access relevant resources.

Conclusion

This chapter has highlighted that co-supervision is a central part of the current doctoral landscape and that although it has become a common expectation in many countries and institutions there is surprisingly little attention paid to understanding how it works. Recent studies have started to address this through focusing on the potential benefits and challenges of co-supervision, and a range of these are explored in the chapter. It seems clear that there are learning opportunities for both supervisor and student if co-supervision is set up effectively. It can provide structured mentorship for more junior supervisors, open up access to a greater variety of knowledge and opportunities for the student and allows for a supportive team structure if things go wrong. It may also help to share workload. On the other hand, when co-supervision is weak or dysfunctional, it can exacerbate the challenges associated with power imbalances, leave the student as the 'piggy in the middle' having to negotiate contradictory feedback and tensions between supervisors. It may also, in some circumstances, add to workload.

Co-supervision is the most common structure of collaborative supervision but in recent years other structures such as team supervision and group supervision have grown in interest and studies have demonstrated that these approaches can also have benefits for the supervisee, the supervisors and the project. They also align more closely with the realities of research projects which are increasingly expected to be interdisciplinary, intersectoral and international. All of these require a greater degree of collaboration than traditional models. As doctoral research continues to expand and develop, it can be expected that collaborative supervision will also grow. In this chapter we have argued that all these models of collaborative supervision share a similar set of challenges, and that to address these, it is necessary that supervisors and students take an intentional approach to setting up and maintaining the relationship.

This final part of the chapter sets out some of the approaches that can be taken to initiating and continuing communication around expectations and roles. We present a discussion tool from Wald et al. (2023) that promotes deeper discussions around expectations between supervisors and students and between supervisors. Mutual trust is an essential element of building an effective co-supervisory arrangement and it should be acknowledged that this takes time and intention to develop. Formal mentoring arrangements between supervisors can also provide a structure for new supervisors to learn and develop and practitioners should consider how to develop these approaches to making co-supervision work effectively in their own environments.

References

Almlöv, C. & Grubbström, A. (2023) '"Challenging from the start": Novice doctoral co-supervisors' experiences of supervision culture and practice', *Higher Education Research & Development*, 43(1), pp. 17–31.

Amundsen, C. & McAlpine, L. (2011) 'New academics as supervisors: A steep learning curve with challenges, tensions and pleasures'. In: McAlpine, L. & Amundsen, C. (eds) *Doctoral education: Research-based strategies for doctoral students, supervisors and administrators*. Dordrecht: Springer, pp. 37–55.

Clegg, K., Houston, G. & Gower, O. (2024) *Doctoral supervision and research culture: What we know, what works and why*. 1st ed. London and New York: Routledge.

Engineering and Physical Sciences Research Council (EPSRC) (2021) *Review of EPSRC-funded doctoral education*. Available at: https://www.ukri.org/wp-content/uploads/2021/10/EPSRC-071021-ReviewDoctoralEducationSupport.pdf (Accessed February 2026).

Grossman, E.S. & Crowther, N.J. (2015) 'Co-supervision in postgraduate training: Ensuring the right hand knows what the left hand is doing', *South African Journal of Science*, 111(11/12), p. 8.

Guerin, C. & Green, I. (2013) '"They're the bosses": Feedback in team supervision', *Journal of Further and Higher Education*, 39(3), pp. 320–35.

Hansson, E. & Schmidt, M. (2023) '"A small pawn in a big game": An exploration of doctoral students' experience of co-supervisory relationships', *Journal of Further and Higher Education*, 47(9), pp. 1169–81.

Kálmán, O., Horváth, L., Kardos, D., Kozma, B., Feyisa, M. & Rónay, Z. (2022) 'Review of benefits and challenges of co-supervision in doctoral education', *European Journal of Education*, 57(3), pp. 1–17.

Manathunga, C. (2011) '"Team" supervision: New positionings in doctoral education pedagogies'. In: Lee, A. & Danby, S. (eds) *Reshaping doctoral education: Changing programs and pedagogies*. London: Routledge, pp. 42–55.

Manathunga, C. (2012) 'Supervisors watching supervisors: The deconstructive possibilities and tensions of team supervision', *Australian Universities' Review*, 54(1), pp. 29–37.

Navé Wald, V., Kumar, V. & Sanderson, L.J. (2023) 'Enhancing co-supervision practice by setting expectations in a structured discussion using a research-informed tool', *Higher Education Research & Development*, 42(3), pp. 757–69.

Olmos-López, P. & Sunderland, J. (2017) 'Doctoral supervisors' and supervisees' responses to co-supervision', *Journal of Further and Higher Education*, 41(6), pp. 727–40.

Pyhältö, K., Tikkanen, L. & Anttila, H. (2023) 'The more the merrier? PhD supervisors' perspectives in engaging in co-supervision', *Innovations in Education and Teaching International*, 61, pp. 1–12.

Robertson, M.J. (2016) 'Team modes and power: Supervision of doctoral students', *Higher Education Research & Development*, 36(2), pp. 358–71.

Robertson, M.J. (2017) 'Trust: The power that binds in team supervision of doctoral students', *Higher Education Research & Development*, 36(7), pp. 1463–75.

Taylor, S., Kiley, M. & Holley, K.A. (eds) (2020) *The making of doctoral supervisors: International case studies of practice*. 1st ed. Abingdon, Oxon, and New York: Routledge.

Taylor, S., Kiley, M. & Humphrey, R. (2018) *A handbook for doctoral supervisors*. 2nd ed. Abingdon, Oxon, and New York: Routledge.

Wilmot, K. (2022) '"Fail early and fail fast': The value of group supervision for doctoral candidates', *Higher Education Research & Development*, 41(6), pp. 2108–21.

7

Modelling Doctoral Supervision

Chris Hughes and Clive Palmer

Supervision and the learning relationship

Is 'supervision' the best way to look at, or model, the learning relationship during a doctorate? The concept of 'supervision' is loaded with master-apprentice connotations, pointing towards power imbalances, oversight and gnawing at issues of responsibility for and ownership of the research. Barnett (2022) speaks of teaching in HE as being a 'provocative matter', a means of 'unsettling', 'disrupting' but also 'inspiring' thinking. Can this really be done by 'supervising'? Surely one needs to get close to the researcher and their research in order to agitate and help bring about the kind of inquiry and learning necessary for achieving a doctorate. This leads us to see the 'supervisory relationship' more along the lines of a coaching relationship. The coach doesn't 'supervise' their athletes, but nor do they do the work for their athletes either. Developing an understanding (during a doctorate), just like acquiring higher-level physical skills and abilities, is hard won and requires a coach who can provoke yet nurture. Simply being a past champion is not the criterion against which we determine who is a good coach. Equally, there's more to 'supervising' a PhD than merely having one yourself. Connectedly, it is people who are 'supervised', not the research itself. This critical point seems too easy to overlook at times and can occur if the learning relationship is misconstrued by thinking that it is the experienced researcher, complete with their own PhD and training, that supervises 'the project' being undertaken by the novice. As educational developers in doctoral education we have advocated that it is helpful to think of the 'P in PhD as being about the Person not the Project' (Palmer et al., 2024), a phrase and emphasis now adopted in a new, nationwide Supervision Survey from the UK Council for Graduate Education (UKCGE, 2024).

Following Taylor's (2019a) invitation to 'think of research supervision as a form of teaching', this is a valuable reminder that students are learners in doctoral programmes, which are assessed units of educational work. Therefore 'supervision' is primarily, a learning and teaching endeavour, the research enterprise that may stem from it being secondary to meeting educational learning outcomes in HE (e.g. QAA, 2020). One inevitable implication of this is that colleagues involved with research supervision may follow the 'model' or practices of supervision that they experienced as doctoral students themselves (Taylor et al., 2017). This, we take up through some critical self-reflections, and the hope that it spurs on some critical thought in the reader.

Chris Hughes

I learned lots, but was I 'supervised'?

There are three main characters in this short story. My co-author Clive was my undergraduate dissertation supervisor and was the nudge that I didn't know that I needed. The recipient of this, Andrew, supervised my PhD. The person who has had the most influence on my recent intellectual development, Leon, was the person who received me as the confused post-doctoral vagabond that I was. All three people have nudged, cajoled, provoked, mentored and shaped me. Writing this chapter comes at a time when I'm moving away to pastures new, and a good vehicle for some critical reflections on supervision might be something by way of a series of letters that I sent to these important people. Did these three people follow a model? Could we model what they did with me?

> *Dear Andrew,*
>
> *I'll be heading off soon and whilst I think we might touch base at times, I wanted to send a little note. I often think of the third time we met; I was terrified of you. I had completed the PhD registration forms and you set me the task of summarising some literature and starting to shape some kind of research question. Walking up to your office I half expected a reality shock. 'Come in you daft t##t'. 'What sort of s##t have you been smoking'? No sooner did I have chance to respond, we were heading out for coffee and a very subtle unpicking of my early naïve writing. You knew that you could do that with me, it helped, it scared*

me, but I'm glad you were like that. There have been times when I have questioned some of the things that you did as a 'supervisor'. I have often wondered whether you could have done more, whether I could have done more, whether you even 'supervised' me at all. I want to say that you didn't supervise, but I now don't think of that as being a problem. I want to thank you for not being the supervisor that I didn't need.

With my students, I don't try to emulate you. There are however times where and when bits of you come out in me. I'm sure "Posner" would have the same thought about "Hector." Equally, I'm thankful that you didn't "Felix" me towards a PhD. I can see lots of this pedagogy in a much better light now and I thank you enormously.
Best wishes,
Chris

Dear Leon,

You saved me. When we met, I was utterly lost and completely disillusioned – intellectually homeless. I'm writing this letter at a time when my career direction is changing in several respects, and I have the opportunity to pause and think about 'supervision'. I 'supervise' students with you, and we will do more in the future, but you have in many respects shaped my future at the same time. I have seen through you a version of 'supervision' very different to those frequently illustrated in the literature; you have 'mentored' me, you "passed the parcel."

Who would have thought what would come from a canoe paddle and a mutual interest in Wittgenstein!? That paddle was of no use whatsoever as you let me, and several others, 'bob about in confusion' until being able to float and 'see our way around' the Investigations. You did all that unsettling for what appears to be no material gain for yourself, thank you.

I certainly wouldn't want to be supervised by Ludwig Wittgenstein, part of me thinks I couldn't handle you! I do however truly value you, and him, seeking to not spare me the effort of thinking for myself.
I'll do my best to "pass the parcel."
Chris

Dear Clive,

There's been no shortage of beer and burgers. One regret I have though is that we haven't had too many random trips and adventures; you know though that the truth is that I'm too much of a wimp.

You were my first supervisor, and you have supervised. Curiously though, you have been someone comfortable with letting me rub off on you. You have had a certain openness to enjoy the ride and let me be

me; you've known how to point me in a particular direction and been comfortable with me taking steps on that route. Not too many people would be so understanding of me when I ramble on (about Caesar salad in this chapter!); you do this because you trust that some good might come from it. Thank you for being that supervisor who puts their trust in their student. You trusted me to make mushrooms on toast in a cave, I trusted you to get us both in and out of the bloody thing.
I can't thank you enough,
Chris

Clive Palmer:

My PhD supervisor was brilliant. He was a teacher to the core who valued the learning relationship. He was an expert in the field my research was in, which was philosophy and international gymnastics. While he openly admits he 'was just following his nose' on what PhD's are, he has definitely shaped the way I support others on their doctorates now. However, he did not have a PhD himself and had no experience of supervising PhDs during his long career in HE – my PhD was his first and last at the end of his career (which accounts for his nose following!). My Director of Studies on the other hand was a geologist who knew nothing about gymnastics, but was very experienced, with forty to fifty completions, at guiding projects through progression boards, ethics, viva examinations, etc. My DoS appreciated the value of my relationship with the topic expert; however, my DoS also knew me very well as a learner. In 1988, leaving the RAF, I signed up to an undergraduate degree that my yet-to-become DoS (I started my PhD in 1999) was programme leader for. My undergraduate degree was dual honours requiring two major projects, and therefore two research supervisors. One supervisor was my yet-to-become DoS [geologist], the other was a highly respected sports coach, expert and consultant in his field. My experience of being supervised by him was absolutely awful. He was dry, overtly business like, detached and dis-passionate. I felt like my learning was getting in his way. At the time I thought this was normal, all I knew was that I did not want to be supervised like that again!

When I look back, this undergraduate experience was highly formative for me regarding how I go about facilitating other's learning through research. The person who provided such a dull and numbing experience of supervision for me did not import his skills as a coach into his educational work of research supervision. He did not have a PhD at the time but was doing one, which may have been the model he visited upon me from his supervisor, if he felt those were appropriate expectations on how to go about things, now we were doing 'research' and not just interacting through classroom teaching. The shift in formality towards 'research' was significant to him, but as the learner, I did not like his shift. My model of helping others to learn through research is an informed choice, born from my experience and how I think I'd like to be treated as a learner.

I am fortunate to have had opportunities to reflect on my experiences of research supervision, receiving it and providing it, which for me have usually turned to the quality of student experience I had myself, or I am able to afford others. For example, some ten years after my PhD I wondered if research supervision was a matter of '20:20 clarity or blurred view of care?' (Palmer, 2011), and then another decade to realize that learning through doctoral research for me is a matter of 'Flippin' switches and floatin' boats' to nurture the conditions for learning to thrive (Palmer, 2024).

REFLECTIVE ACTIVITY 6.1: UNDERSTANDING THE SUPERVISEE EXPERIENCE

Step 1: Personal reflection

Take a moment to think about your own experiences as a supervisee.

Consider the following questions:

What qualities did you appreciate most in your past supervisors?

Were there any supervisory styles that challenged you or made your experience difficult?

How did feedback (both positive and constructive) impact your motivation and growth?

Were expectations and goals clearly communicated to you? How did that affect your performance?

Did you feel supported and encouraged to take on new challenges?

Step 2: Identifying key themes

From your reflection, identify three key themes that influenced your experience as a supervisee. For each theme, consider:

How did this aspect impact your growth and learning?

How does this experience shape the way you supervise others today?

Step 3: Application to your current role

Now, think about your current supervision style:

Do you provide the kind of support and guidance that you valued as a supervisee?

How do you handle feedback and communication with those you supervise?

What improvements can you make to create a more positive and growth-oriented environment for your supervisees?

The act of modelling: Shaping and influencing

Upon which model of models should we speak about 'modelling supervision'? Is there any way to model the kinds of valuable things being illustrated above? Models, frameworks and concepts are everywhere, but what exactly do we mean when we speak about models, and, more specifically, modelling supervision? Does 'modelling supervision' even make sense? There are perhaps two distinct ways to see the problem of/with models, let's lay them out with two questions:

1 Is supervision **the model** for the things done when assisting the learning of doctoral candidates? Or
2 Are the things done when assisting the learning of doctoral candidates **modelled**, and then called supervision?

A similar dynamic is brought out by thinking about the difference between 'models of' and 'models for' things. In a sense both these questions focus on things that overlap but the questions help bring about a feature of models that is at times rather abstract, distracting and arguably unhelpful.

Towards question 1, the UKCGE Good Supervisory Practice Framework (Taylor, 2019b), though not a 'model', is, we believe, the most accessible, well-framed, considered 'model' for shaping the learning relationship in doctoral study. The ten areas of the GSPF give some structure to supervision practice nationally where there was little before in this area of Higher Education. The GSPF spans from the recruitment phase right through to examination and beyond, basically pointing to common areas of learner needs and encouraging supervisor reflections on key topics arising throughout the life-course of a doctoral programme.

The GSPF criteria include:

1 Recruitment and selection
2 Supervisory relationships with candidates
3 Supervisory relationships with co-supervisors
4 Supporting candidates' research projects
5 Encouraging candidates to write and giving appropriate feedback
6 Keeping the research on track and monitoring progress
7 Supporting candidates' personal, professional and career development
8 Supporting candidates through completion and final examination
9 Supporting candidates to disseminate their research
10 Reflecting upon and enhancing practice.

The GSPF is born from years of experience in teaching at doctoral level, with the intention of enabling others with less experience in doctoral supervision to identify areas of good practice, rather than just blindly 'having a go'. That said the GSPF is still just a generalized set of areas to consider about practice, it cannot tell us what to do, and nor does it seek to.

Towards question 2, the query is whether teaching actions can be shaped or modelled to meet the needs of the individual learner. There are many theorists who have spent their life's work in search of clarity on this matter, setting out their models to explain it. Some notable examples are:

- Dewey's (1938) – Experiential Learning
- Piaget's (1964) – Stages of Cognitive Development
- Vygotsky's (1967) – Zone of Proximal Development
- Kolb's (1984) – Learning Style Inventory
- Myer's-Briggs (1962) – Personality Type Indicator Assessment
- Belbin (1993) – Team Role Characteristics
- Bloom's (1956) – Taxonomy of Learning
- Mosston's (1966) – Spectrum of Teaching Styles

From the richness of these theorists' work to delve into the nuances of the learning and teaching experience, their models often become more complex and overlapping in what they are attempting to explain. However, the models they present are fixed in that theorist's view of the world, and their view

REFLECTIVE ACTIVITY 6.2: THINKING ABOUT THE GSPF CRITERIA

How do you ensure that you select candidates whose research interests align with your expertise and institutional capacity?

How do you establish a productive and supportive relationship with your candidates? Can you identify any challenges you have faced in supervision? How have you addressed them?

How do you navigate relationships with co-supervisors to ensure a collaborative approach? Reflect on a time when differences in supervisory styles arose. How did you handle them?

What strategies do you use to guide candidates in developing their research projects? How do you balance providing direction while fostering candidates' independence?

How do you encourage candidates to develop strong writing habits? Reflect on the effectiveness of the feedback you provide – how do you ensure it is constructive and actionable?

What methods do you use to track and assess candidates' progress? Have you encountered instances where a candidate struggled to stay on track? How did you intervene?

In what ways do you support candidates in developing their professional and career skills? Reflect on an instance where you guided a candidate beyond their research – what was the outcome?

How do you prepare candidates for their thesis defence or final examination? What strategies have you found effective in managing candidates' stress and anxiety around completion?

How do you encourage candidates to publish or present their research? Reflect on how you have helped candidates develop confidence in sharing their work with a wider audience.

What steps do you take to reflect on and enhance your supervisory practice? Identify one area of improvement in your supervisory approach and outline steps to address it.

of learning, not to mention a given theorist's preference for plotting indices, creating measures, scoring statements and giving definitions to substantiate their particular model of learning. This, all the while, the learner is a constantly moving and evolving social being. Achieving one score and a label or being a particular type of this or that learner can never be a full or accurate account of the learner as they develop, and that is maybe the point, as good learners are developing and changing rapidly – such a learner is evident in our reflections above. These models tell us things about the observable, general characteristics of learners, which the teacher, if a given theory appeals to them, can apply in their thinking, to interpret freely and make any assessment they feel appropriate about a learner in a given situation. On this basis, it has to be wondered how useful these theories are to model our actions as teachers, given that many of them have been the foundation of educational training through the twentieth and twenty-first centuries.

However, caution: There is no model to be found in this chapter about models. If a model is something that you require, we invite you to ask yourself the question, for what purpose might it be required? Only then might you be better equipped in your pursuit. Instead, what we offer is something far more modest but potentially more helpful to supervisors and those being supervised. We are encouraging a critical reflection on the nature of models against the backdrop of our own reflections – we are showing rather than telling.

Let's take a step back and look at some features of models that require careful thought. Take concepts like leadership, management, teaching, coaching, parenting and, for present purposes, supervision. Here, some things that might be 'modelled' (by various means of representation) are data, findings, themes, trends, connections, processes, etc. These models are meant to provide a representation, clarification, simplification, abstraction, etc., for us to better see something that is occasionally difficult to grasp. Such models might depict a feature of the whole (communication *in* leadership) or, perhaps, a schematic of the whole (Leadership). Such models might at times be about the thing (Teaching) in the general sense, or in a more contextual sense (teaching X to Y). Nevertheless, the goal is always to render clear and simple something that might not always be seen clearly. Now, reflecting upon your practice and reading of literature, do these kinds of models succeed in achieving their aim? Is the aim even worthwhile? The problem here is related to Graham McFee's stance on the providing of definitions in a quest for 'definiteness', that once a definition is set out, the definition itself has to be explained and re-defined. What was meant to be concise and clear, got longer and often murkier (McFee, 1992, p. 16).

There is another sense of model that offers a more pliable and useful grammar. Built into the grammar of model as previously described (representation, simplification, etc.) is a certain rigidity and scientism. Such models need to convey a solidity which, for the presumed lucky recipient, offers something concrete by way of representation – 'this is a model of that', for example, a model car, train set, house, etc., come to mind – they might not be replicas, but they are predicated on modelling the thing as a thing as it is, but without ALL its features and properties. It's hard to see this being particularly useful for processes, like teaching, learning and supervision, but there is no doubt for many a temptation to depict and model processes as material things. There is also at times an allure for such depictions by way of models, there can be a certain sense of reassurance by 'having a model'. Both supervisors and students can occasionally find reassurance in models (model feedback, model chapters, model/mock questions and model answers). However, might models stifle learning? Did Wittgenstein have something like this in mind when he insisted, we think for ourselves? There is also the idea of a model as a sign – things fall into place and we know what to do when we see the sign. Models of all sorts strive for this kind of generality and even reproducibility in action, but can it apply to individual thinking? There is also the concept of a model as a map – a surveyable representation. But while the map sets out the geography or topography, it does not decide for us where we might want to go.

All models have limitations, and this must be remembered. For models to be models they must omit certain elements, features, properties or aspects. A model that was indistinguishable from the real thing would cease to be a model; it would be another real thing. In that way, there is a window of possibility for models – too much generality at one end, or excessive particularity at the other end, then things become abstract with little applicability, representation and practical use. This window between generality and particularity appears to be a problem for modelling supervision, where it is perfectly feasible to set out a framework of recognizably good, but basic, features of practice in teaching others on doctoral programmes, such as the UKCGE Good Supervisory Practice Framework (Taylor, 2019b), but, that framework cannot tell you how to supervise a particular person in a particular circumstance.

For something to be a 'model of', or 'for' something then it needs to have, at its very least, some kind of structural feature. A model airplane for example does not require the capacity for flight for it to be a model; it must however have some similarity with a real plane that can fly (proportion, arrangement, scale, etc.) for it to be of any use as a model. An architectural model house is never meant to be habitable; but to assist in the design process, though, it does require the implementation of certain building/engineering concepts and principles for it to be of any practical or aesthetic use. The model might well fall down but the idea is that the model helps to design a house that stays up. Let's take things back to supervision – whatever the model might look or be like, there are certain concepts, that need to be properly understood, factored in and sensibly arranged for the model-to-model supervision.

Caesar salad and supervision

We noted earlier that we are not offering anything in the form of a model. Instead, we are encouraging critical reflection on the range of concepts that need to be 'baked in' so to speak. In that sense, a helpful way to look at this is by thinking about something altogether quite different. For a salad to be a Caesar salad it needs to conform to certain rules; it must have certain things in it, period. For many, that might sound like rigid stipulation, but that is just how things are if we wish for something more definite or specialized. You might ask the waiter for a Caesar salad without the anchovies and be happy with the result, and it will still say 'Caesar Salad' on the bill, but, in a very important sense, you haven't eaten or paid for a Caesar salad. Now let's jump back to supervision. What would it be to supervise someone doing a doctorate and the supervisor set the research question(s)? – just like omitting the anchovies. Here, the opportunity for the learner to design the question(s) is omitted, so could we model supervision on this premise ... that key things are being left out? Persisting with this line of thought, could we model supervision on it being the case that supervisors give to their students 'understanding'? Of course not. Could we model supervision along the lines of 'students being absolutely independent'? Well, we could bake into all such models certain notions of question design, developing an understanding and independence, etc., but if we baked in *these* notions with conceptual misunderstanding, then all we have is something that we might (wrongly) call a 'model of supervision'.

Back to Caesar salad for a minute, the presence of parmesan and croutons is rather pivotal too – anchovies aside for a second. At different sorts of establishments, with creative licence, yet a degree of restraint, the parmesan could be shaved, it could be made into crisps, it could be turned into a fancy foam or even a jelly. The crouton could be sourdough, they could be wafer like or they could be covered in the parmesan to make lovely little cheese-on-toast like nibbles. Certain things being equal, we are in a sense only limited by our own skill and imagination here, but there is a conceptual limit as we've tried to explain. Supervision is the same in that sense. Just as you can't have a smooth minestrone soup, you can't have an entirely supervisor-led doctoral education or a learning relationship where the supervisor passes on 'understanding'. No model could ever cater for, prescribe or forecast the subtleties of learner-teacher interactions as they progress through a doctoral programme, each often learning from the other along the way. So, with these thoughts in mind, a model of supervision, should this still be something needed or wanted, must have a certain degree of structural integrity (concepts) but with a pedagogical pliability. You would need to know what supervision is (conceptually) before you model it – the problem of defining the definition again.

Conclusion: Three recommendations

If we were to suggest a 'model of good practice' our three recommendations would be to consider that people tend to learn more effectively when challenges are shared with contemporaries around them. Doctoral learners are not in competition with each other and there is much to gain from the synergy of sharing their expertise. Such an action brings learners together in projects with the pedagogical stance of the supervisor and we advocate strongly for the establishment of **communities of learning** from the start of a doctoral programme (e.g. Hughes & Palmer, 2023; Palmer & Hughes, 2023; Palmer et al., 2024). This has the added benefit of **breaking down isolation** in doctoral learning, even if the candidate is a remote or distance learner, perhaps in another country, they can still experience being included in something larger than them alone. Our final recommendation is to remember there is a **natural power imbalance** when a person signs up to become a doctoral candidate – that by definition, a student can only be 'a student' if there is 'a teacher' present. The teacher or supervisor in our case is the essential element in the educational equation to lay claim to being a 'university', itself a seat of learning.

References

Barnett, R. (2022) *The philosophy of higher education: A critical introduction.* Abingdon: Routledge.

Belbin, M. (1993) *Team roles at work.* Oxford: Butterworth-Heinemann.

Bloom, B.S. (1956) *Taxonomy of educational objectives, handbook: The cognitive domain.* New York: David McKay.

Dewey, J. (1938) *Experience and education.* New York: Macmillan Company.

Hughes, C. & Palmer, C. (2010) 'Examining a coaching philosophy through ethnographic principles – winter with Woolton', *Journal of Qualitative Research in Sports Studies*, 4(1), pp. 23–48.

Hughes, C. & Palmer, C. (2020) 'One foot in the cave – a sensorial adventure of a first-time caver', *Journal of Qualitative Research in Sports Studies*, 14(1), pp. 335–54.

Hughes, C. & Palmer, C. (2023) 'PGR supervision and learning: A collaborative development', *SOLSTICE and Centre for Learning and Teaching (CLT) Conference*, Edge Hill University, Ormskirk, UK, 14–15 June.

Kolb, D.A. (1984) *Experiential learning: Experience as the source of learning and development*. Englewood Cliffs, NJ: Prentice Hall.

McFee, G. (1992) *Understanding dance*. London: Routledge.

Mosston, M. (1966) *Teaching physical education: From command to discovery*. Ohio: Charles E. Merrill Books.

Myers, I. (1962) *The myers-briggs type indicator: Manual*. Palo Alto, CA: Consulting Psychologists Press.

Palmer, C. (2011) 'Supervision: 20:20 clarity or blurred view of care?' *Journal of Qualitative Research in Sports Studies*, 5(1), pp. 159–70.

Palmer, C. (2024) 'Flippin' switches and floatin' boats: Nurturing the conditions for learning to thrive (chapter 1: case study 1.2)'. In: Polkinghorne, M., Taylor, J. & Knight, F. (eds) *Innovative approaches to doctoral supervision: Selected case studies*. Cheltenham: Edward Elgar Publishing.

Palmer, C. & Hughes, C. (2023) 'An interactive workshop to promote good practice in PGR/doctoral supervision pathways to formal recognition from the UK Council for Graduate Education', *Learning and Teaching Week*, Edge Hill University, Ormskirk, UK, 6 July.

Palmer, C., Hughes, C. & Sprake, A. (2024) '"Getting on with strangers": Collaborations, expectations, and doctoral relations', *6th International Conference on Developments in Doctoral Education and Training*, UKCGE, Bath, 21–22 March.

Palmer, C., Sprake, A. & Hughes, C. (2023) 'Managing the expectations of doctoral students and their supervisors', *Encyclopedia*, 3, pp. 1474–88.

Palmer, C., Sprake, A. & Hughes, C. (2024) *You expect me to do what? PhD by portfolio: research showcase and development event for candidates and supervisors*. Research and Knowledge Exchange Festival, UCLan, 8 February.

Piaget, J. (1964) 'Cognitive development in children: Development and learning', *Journal of Research in Science Teaching*, 2(1), pp. 176–86.

QAA (2020) *Characteristics Statement: Doctoral Degree*. Quality Assurance Agency for Higher Education. Available at: https://www.qaa.ac.uk/docs/qaa/quality-code/doctoral-degree-characteristics-statement-2020.pdf (Accessed 2 July 2024).

Taylor, S. (2019a) 'Thinking of research supervision as a form of teaching'. In: Taylor, S. (ed.) *Enhancing practice in research supervision – Research supervisors network: Resource*. UK Council for Graduate Education, pp. 6–9.

Taylor, S. (2019b) *Good supervisory practice framework*. Lichfield: UK Council for Graduate Education (UKCGE).

Taylor, S., Kiley, M. & Humphrey, R.A. (2017) *Handbook for doctoral supervisors*. 2nd ed. Abingdon: Routledge.

UKCGE (2024) *The UK Research Supervision Survey (UKRSS 2024)*. UK Council for Graduate Education. Available at: https://research.shift-insight.co.uk/UKRSS (Accessed 2 July 2024).

Vygotsky, L.S. (1967) 'Play and its role in the mental development of the child', *Soviet Psychology*, 5(3), pp. 6–18.

8

Online Supervision of Distance Doctoral Researchers

Brett Bligh

Introduction

Online doctoral supervision is not merely a technological concern, although technology is certainly an important consideration. It requires rethinking and reconfiguring supervisory practices and environments (Huet & Casanova, 2020). All doctoral educators – even the sceptical, or those who supervise online rarely – should explore these issues, using the opportunity to reflect on their taken-for-granted ways of working (Roumell & Bolliger, 2017).

Many discussions of online supervision proceed from the potential for opening doctoral education:

- reaching non-traditional populations of doctoral students: working professionals, part-time and/or mature students, and those with family commitments or living in rural settings (Erichsen et al., 2014; Huet & Casanova, 2020);
- providing international possibilities, for students in countries where doctoral education is underdeveloped, to gain advanced qualifications from 'globally recognised universities' (Nasiri & Mafakheri, 2015);
- enabling doctoral students to undertake extended research in disparate locations, and thereby allowing them to confront global challenges (Stevens et al., 2021).

The quantity of online doctoral provision has been increasing for many years (Roumell & Bolliger, 2017), though this increase has accelerated in the wake of the Covid-19 pandemic (Stevens et al., 2021). Institutional provision is disproportionately concentrated in a universities from a few countries (UK, United States, Australia) (Huet & Casanova, 2020), and in particular disciplines – especially in 'professions' where graduates spend years in practice before some decide to return for postgraduate education (Albion & Erwee, 2011). Scholarly knowledge on the topic is underdeveloped in both scale and depth (Gray & Crosta, 2019; Guerin & Aitchison, 2021; Huet & Casanova, 2020) and disproportionately focuses on provision in education fields (Erichsen et al., 2014; Lee et al., 2022).

In this chapter, we explore the situation where research supervisors and students work at distance from each other, with supervision mediated by online technologies (cf. Huet & Casanova, 2020). The students (and sometimes supervisors) also usually work at distance from the awarding institution, with their wider network of research relationships also mediated online. In reality, there is no hard dichotomy between 'online' and 'traditional' doctoral education, but rather a spectrum of different approaches and situations (Erichsen et al., 2014).

We avoid assuming that online doctoral education is somehow an inferior version of traditional doctoral study (Wisker et al., 2021). It is, instead, a qualitatively new development in doctoral practice. Yet it does remain distinctively *doctoral* education. Other forms of online learning, such as blended learning for undergraduates, or MOOCs, are poor analogues. The situation might better be understood by analogy with the tradition of distance learning in adult education (Nasiri & Mafakheri, 2015; Torka, 2021).

In the following sections, we reflect on the issues of becoming an online supervisor, establishing online supervisory relationships, conducting online supervision meetings, engaging with online technologies and supporting online doctoral students to experience a sense of community. First, however, it is necessary to address the broader context.

Contexts of online doctoral supervision

As mentioned above, online doctoral student populations are noticeably diverse, with scholars discussing issues of gender, ethnicity, ability and international cultural background (Nasiri & Mafakheri, 2015; Roumell & Bolliger, 2017; Stevens et al., 2021). Many online doctoral students study part-time while working, funding their studies from their salary or with financial support from employers. Undertaking their doctorates as mature students, working through evenings and weekends, escaping to study in coffee shops, navigating hectic professional and family lives, such students often work very hard but still have lengthy completion times (Erichsen et al., 2014). A key motivation for many such students is to study with flexibility (Nasiri & Mafakheri, 2015). Conversely, the institutional motivation for offering online doctoral provision is often to recruit full-time professionals as students, using technology to offer programmes that minimize disruption to their working lives (Lee et al., 2022).

We should appreciate, then, that online doctoral students are adults of considerable prior accomplishment – in academia, career and perhaps family life (Torka, 2021). Many actively develop strategies for enhancing their experience and overcoming obstacles (Sussex, 2008) and feel that they demonstrate more focus, commitment and self-discipline than their traditional counterparts (Erichsen et al., 2014). Informed by their life experiences, online doctoral students may engage with unconventional research projects, with their professional status sometimes providing an opportunity to pursue those projects in impactful ways (Kumar & Johnson, 2017).

Common issues do exist for such students, however. As Sussex (2008) observes:

> The student is separated from (a) regular personal advisory meetings, as well as emergency on-demand personal contact, with the supervisor; (b) the supporting and collegial student networks which an on-campus, and perhaps in-college, environment can provide, and (c) the infrastructure of the home institution in its many forms – including libraries, space and room, and technology.
>
> (pp. 121–2)

Online doctoral students may feel a profound sense of isolation, since others in their lives (family, friends, work colleagues) may not understand their doctoral motivations and experiences (Erichsen et al., 2014), and they often miss out on the informal interactions within institutions which typically help doctoral students to build relationships and share knowledge (Wisker et al., 2021). As Kumar and Johnson (2017) put it, they are not 'surrounded by the culture of academia' (p. 208). This is an important well-being issue (Stevens et al., 2021). It may also narrow these students' perception of their studies, with wider aspects of university life – even where made available online – viewed as 'distractions' (Wisker et al., 2021). Supervisors may therefore need to help online doctoral students understand the wider developmental opportunities of the doctorate.

In this context, a wide range of online professional relationships are crucial. Online doctoral students have distinct requirements for administrative and pastoral support (Albion & Erwee, 2011), with institutions often poor at anticipating or meeting these needs (Guerin & Aitchison, 2021). Specialist support staff are important for online doctoral provision (Nasiri & Mafakheri, 2015), without which supervisors face disproportionate workload burdens. For this reason, online supervisors may often lobby for better support within their institutions.

Nonetheless, the supervisory relationship remains central. The supervisor is not only a mentor for online students' doctoral project, but also a guide supporting their interactions with the rest of the institution.

Being an online supervisor

Being an online doctoral supervisor is not easy. The role is poorly understood in the literature (Huet & Casanova, 2020), and institutional guidance and support is typically scant (Roumell & Bolliger, 2017). Understandably, then, many start by trying to transfer existing practices – developed for co-present supervision and often inherited from their own doctoral experiences (Maor et al., 2015; Wisker et al., 2021) – to the online context.

Doing so is hazardous. While existing expertise is hard-won and valuable (Kumar & Johnson, 2017; Roumell & Bolliger, 2017), and many progression requirements are similar for all doctoral students (Lundgren-Resenterra & Crosta, 2019), attempts to transfer co-present practices to online doctoral education are seldom entirely successful (Torka, 2021). Below, we reflect on how supervising online doctoral students is distinctive.

Firstly, doctoral supervisors often connect with their online students differently (Torka, 2021). Such students require 'rapid, comprehensive, non-ephemeral and intellectually and personally appropriate' forms of communication (Sussex, 2008), and so online supervision can be experienced as relatively more continuous and less episodic. More aspects of supervisors' and supervisees' lives, moreover, can easily become more entangled. Where video meetings and short messaging arise within domestic settings, the result can be a 'pedagogical homeliness', requiring that 'supervisors and candidates recognise, allow and acknowledge the tensions, paradoxes, vulnerability and exposedness that their homes express' (Wisker et al., 2021, p. 618).

Online supervisory relationships may also involve using more diverse forms of engagement (Torka, 2021). Supervisors and online doctoral students can benefit from exploring together:

- new ways of working collaboratively (Sussex, 2008);
- new understandings of the emerging needs of *both* parties for supervisory involvement and contact (Kumar & Johnson, 2017); and
- new technological possibilities (Palmer & Gillaspy, 2021).

The above must rest on a foundation of explicit, clear communication. Online communication is prone to misunderstandings, and supervisors should strive to avoid assumptions about contextual situations, cultural norms or prior knowledge. Instead, they should be direct about priorities: such as the 'hidden curriculum' of what doctoral students should *really* be doing; and wellness issues, including actively encouraging students to take days *off* (Roumell & Bolliger, 2017; Stevens et al., 2021). Supervisor communication can often feel highly structured – by comparison with campus-based doctoral supervision, there may be more asynchronous communication about planning, and synchronous meetings may focus more on the supervisor's advice (Torka, 2021).

It is crucial to appreciate that online supervisors serve as *mediators* between online doctoral students and the wider institution, campus and programme. They frequently help online students, who often remain unaware of information provided via institutional channels, to navigate the programme structure (Jacobsen et al., 2021), and may attempt to compensate for shortcomings in the support networks which other PhD students develop on-campus (Kumar & Johnson, 2017). Nasiri and Mafakheri (2015) discuss how online doctoral supervisors 'represent the whole university system for a distance student' (p. 1965). Doing so does not involve demonstrating only compliance. It can involve modelling healthy behaviour, such as answering emails promptly but *not* at weekends (Roumell & Bolliger, 2017). It can also involve showing students how to resist and fight aspects of the university system or academic culture – those 'sneaky ploys' we use to exert our own agency, make time for our priorities and keep our research interesting (Palmer & Gillaspy, 2021).

Online supervisors themselves often experience intense workloads (cf. Sussex, 2008), receiving messages day and night and having online tutorials lined up like a job queue in a call centre (Palmer & Gillaspy, 2021). Written feedback is important but time-consuming, with some students expecting unrealistic turnaround times (Roumell & Bolliger, 2017). There is often a heavy administrative burden – including where engaging with institutional systems on behalf of students (Nasiri & Mafakheri, 2015).

Online supervisors will, of course, develop ways of coping. Examples include 'more time-efficient interaction strategies such as virtual office hours, peer live meetings, a stricter schedule for submissions and feedback, and mandatory induction sessions' (Nasiri & Mafakheri, 2015, p. 1968). They may also develop their *own* technological systems for productivity, monitoring and student engagement (Palmer & Gillaspy, 2021), sometimes supplanting standard institutional tools and approaches. They should develop friendly working relationships with technical and administrative professionals, useful for fielding unconventional requests (Nasiri & Mafakheri, 2015). They will often choose to lobby for better recognition of their actual workload.

It can be very useful to discuss supervision experiences, anxieties and forms of working with other online doctoral supervisors, whether informally or in a more definite community established for the purpose. Huet and Casanova (2020) suggest that this might be done online, thereby providing useful insight into analogous student experiences.

Establishing online supervisory relationships

By now, it should be clear that online doctoral supervision involves a complex and ongoing relationship, and far more than a sequence of online meetings.

The starting point for this relationship can be difficult. Online doctoral students are less likely to choose their supervisors by carefully considering their expertise or identity, and may even be allocated institutionally, which can be a source of friction (Gray & Crosta, 2019). Many such students initially know little about their supervisors' professional profile and institutional status (Erichsen et al., 2014), and their interests may not match in terms of topic or methodology (Gray & Crosta, 2019). Some supervisors, conversely, may feel disappointed at a lack of potential for collaborative research or for the student's project to contribute to their research programme (Roumell & Bolliger, 2017). There is an urgent need for initial, informal conversations about the parties' respective motivations (Huet & Casanova, 2020) and to become 'professionally, personally and possibly socially well acquainted' (Sussex, 2008, p. 124).

Early supervisory interactions will address functional concerns: how (and how often) to meet, how to arrange meetings, reasonable work schedules, communication response times and so on (Lundgren-Resenterra & Crosta, 2019; Stevens et al., 2021). They should also consider the wider interactions a student might pursue (Torka, 2021), such as nurturing peer relationships (Jacobsen et al., 2021), research training (Wisker et al., 2021) and how training courses are places to meet peers as well as developing skills (Guerin & Aitchison, 2021). Mental health can be a challenging issue for online doctoral students, and supervisors should outline where professional support can be found and emphasize that it *is* appropriate to share such struggles within the supervisory relationship (Stevens et al., 2021). These functional discussions should lay foundations for a collegial, reciprocal and exploratory relationship of trust (Jacobsen et al., 2021). Where appropriate, topics of cultural disharmony and different international expectations might provide a basis for open and honest dialogue (Gray & Crosta, 2019).

Online supervisory relationships rely on clear structures and narratives (Huet & Casanova, 2020; Kumar & Johnson, 2017). Supervisors should outline processes and timelines, delineate accountability measures, and communicate expectations of students for proactive communication and of themselves for responding and providing feedback (Erichsen et al., 2014; Guerin & Aitchison, 2021). It is useful to clarify that the student *owns* their doctorate and must take independent responsibility for it (Albion & Erwee, 2011; Roumell & Bolliger, 2017). It will also be useful to have frank conversations about what is convenient for both parties, for example, about appropriate times to meet.

Online supervisors should offer a sense of 'remaining connected' (Lundgren-Resenterra & Crosta, 2019), thereby making the supervisory relationship seem 'less remote' (Sussex, 2008). Doing so is as much about establishing trust as skill development or feedback (Wisker et al., 2021). With sufficient quality and frequency of advice and interaction, genuine supervisory connections *can* be established online (Gray & Crosta, 2019; Torka, 2021). It is important to devote effort to managing online environments and communicative arrangements with students (Wisker et al., 2021), finding lifelines for maintaining informal relationships which substitute for the corridor conversations and 'open doors' of more traditional settings (Palmer & Gillaspy, 2021). Doing so should respect students' different preferences and autonomy; yet, even where a student inclines towards asynchronous communication, periodic 'check-in' meetings remain important for sustaining supervisory connections (Stevens et al., 2021).

One useful mechanism involves establishing recurrent interactions. Synchronous meetings must be held frequently enough to maintain momentum (Huet & Casanova, 2020; Roumell & Bolliger, 2017), and may usefully become embedded in recurrent routines wherein supervisors first provide annotated feedback on a document before reflecting on key points in the meeting (Kumar & Johnson, 2017). Maintaining suitable routines can help avoid domino effects, where delays or forgotten commitments spiral into bigger problems (Nasiri & Mafakheri, 2015). Yet the patterns should be reviewed periodically as students' requirements change (Erichsen et al., 2014).

Synchronous meetings only partially fulfil the need for connection of online doctoral students. Indeed, we might view the supervisory relationship as a process supported mainly by asynchronous communication but punctuated by moments of synchronous, specialized pedagogical intervention (Maor et al., 2015). Means of asynchronous communication might include annotated documents (Wisker et al., 2021), voice monologues (Sussex, 2008) and text chat (Maor et al., 2015). These means present possibilities for maintaining supervisory 'presence' (Rockinson-Szapkiw, 2012), and the resulting artefacts can be reviewed and searched by students later (Kumar & Johnson, 2017; Sussex, 2008). Yet they can also be overwhelming and confusing for both parties (Nasiri & Mafakheri, 2015). Mutual agreement and ongoing communication about the blend of shared 'places' for interacting and sharing documents can be very useful (Guerin & Aitchison, 2021; Palmer & Gillaspy, 2021).

Online supervisors should remain aware that their students' circumstances will change as the parties collaborate; for example, during periods of challenging family commitments, intense professional work (Guerin & Aitchison, 2021) or depression (Stevens et al., 2021). Since online doctoral students often undertake projects which dovetail with their work context, changes in that context can impact progress significantly (Kumar & Johnson, 2017). Framing communication supportively will be important in such circumstances, with supervisors wishing to proactively check on students (Roumell & Bolliger, 2017) while avoiding 'badgering' them (Albion & Erwee, 2011). Intervening at such moments is easier where a sense of connection and trust has been established beforehand.

Finally, while online doctoral students choose to study at distance for valid reasons, supervisors should not assume that in-person meetings are always impossible (Erichsen et al., 2014). Occasional co-present meetings can be useful, especially at critical points such as familiarizing the parties involved, dealing with 'troughs' of progress or immediately prior to submission (Sussex, 2008). In some cases, for instance where there is a cluster of supervisees in a given location, it may be possible for the supervisor to travel to meet students if institutional support is available (Albion & Erwee, 2011).

RESEARCH BRIEFING 8.1: DECOLONIZATION AND ONLINE SUPERVISION. MANATHUNGA'S BOOK ON REIMAGINING TIME, PLACE AND KNOWLEDGE IN INTERCULTURAL SUPERVISION

Manathunga (2014) states: "Place plays a hugely significant role in supervision, especially when students and supervisors come from different places" (p. 39). In an age of decolonization within higher education, including doctoral supervision, we should by now be acutely aware of the importance of place-based knowledge for indigenous philosophies and knowledge communities. What are the implications for doctoral supervision and decolonialization where the place of engagement is online? Writing over a decade ago, one of the most thoughtful voices on decolonial and intercultural postgraduate supervision, Catherine Manathunga, referred to then-dominant meeting platform Skype as a "non-place" (p. 46). At this time, the high-quality online doctoral programmes we see today were in their infancy, and largely overlooked by people writing about higher education. It was also a time before Covid-19 made so many more people familiar with working, talking and interacting through online platforms.

Online supervision has woven together three concurrent developments over the past decade:

1. the development of high-quality online doctoral programmes by institutions;
2. a greater familiarity with the online space as one where we talk and engage; and
3. an increasing call for decolonization within higher education and recognition of indigenous knowledges.

As the central aim of much doctoral work is a direct contribution to a body of knowledge, sensitivity to different ways of knowing the world is essential. Manathunga, referring to the esteemed international scholar Fazal Rizvi, states that when asked to speak on the issue of 'east meets west' the most important thing to consider is neither 'east' nor 'west', but *meets*. We therefore think it is timely to consider decolonization and the implications for when we *meet* in the space of online doctoral supervision.

We want to encourage reflection on Manathunga's work on intercultural supervision, and in a sense reimagine it in the context of the above developments. Given our commitment to decolonialization, can and should we rethink online supervision as a non-place?

In keeping with Manathunga's lead, this briefing will not provide 'tips'. Decolonization requires a deeper, more thoughtful and reflective way of considering these issues.

REFLECTIVE ACTIVITY 8.1. INTERCULTURAL LEARNING

Considering online supervision, we fully understand that to describe the 'online' as a place, can completely undermine the visceral importance of land, earth, dust, sea, skies and mountains to indigenous understandings of place, and the attendant place-based knowledges. This foundational importance of place underpins all indigenous knowledge, and also the simple proposition that true decolonialization must involve reparation of land (Manathunga, 2014).

Following Manathunga's lead, we do not get into strained debates about the difference between place and space, but comfortably use the terms interchangeably. We cannot, however, blithely say that the online supervision space is a place like any other, real in the same ways as the Australian outback, the savannah of Africa or the plains of north America.

A key idea to help bring a decolonial understanding to our online supervisory practices comes from Manathunga, who cites Bhabba's idea of a "third space" where different epistemological understandings come together to communicate, negotiate and learn. If we conceive the online supervisory space as a third space in this way, we strive to find a place to coexist without making any claims of either appropriation or dismantling of the foundations of indigenous place-based learning and the notion of place in very real mountains, rivers and so forth.

We suggest that third space is an important way of thinking, warmer and more rewarding than the idea of non-space for online doctoral supervision. Online supervision should be a third space which acknowledges and respects other notions of space.

Online supervision meetings

While supervision meetings are but one element of online doctoral supervision, they are significant for addressing important problems, determining strategy and upcoming actions, and setting the tone of the relationship. In some ways, online supervision meetings are not categorically different from their campus-based counterparts, although they may be more 'structured' and have more focus on the supervisor (Torka, 2021). Yet such meetings, typically conducted via video conferencing, should aim to support the wider online doctoral process.

An initial issue is scheduling, with the frequency of meetings determined by student and supervisor preferences but also institutional rules. The timing and frequency of meetings can affect students' persistence and completion rates (Gray & Crosta, 2019), perhaps by overcoming communication challenges and feelings of isolation (Huet & Casanova, 2020). Yet finding mutually convenient times to meet can be challenging, given time differences and work-life commitments. It can be useful to schedule meetings regularly, while arranging meetings to facilitate following-up on asynchronous feedback can allow students to 'clarify their understanding of the supervisor's comments and suggestions' (Guerin & Aitchison, 2021).

Such meetings are fundamentally about rich, real-time conversations – often resourced by artefacts like manuscripts – and sharing motivations and challenges (Stevens et al., 2021). Many will address a specific issue or piece of work on which the student is currently focused, with supervisors giving feedback and reassurance.

Online doctoral supervision meetings can feel 'structured', which potentially accentuates the power of the supervisor (Torka, 2021). Supervisors should reflect on how the structure they adopt fosters desirable interactions, for example, a 'sandwich model' might position detailed intellectual work *between* supportive personal interactions (Wisker et al., 2021). It can be useful to reserve time at the start of meetings to discuss personal issues and perhaps check on the student's wellness (Stevens et al., 2021). Meetings might conclude by planning and exploring strategy – to direct the upcoming actions of the student, but also to explicitly demonstrate the practice of disaggregating academic work (Guerin & Aitchison, 2021).

The use of online technologies is explored in more detail below. But screen sharing functions in videoconferencing tools are particularly useful for allowing common reference to students' work and supervisors' comments (Wisker et al., 2021). They might also occasionally be used (somewhat awkwardly) to demonstrate processes or skills, such as using data analysis software (Kumar & Johnson, 2017). Yet screen sharing might also reinforce power relations, since supervisors usually determine whether and how to share screens. Reflection and discussion are therefore advised, and technical solutions might be considered – such as viewing online boards or shared documents which both parties can edit (Guerin & Aitchison, 2021). Recording such meetings for later reference can be useful for students (Palmer & Gillaspy, 2021).

Supervisors should bear in mind some potential difficulties in online meetings. These are, of course, not purely virtual events, with participants having to find suitable physical spaces for holding video calls (Wisker et al., 2021). Pets, children and spouses can enter into meetings, which can interrupt the flow but also defray an overly formal tone. Supervisors and students may not experience the same meeting in the same way, with supervisors worrying more than students about voice tone and body language (Kumar & Johnson, 2017). There is a danger of monologue, which may not be a good use of meeting time; reflective commentaries can instead be recorded. But even genuine interaction can become relentless. As Palmer and Gillaspy (2021) note, 'screen presence seems to elicit constant dialogue [...] where there are not empty spaces for thinking' (p. 674). This may serve to partly explain why online meetings are often perceived as exhausting (Torka, 2021), with phenomena such as 'Zoom fatigue' affecting the attention levels of students and the work lives of supervisors (who may host meetings in succession). The stability or bandwidth of internet connections can also be difficult, especially given the international geographical spread of online doctoral students (Wisker et al., 2021).

Online technologies and doctoral supervision

Online doctoral supervisors and students vary in expertise and enthusiasm for online technology, and in access to it. Yet such technologies are their core means of overcoming what Maor et al. (2015) call the 'tyranny of distance' (p. 174). Supervisors must usually take the lead in engaging with such technologies, and often in choosing which tools and functions to use (Wisker et al., 2021).

Research typically emphasizes how *multiple* technologies are used (Guerin & Aitchison, 2021; Jacobsen et al., 2021; Kumar & Johnson, 2017; Lee et al., 2022), typically combined according to the different interaction and communication modalities they offer (Erichsen et al., 2014). A distinction is usually made between asynchronous and synchronous tools, with the latter permitting more authentic, critical dialogue, yet less flexibility in scheduling (Lee et al., 2022). Sussex (2008) has suggested that such tools can be further differentiated according to whether they cater for written or spoken communication, while Lee et al.'s (2022) typology foregrounds which learning tasks are supported – such as supervision, writing and data analysis (p. 46).

In Table A, we consider a range of goals for online doctoral supervision, and how these goals are related to different technologies in published papers. The goal of maintaining contact with students, for example, is typically accomplished using email, while meeting 'together' is associated with videoconference platforms. In each case we consider the technology's role and commonly discussed issues. The table addresses common goals and technologies first, before turning to more specialist ones, and retains a narrow focus on supervision rather than considering how online doctoral students might use technologies for purposes like data analysis.

Table A Online technologies and the goals of online doctoral supervision

Goal	Online technologies	Roles and issues
Maintaining contact (Albion & Erwee, 2011; Lee et al., 2022; Nasiri & Mafakheri, 2015; Palmer & Gillaspy, 2021; Roumell & Bolliger, 2017)	Email Scheduling tools (Outlook, Doodle)	• A familiar foundation • Reducing the psychological distance experienced by students • Modelling acceptable response times • Useful for scheduling meetings • Focus on consultative and administrative interactions
Meeting 'together' (Guerin & Aitchison, 2021; Kumar & Johnson, 2017; Palmer & Gillaspy, 2021; Roumell & Bolliger, 2017; Stevens et al., 2021; Sussex, 2008; Torka, 2021; Wisker et al., 2021)	Videoconference (e.g. Zoom) • Sharing functions • Recording functions Telephone if needed	• Simulating a table discussion • Both parties demonstrate thinking processes • Looking together at artefacts, but with restricted views • Recording meetings • Scheduled in advance, acknowledging time zone differences • Requires a suitable, quiet space to talk • Negotiating control of meeting tools • Fatigue • Bandwidth and internet issues
Extensive written feedback (Guerin & Aitchison, 2021; Jacobsen et al., 2021; Kumar & Johnson, 2017; Nasiri & Mafakheri, 2015)	Email Document annotation Shared documents, collaborative writing tools (e.g. Google Docs)	• Longer, detailed, considered feedback • Tracking comments and progress across rounds of revision • Danger of misunderstandings and out-of-context comments • Managing expectations about response times • 'Accepting' comments without reflection

Goal	Online technologies	Roles and issues
Supporting longitudinal reflection and documenting progression (Kumar & Johnson, 2017; Palmer & Gillaspy, 2021; Stevens et al., 2021)	Virtual spaces (e.g. Teams) Emails, documents Institutional recording platforms	• Documenting decisions and deadlines • Sharing and storing annotated documents and meeting recordings so they can be found later • Meeting summaries as resource for reflection • Documenting that a meeting was held • Decide what records to share with whom • Multiple spaces for different purposes
Ambient messaging (Palmer & Gillaspy, 2021; Sussex, 2008)	Instant messaging tools (Teams, LinkedIn, Facebook)	• Short text communications • Fast replies expected • Scrolling back through chat transcript • Groups can chat
Reflective commentary (Rockinson-Szapkiw, 2012; Roumell & Bolliger, 2017; Sussex, 2008)	Sending audio/video files Screencast platforms	• Monologue of supervisor's voice and perspective • Tutor answers questions or respond to work at length • Can be created relatively quickly • Recorded and so not ephemeral • Useful paralinguistic cues • Perceptions of instructor enhanced
Open ended group interaction (Lee et al., 2022; Maor et al., 2015; Nasiri & Mafakheri, 2015; Palmer & Gillaspy, 2021)	Social media/ productivity platforms (LinkedIn, Teams, Discord, X, WhatsApp) Virtual portfolio platforms VLE areas (Canvas, Moodle) Virtual worlds (Second Life, World of Warcraft)	• Community of scholars • Informal with little agenda • Exploring research and supervision issues • Collaborative learning • Collegial dialogue and connection • Collaborative writing

The table conveys that a wide range of technologies is discussed in the research. Online supervisors will benefit from reflecting periodically on the possibilities for their practice. Yet supervisors will not use all of these technologies, or even necessarily the same tools with different students; the needs of the supervisory relationship should drive the choice of technologies, rather than vice versa (Albion & Erwee, 2011). While students do sometimes desire more varied online communication (Erichsen et al., 2014), the range of tools used typically remains limited (Lee et al., 2022). Supervisors may wish to become familiar with a specific range of tools (Kumar & Johnson, 2017). Within particularly supervisory relationships, supervisors and students may agree initially to use a smaller set of tools and then consider other options as needs arise.

The experience of being an online supervisor can benefit from being *open* to new technological possibilities. Supervisors sometimes feel – legitimately – that online technologies constrain their practices, but sometimes a lack of persistence or awareness of options can itself restrain opportunities to 'flex' towards more varied possibilities (Palmer & Gillaspy, 2021). Where doctoral students are more knowledgeable about technology than their supervisors, this can be an interesting opportunity for open dialogue.

Supporting online doctoral students to experience academic community

Supervisors have a responsibility to reflect on how their online supervisees experience academic community and how to support them to seek and engage with particular communities. While doing so can help students address isolation, procrastination and stress (Erichsen et al., 2014; Maor et al., 2015; Sussex, 2008), it is more than a remedial concern. Understand and working in academic communities, debating and critiquing ideas, and forming connections with other scholars are important developmental issues for those pursuing a doctorate (Guerin & Aitchison, 2021; Lee et al., 2022; Wisker et al., 2021). Supporting students in these endeavours takes time and effort, although conversely it may also serve to reduce a student's reliance on their supervisors (Nasiri & Mafakheri, 2015).

Some approaches can be modest but useful. Supervisors might, for example:

- organize online group supervision meetings, to forge links between students and reduce repetition of some information (Nasiri & Mafakheri, 2015; Stevens et al., 2021);

- share resources between students by email, promoting interchange (Palmer & Gillaspy, 2021); or
- encourage students to support each other's writing (Guerin & Aitchison, 2021).

More ambitiously, supervisors might set up online, informal spaces. One published example is 'Clive's Learning Shack' (Palmer & Gillaspy, 2021), a Microsoft Teams space containing paper recommendations, reflective discussions about progress and a 'virtual gallery' of students' research interests. Email lists or social media groups (e.g. on Facebook) have also been useful for pursuing such goals (Nasiri & Mafakheri, 2015).

Another approach involves connecting online students to existing departmental or institutional initiatives, such as attending research seminars online (Guerin & Aitchison, 2021). Supervisors should also reinforce that students should not overlook existing university support, such as research training courses (where they might connect with campus-based students) and library services (Nasiri & Mafakheri, 2015).

Where there is a critical mass of online doctoral students, dedicated online communities can be powerful. Some online doctoral programmes organize students into cohort groups for mutual support (Lee et al., 2022; Stevens et al., 2021), with such groups sometimes meeting in person to strengthen social bonds (Jacobsen et al., 2021). A variety of online support groups for different purposes might be created (Lee et al., 2022), for instance, for sharing joint interests in topics or methodologies (Jacobsen et al., 2021). Consideration should be given to whether groups are aimed at *all* PhD students or online students only (Albion & Erwee, 2011). With appropriate support, academics might coordinate particular communities as part of their workload (Nasiri & Mafakheri, 2015), though other networks might be student-led (Lee et al., 2022). The role and extent of supervisor involvement vary, and might involve merely indicating the possibilities and checking on experiences.

Supervisors will also find it useful to encourage students to engage in opportunities outside the university. Online doctoral students might engage in-person with conventional academic conferences and events, and researchers and institutions, which are 'local' to where they live (Nasiri & Mafakheri, 2015), and engage with other researchers via social media (Palmer & Gillaspy, 2021). They might also consider attending online conferences and courses (Wisker et al., 2021) and participating in international networks of doctoral students (Maor et al., 2015).

Conclusion

This chapter has explored the context of online doctoral supervision, highlighting its particular relevance to non-traditional doctoral students and the demanding expectations often placed on supervisors. We have discussed how supervision in this context demands sustained engagement and positions supervisors as mediators between students and their institutions.

We have also examined the central role of technology in shaping communication, supervision practices and the student's engagement in academic community. As online supervision continues to develop, it will present both challenges and exciting opportunities for fostering meaningful, supportive and academically rigorous relationships between supervisors and doctoral students, and for opening doctoral education to students across the globe.

References

Albion, P. & Erwee, R. (2011) 'Preparing for doctoral supervision at a distance: Lessons from experience', *Society for Information Technology & Teacher Education International Conference (SITE 2011)*, Nashville, Tennessee, USA.

Erichsen, E.A., Bolliger, D.U. & Halupa, C. (2014) 'Student satisfaction with graduate supervision in doctoral programs primarily delivered in distance education settings', *Studies in Higher Education*, 39(2), pp. 321–38. https://doi.org/10.1080/03075079.2012.709496

Gray, M.A. & Crosta, L. (2019) 'New perspectives in online doctoral supervision: A systematic literature review', *Studies in Continuing Education*, 41(2), pp. 173–90. https://doi.org/10.1080/0158037x.2018.1532405

Guerin, C. & Aitchison, C. (2021) 'Doctoral writing and remote supervision: What the literature tells us', *Innovations in Education and Teaching International*, 58(6), pp. 624–34. https://doi.org/10.1080/14703297.2021.1991429

Huet, I. & Casanova, D. (2020) 'Exploring the professional development of online and distance doctoral supervisors', *Innovations in Education and Teaching International*, 58(4), pp. 430–40. https://doi.org/10.1080/14703297.2020.1742764

Jacobsen, M., Friesen, S. & Becker, S. (2021) 'Online supervision in a professional doctorate in education: Cultivating relational trust within learning alliances', *Innovations in Education and Teaching International*, 58(6), pp. 635–46. https://doi.org/10.1080/14703297.2021.1991425

Kumar, S. & Johnson, M. (2017) 'Mentoring doctoral students online: Mentor strategies and challenges', *Mentoring & Tutoring: Partnership in Learning*, 25(2), pp. 202–22. https://doi.org/10.1080/13611267.2017.1326693

Lee, K., Zawacki-Richter, O. & Cefa Sari, B. (2022) 'A systematic literature review on technology in online doctoral education', *Studies in Continuing Education*, 46(1), pp. 38–64. https://doi.org/10.1080/0158037x.2022.2135499

Lundgren-Resenterra, M. & Crosta, L. (2019) 'Beyond personal expectations: Research supervision framed as a collective endeavour in online structured doctoral programmes', *International Journal of Doctoral Studies*, 14, pp. 703–20. https://doi.org/10.28945/4439

Manathunga, C. (2014) *Intercultural postgraduate supervision: Reimagining time, place and knowledge*. London: Routledge.

Maor, D., Ensor, J.D. & Fraser, B.J. (2015) 'Doctoral supervision in virtual spaces: A review of research of web-based tools to develop collaborative supervision', *Higher Education Research & Development*, 35(1), pp. 172–88. https://doi.org/10.1080/07294360.2015.1121206

Nasiri, F. & Mafakheri, F. (2015) 'Postgraduate research supervision at a distance: A review of challenges and strategies', *Studies in Higher Education*, 40(10), pp. 1962–9. https://doi.org/10.1080/03075079.2014.914906

Palmer, C. & Gillaspy, E. (2021) 'Digital shifting in doctoral supervision: Different routes to the same destination', *Innovations in Education and Teaching International*, 58(6), pp. 672–81. https://doi.org/10.1080/14703297.2021.1991428

Rockinson-Szapkiw, A. (2012) 'Should online doctoral instructors adopt audio feedback as an instructional strategy? Preliminary evidence', *International Journal of Doctoral Studies*, 7, pp. 245–58. https://doi.org/10.28945/1595

Roumell, E.A.L. & Bolliger, D.U. (2017) 'Experiences of faculty with doctoral student supervision in programs delivered via distance', *The Journal of Continuing Higher Education*, 65(2), pp. 82–93. https://doi.org/10.1080/07377363.2017.1320179

Stevens, D., Chetty, R., Jones, T.B., Yallew, A. & Butler-Henderson, K. (2021) 'Doctoral supervision and COVID-19: Autoethnographies from four faculty across three continents', *Journal of University Teaching and Learning Practice*, 18(5). https://doi.org/10.53761/1.18.5.6

Sussex, R. (2008) 'Technological options in supervising remote research students', *Higher Education*, 55(1), pp. 121–37. https://doi.org/10.1007/s10734-006-9038-0

Torka, M. (2021) 'The transition from in-person to online supervision: Does the interaction between doctoral advisors and candidates change?' *Innovations in Education and Teaching International*, 58(6), pp. 659–71. https://doi.org/10.1080/14703297.2021.1993959

Wisker, G., McGinn, M.K., Bengtsen, S.S.E., Lokhtina, I., He, F., Cornér, S., Leshem, S., Inouye, K. & Löfström, E. (2021) 'Remote doctoral supervision experiences: Challenges and affordances', *Innovations in Education and Teaching International*, 58(6), pp. 612–23. https://doi.org/10.1080/14703297.2021.1991427

PART THREE

Fostering Inclusive and Supportive Doctoral Environments

9

Supervising a Diverse Doctoral Student Body

Fiona Hallett

Introduction

This chapter examines the role of higher education institutions in supporting diverse doctoral student populations, focusing on inclusive policies, culturally responsive pedagogy and equitable educational environments. It explores how these elements can foster cultures of (in)visibility (Deem, 2022) while addressing barriers faced by underrepresented students, such as financial challenges, academic preparedness and marginalization. By investigating institutional responsibility and student diversity, this chapter aims to provide insights into how universities can better support all students and what this means for supervision.

Diversity in doctoral education extends beyond traditional views of academic enrichment and workforce preparation; it represents an ethical imperative rooted in equity and justice. Historically, access to higher education has been uneven, with systemic barriers disproportionately affecting marginalized populations. This inequity is especially pronounced in doctoral education, where gatekeeping mechanisms often reinforce these barriers. Access to, and success within, these programmes remain skewed towards privileged groups, requiring interventions to dismantle structural obstacles. This is not to suggest that such challenges are limited to marginalized groups; the point here is that historically marginalized groups, or international students studying away from home, require supervisors and mentors to look beyond their own experiences.

For example, concerns have been noted that underrepresented students may feel pressured to conform to the norms of perceived 'elite' groups, as the prevailing academic culture often emphasizes specific standards of excellence and practices that may not align with diverse backgrounds and experiences (McArthur, 2021). This pressure to assimilate can lead to a sense of alienation, where students may suppress their unique identities and perspectives in order to fit into an environment that values conformity over individuality.

In this regard, the concept of tacit assumptions surrounding 'doctorateness', as articulated by Trowler (2022), enables a reconsideration of what 'research' signifies for both doctoral candidates and their supervisory teams. These unarticulated assumptions influence the expectations and practices embedded within doctoral education, often dictating what is regarded as acceptable or legitimate within the research process. Such assumptions encompass various factors, including the perceived value of specific methodologies, the importance attributed to particular forms of knowledge production and the expectations surrounding scholarly engagement.

This phenomenon is particularly concerning in the context of diverse doctoral populations, where the backgrounds and lived experiences of students may not align with conventional notions of 'doctorateness'. Consequently, previously marginalized students may encounter significant challenges in navigating implicit doctoral expectations, leading to feelings of inadequacy and, potentially, inhibiting innovation and critical thinking, as students might refrain from questioning established norms or pursuing unconventional research topics.

By addressing and redefining what 'research' signifies within this context, higher education institutions can promote a more equitable and supportive environment that recognizes and values the myriad perspectives and methodologies that enrich academic discourse. Such an endeavour will not only enhance the educational experiences of all doctoral candidates, but also contribute to the advancement of knowledge in a manner that is inclusive and representative of the diversity within the scholarly community.

This chapter is organized into three sections: challenges facing diverse doctoral student populations; culturally responsive pedagogy; and strategies for building an inclusive academic climate. Each section will explore approaches to supporting diversity in doctoral education and their broader implications for equity in the sector.

RESEARCH BRIEFING: 9.1: DIVERSIFICATION OF DOCTORAL PROGRAMMES

One aspect of the tremendous changes in doctoral education over recent decades is the increased diversification in doctoral populations. This has global relevance and has been observed in a wide variety of different international contexts as highlighted through a series of case studies included in the 2023 special issue of Innovations and Teaching International on the changing landscapes in Doctoral Education. As Taylor (2023) explains in the introduction to the series there are a number of possible factors behind the changes in doctoral populations which have led to a trend of both international diversification (*candidates studying in a countries other than that of their origin*) and domestic diversification (*a move away from a traditional view of a PhD candidate as white, male, able bodied and full time*). In their case study on the UK context, Taylor and Wisker (2023) explore these factors in more detail, drawing from figures over the last two decades which illustrate a modest increase in female candidates, a relatively significant increase in Black and Ethnic Minorities (BAME), a large increase in candidates who record a known disability and a suggestion that the age of candidates is also increasing. They show that the proportion of international candidates has risen substantially over the time period. Across this is an acknowledgement that the mode of study continues to change, with a greater number of part time possibilities for doctoral candidates.

Challenges facing diverse doctoral student populations

Despite efforts to promote diversity and inclusion in higher education, doctoral students from underrepresented groups continue to encounter significant challenges in their academic pursuits. This section examines the primary challenges faced by marginalized students, focusing on financial obstacles, academic and social difficulties, and the mental health impacts of marginalization.

Barriers to access, retention and recruitment

Financial challenges are among the most significant obstacles for under-represented doctoral students. In many national contexts, rising tuition fees and living expenses have rendered higher education increasingly inaccessible for low-income individuals. Limited scholarships and financial aid exacerbate this strain, often forcing students to accumulate debt or juggle multiple jobs, placing them in precarious positions.

For many low-income students, the prospect of accruing debt deters them from pursuing doctoral studies. This barrier disproportionately affects first-generation students, and other marginalized groups, reinforcing educational disparities. Retention is also a critical issue; research indicates that underrepresented racial and ethnic groups, along with first-generation college students, have lower retention rates compared to their more privileged peers (Rost & Krahenbuhl, 2023). Contributing factors include inadequate financial support, limited mentorship, feelings of isolation and experiences of discrimination, all of which undermine students' sense of belonging.

Academic and social challenges

In addition to financial obstacles, marginalized doctoral students face various academic and social challenges. Language barriers pose significant difficulties for international students or those from non-English-speaking households, complicating their engagement in academic discourse, research writing and seminar participation.

Bastalich and McCulloch (2024) stress the need to critically assess the ways in which conventional narratives can oversimplify professional trajectories and overlook diverse experiences. Such oversight may result in what Bahack and Addi-Raccah (2022) recognize as imposter syndrome experienced by first- and continuing-generations' doctoral students.

This is, perhaps, understandable when students may be the first in their family to complete a research degree, let alone a first degree. However, we must also acknowledge that imposter syndrome is not limited to those who are the first in family to study at university. There is a plethora of reasons for such feelings.

Nevertheless, imposter syndrome can be complicated by the fact that students from marginalized backgrounds often confront microaggressions and implicit biases from peers, faculty and staff. These subtle, often unintentional comments or behaviours can create a hostile environment, eroding students' confidence and contributing to feelings of frustration, anxiety andalienation.

The mental health impact of marginalization

The discrimination and marginalization some doctoral students experience significantly impact their mental health. Navigating an unfamiliar academic environment can lead to chronic stress, anxiety and depression, which negatively affect academic performance and overall well-being.

Unfortunately, many university support structures lack culturally knowledgeable mental health services, compounding the issue. Students from marginalized groups may hesitate to seek help if they believe their unique challenges will not be understood. This reluctance can create a cycle of avoidance, leading to deteriorating mental health and exacerbated feelings of alienation and failure.

REFLECTIVE ACTIVITY 9.1: NAVIGATING THE BARRIERS OF DOCTORAL EDUCATION

Consider the case of Maria, a first-generation Latina doctoral student from a low-income background. Maria was accepted into a prestigious doctoral programme in sociology, but from the outset, she faced numerous barriers that threatened her ability to succeed. Financially, Maria struggled to cover tuition and living expenses, relying on a combination of loans, part-time work and limited scholarship support. Despite working nearly full-time, she still found herself accumulating significant debt, which added to her stress and anxiety.

Academically, Maria faced additional challenges. As a non-native English speaker, she struggled to keep up with the rapid pace of academic discourse, and her writing often took her twice as long as her peers. Though she was passionate about her research on racial inequality in education, she frequently encountered microaggressions from classmates and professors who questioned the validity of her work or implied that her focus on race was not rigorous enough for doctoral research. These perceived dismissals left her feeling isolated and unsure of her place within the academic community.

Socially, Maria found it difficult to connect with her peers, most of whom came from more privileged backgrounds and did not share her life experiences. She also felt guilty for not being able to spend as much time with her family, who relied on her financial support. The constant balancing act between academic demands, financial pressures and family obligations took a significant toll on Maria's mental health. She experienced chronic stress and anxiety, but when she sought help from the university counselling centre, she found that the counsellors lacked an understanding of the cultural and socioeconomic challenges she faced.

Questions for reflection:

What specific institutional policies or practices could have alleviated Maria's financial burden during her doctoral studies?

How can universities better support students facing microaggressions and implicit bias from peers and faculty?

What role can culturally competent mental health services play in supporting the well-being of doctoral students like Maria?

In what ways can institutions create a more inclusive academic environment that fosters belonging for students, including those from marginalized backgrounds?

Culturally responsive pedagogy

RESEARCH BRIEFING 9.2

In 1995, Gloria Ladson-Billings introduced the concept of Culturally Relevant Pedagogy (CRP), a transformative educational approach designed to bridge the gap between students' cultural identities and the learning process. CRP rests on three foundational pillars: academic achievement; cultural competence and socio-political or critical consciousness. These pillars highlight the importance of not only fostering student success but also cultivating an environment where students can thrive as whole individuals – bringing their full selves, including their cultural backgrounds, into both the classroom and the larger world. Ladson-Billings envisioned a teaching model where students would engage deeply with their own cultural narratives while critically examining the world around them, ensuring that education becomes a tool for both personal empowerment and social change. Whilst her work focused on reshaping schools and teacher education, its relevance for higher education cannot be overstated.

Nearly two decades later, in 2012, Django Paris expanded upon Ladson-Billings' ideas with the introduction of Culturally Sustaining Pedagogy (CSP). While CRP encourages responsiveness to students' cultural backgrounds, Paris argued that this wasn't enough. He proposed that our educational approaches should go further – they should sustain the cultural and linguistic practices of the communities students come from. CSP, Paris explained, is about more than offering students access to dominant cultural competence; it is about empowering them to maintain their own cultural identities in tandem with learning the skills necessary to navigate and succeed in mainstream society. His vision called for an educational system that celebrates students' heritage while preparing them for the world beyond the classroom, rejecting assimilation and fostering a vibrant coexistence of diverse cultures.

This evolution in pedagogy came at a time when educators were increasingly aware of the need for more inclusive practices, particularly in an era of growing diversity and globalization. However, the events of 2020, when the Covid-19 pandemic disrupted education systems globally, brought to the surface new challenges that required urgent attention.

In response to these challenges, Pacansky-Brock and colleagues (2020) began exploring what it means to practice humanizing, culturally responsive online teaching, particularly in higher education. Their work came at a critical juncture: the rapid shift to online learning left many institutions scrambling to maintain connections with their students in meaningful ways. The pandemic exposed gaps in traditional educational frameworks, particularly in the ability to connect with students emotionally and socially in a remote setting. Pacansky-Brock et al. (2020) emphasized the need for institutions to value the students they serve by creating learning environments that are not just functional but deeply authentic. They argued for educational practices that prioritize students' mental, emotional and academic needs, offering pathways for them to achieve their academic goals while feeling seen and supported.

As the pandemic unfolded, Ladson-Billings (2021) reflected on its unforeseen impact on students' well-being. 'Perhaps not unanticipated but surely unplanned for' she observed, was the extent to which the pandemic and remote learning intensified students' social, emotional and mental health needs (p. 75). The crisis magnified existing inequalities, highlighting the need for pedagogical models that account for the whole student, not just their academic performance.

Django Paris, writing again in 2021, echoed these sentiments, pointing out that the pandemic laid bare the shortcomings of the education system. He noted that the global pandemic had revealed just how far education was from achieving its potential. 'We are far from where we need to be', Paris claimed, 'if we are to work in productive opposition to the system that employs us, as we regenerate, reclaim, and reimagine an education system that sustains us' (p. 372). His words called for educators to rethink the role of education in society, to use this moment of disruption as an opportunity to rebuild an education system that does not simply adapt to the challenges but fundamentally transforms to meet the needs of all learners.

A significant aspect of Culturally Responsive Pedagogy in doctoral education is the deliberate diversification of curricular content to reflect a broad spectrum of voices, scholars and perspectives. Traditionally, doctoral programmes have been grounded in Eurocentric paradigms, which often marginalize the contributions of scholars from underrepresented groups, including African American, Latinx, Indigenous and Asian American communities. This narrow focus not only limits the intellectual scope of academic inquiry but also reinforces structural inequalities within the academy.

By integrating the work of scholars from these historically marginalized groups into aspects of study such as course readings, research frameworks and new methodological approaches, faculty can expand students' intellectual horizons. This inclusion broadens the scope of academic discourse and promotes a more comprehensive understanding of the world, encouraging students to engage with knowledge systems that reflect diverse cultural experiences. For students from underrepresented backgrounds, seeing their own cultures, histories and identities reflected in the curriculum creates a sense of validation and belonging within the academic space. It sends a powerful message that their perspectives are valued and that they, too, have a place in shaping the future of their disciplines.

Culturally Responsive Pedagogy also stresses the importance of encouraging doctoral students to draw upon their cultural backgrounds and lived experiences when developing research questions, methodologies and theoretical frameworks. This approach positions students not as passive recipients of established knowledge, but as active creators of new knowledge that is deeply relevant to their communities and personal narratives.

This diversification of perspectives is not merely an act of inclusion, it fundamentally enriches scholarly work. By encouraging students to incorporate their cultural and experiential lenses, doctoral programmes become spaces for innovative research that reflects the complexities of the global society. The blending of diverse perspectives allows for the development of new methodologies, the questioning of established theories and the creation of knowledge that is more inclusive and applicable to a wider range of social contexts.

It is increasingly difficult to justify the continued reliance on a singular, Western epistemological framework in doctoral education, especially when the student body is so diverse (Manathunga et al., 2021; Mugari, 2021). The persistence of this narrow approach fails to reflect the global and multicultural realities of today's academic community. In order to foster a more equitable and intellectually vibrant academic environment, it is essential for doctoral programmes to embrace a multiplicity of knowledge systems. By doing so, they not only create space for students from diverse backgrounds to thrive but also contribute to the ongoing transformation of higher education into a more inclusive and dynamic field.

In the context of doctoral education, Culturally Responsive Pedagogy is not a static concept, but one that requires ongoing reflection, adaptation and engagement with emerging research and student needs. Doctoral programmes are uniquely situated to advance Culturally Responsive Pedagogy by integrating it into both the formal academic curriculum and the informal mentoring relationships that are so central to the doctoral experience. Faculty and advisors must remain attuned to the diverse cultural and intellectual experiences of their doctoral students and be willing to adapt their practices to support the development of scholars from all backgrounds. This dynamic and reflective approach to CRP not only enhances the educational experience for doctoral students but also enriches the intellectual and research capacities of the academic community as a whole.

As we move forward, the ideas presented by Ladson-Billings, Paris and Pacansky-Brock remind us that education must not only evolve in response to societal changes but also work actively to sustain and uplift the diverse cultures and identities of students. This means creating systems that don't just accommodate difference but celebrate it, where learning is as much about maintaining cultural integrity as it is about achieving academic success. In a post-pandemic world, the task is not merely to repair the damage done but to seize the opportunity to rebuild an educational landscape that is truly inclusive, equitable and sustainable for future generations.

Building an inclusive academic climate

The promotion of inclusive pedagogies within higher education classrooms, often pursued through the implementation of practical strategies, activities and techniques, is frequently perceived as a straightforward and measurable method for HE leaders to showcase their commitment to inclusion. However, as Stentiford and Koutsouris (2021, p. 2258) point out, such a reductionist approach falls short of creating genuinely inclusive climates. The endeavour to establish an inclusive campus environment requires a sustained commitment to cultivating a culture that embodies inclusivity, respect and belonging across all institutional levels.

Institutional leadership plays a critical role in shaping an atmosphere of inclusivity within the academic setting. University leaders must not only provide vocal and visible support for diversity initiatives but also engage in meaningful actions that reflect this commitment. The unequivocal articulation that discrimination, harassment and bias are intolerable must extend beyond rhetoric; it must be integrated into institutional policies and practices. This involves establishing clear, accessible and effective mechanisms for reporting and addressing incidents of discrimination. Without these mechanisms, the very foundations of an inclusive environment remain precarious.

Despite substantial efforts to advance inclusivity, incidents of discrimination and bias persist in many academic environments, indicating a systemic failure to address the underlying structures that perpetuate inequity. These incidents can manifest in various forms, including microaggressions, overt acts of racism and sexism, and institutional policies that unintentionally disadvantage specific groups. Such manifestations of discrimination significantly hinder the academic success and emotional well-being of students, particularly those from historically marginalized backgrounds.

The development of inclusive environments is inherently subjective and complex. While practical modifications, such as improving the accessibility of educational materials or establishing specific student societies, are important initial steps, they often do little to dismantle the deeply entrenched and historical exclusions faced by vulnerable individuals and marginalized groups (Slee, 2019). This superficial approach to inclusivity risks creating an illusion of progress while failing to confront the pervasive systemic barriers that continue to marginalize certain student populations.

Fostering a culture of open dialogue surrounding diversity, equity and inclusion is essential for effectively addressing systemic discrimination. Institutions must establish forums that allow doctoral students, faculty and staff to share their experiences, concerns and recommendations for improvement. However, merely creating these forums is not enough; they must be positioned as genuine spaces for dialogue, where all voices are not only heard but actively valued. Such discussions can enhance awareness of the challenges faced by all doctoral students and promote collaborative efforts to forge a more inclusive campus climate and, as Nori et al. (2020) argue, enable doctoral students to look beyond 'imposter syndrome' beliefs.

Redesign of induction

Induction is a crucial part of the student journey; however, frequently the approach to induction is based on giving information on process, procedure and practical aspects. While all of this is necessary, this volume of information at an early stage of the degree can be overwhelming and only superficially encourages the new student to reflect and assess their own expectations and how they align with those of their institution, supervisor and peers. This can also have the often-unconscious effect of perpetuating closed dialogue around inclusivity and the variation in the student population, and further when there is discussion of the doctoral experience, the focus tends to be on the need for independence, self-reliance and the challenges which can be faced.

McCulloch and Bastalich (2023) explain the results of a different approach that they took to designing doctoral induction. In this they focused on collection of the perceptions of entry stage doctoral candidates on expectations of doing a research degree. They did this over three separate orientation days in an Australian university. Participants were given prompts and asked to use metaphors to discuss their perceptions. The intention here was to avoid any predetermined parameters around expectations on doctoral study. Students were given the following prompts:

1. My PhD is like ... because ....
2. If a film were to be made of my PhD experience, I (the research student) would be played by (insert actor's name) ... because ....
3. I think my supervisor expects me to ...
    1. ... ...
    2. ... ...
    3. ... ...
    4. ... ...

The results were fascinating as responses demonstrated the intensely personal approach to understanding expectations and culture in doctoral study. They concluded,

> ... there is a need to introduce new inflections including the pleasures and benefits involved in learning new knowledge, skills, and language, and of thereby achieving a new level of intellectual sophistication. Part of this would be to encourage candidates to consider the doctorate as an enhancement of existing professional identities, and as a course of study that can be managed in parallel with personal and professional obligations.
> (2023, p. 695)

This emphasis on candidate lived experience, they argue would help reduce anxiety, place importance on the relational aspects and emphasize the positive aspects of doing of a doctoral degree.

REFLECTIVE ACTIVITY 9.2: RETHINKING INDUCTION

1 **Your current approach**
- How do you currently approach induction with your doctoral candidates?
- What kinds of information, values or expectations do you tend to prioritize?
- To what extent is your induction shaped by institutional norms versus student needs?

2 **Lived experience and inclusivity**
- Reflect on the diversity of your doctoral students. How do you acknowledge or incorporate their varied backgrounds, experiences and aspirations?
- Are there aspects of your induction process that could unintentionally reinforce assumptions about who doctoral students are or how they should behave?

3 **Reframing expectations**
- Consider the messages you communicate (explicitly or implicitly) about independence, resilience and challenge. How might you also highlight growth, enjoyment and development of professional identity?
- What assumptions do you make about what students expect from supervision and how do you check those assumptions?

4 **Action planning**
- Identify one specific change you could make in your next induction conversation to better foreground student experience and relationality.
- What kinds of open-ended questions, prompts or activities could you introduce to encourage meaningful dialogue?

Conclusion

In the context of the contemporary global economy, employers increasingly seek individuals who can navigate diverse cultural environments, collaborate with people from varied backgrounds and approach problems from multiple perspectives. This demand places a growing responsibility on higher education institutions to ensure their pedagogical practices foster these competencies. However, it also raises an important question: are these institutions genuinely committed to inclusivity, or are they merely responding to external pressures to produce 'market-ready' graduates? Prioritizing inclusivity in pedagogical practices should not simply be seen as a strategic response to labour market demands. Rather, it offers an opportunity to enrich the educational experiences of all students while challenging the systemic inequities that persist within academia and society at large. In this sense, the commitment to inclusivity must move beyond rhetoric and become a catalyst for meaningful change towards a more equitable and socially responsive higher education system.

Supervising a diverse doctoral student body is one context where this commitment can be enacted in meaningful ways. Given the variety of backgrounds, experiences and expectations that students bring to doctoral study, self-reflection plays a vital role in enhancing supervision and, by extension, the overall educational experience. Regular review enables supervisors to recognize how their own assumptions, biases and pedagogical habits influence their interactions with students. This awareness is not merely personal but deeply pedagogical, supporting the development of more responsive and inclusive supervisory practices that are attuned to individual student needs.

Addressing the specific challenges faced by doctoral candidates, such as cultural differences, varying levels of academic preparedness and experiences of marginalization, requires supervisors to continually adapt and refine their mentoring strategies. Reflecting on interactions with students can help identify barriers to learning and progression, and this awareness can guide more tailored and effective support. For instance, being mindful of a student's cultural background may inform how feedback is framed, how expectations are communicated or how progress is measured.

An understanding of the power dynamics that shape doctoral education is equally important. Supervisors hold significant influence over their students' academic trajectories, making it vital that they consider how this power is exercised. Acknowledging one's positionality and being open to feedback foster a supervisory relationship based on mutual respect and shared responsibility. In doing so, supervisors can contribute to more equitable academic environments and be better positioned to advocate for systemic changes that benefit the broader doctoral community.

This approach also sets an important example for doctoral students. When students observe supervisors engaging in honest self-assessment and adapting their practices, they are more likely to develop similar habits of reflection in their own academic and professional lives. This, in turn, nurtures a culture of inquiry, critical thinking and resilience. Cultivating these qualities within the supervisory relationship not only supports students' immediate success but also equips them to navigate the complexities of academic and professional environments in the long term.

References

Bahack, H. & Addi-Raccah, A. (2022) 'PhD first-generation and continuing generation students' academic experience and strengths', *Higher Education*, 84(4), pp. 909–25. doi:10.1007/s10734-021-00798-7

Bastalich, W. & McCulloch, A. (2024) 'Doctoral induction: Sociocultural context and the transition to the research degree', *Innovations in Education and Teaching International*, pp. 1–13. doi:10.1080/14703297.2024.0000000 *(placeholder DOI – replace if available)*.

Deem, R. (2022) 'On doctoral (in)visibility and reframing the doctorate for the twenty-first century', *European Journal of Higher Education*, 12(4), pp. 373–92. doi:10.1080/21568235.2022.2042841

Ladson-Billings, G. (1995) 'Toward a theory of culturally relevant pedagogy', *American Educational Research Journal*, 32(3), pp. 465–91. doi:10.3102/00028312032003465

Ladson-Billings, G. (2021) 'I'm here for the hard re-set: Post-pandemic pedagogy to preserve our culture', *Equity & Excellence in Education*, 54(1), pp. 68–78. doi:10.1080/10665684.2020.1863883

Manathunga, C., Qi, J., Bunda, T. & Singh, M. (2021) 'Time mapping: Charting transcultural and First Nations histories and geographies in doctoral education', *Discourse: Studies in the Cultural Politics of Education*, 42(2), pp. 226–44. doi:10.1080/01596306.2019.1690986

McArthur, J. (2021) 'The inclusive university: A critical theory perspective using a recognition-based approach', *Social Inclusion*, 9(3), pp. 6–15. doi:10.17645/si.v9i3.4220

McCulloch, A. & Bastalich, W. (2023) 'Commencing research students' expectations and the design of doctoral induction: Introducing inflections of collaboration and pleasure', *Journal of Further and Higher Education*, 47(5), pp. 687–98. doi:10.1080/0309877X.2022.2123541

Mugari, Z.E. (2021) 'The decolonial turn: Reference lists in PhD theses as markers of theoretical shift/stasis in media and journalism studies at selected South African universities', *London Review of Education*, 19(1), pp. 1–15. doi:10.14324/LRE.19.1.03

Nori, H., Peura, M.H. & Jauhiainen, A. (2020) 'From imposter syndrome to heroic tales: Doctoral students' backgrounds, study aims, and experiences', *International Journal of Doctoral Studies*, 15, pp. 517–39. doi:10.28945/4637

Pacansky-Brock, M., Smedshammer, M. & Vincent-Layton, K. (2020) 'Humanizing online teaching to equitize higher education', *Current Issues in Education*, 21(2 (Sp Iss). Retrieved from https://cie.asu.edu/ojs/index.php/cieatasu/article/view/1905

Rost, J., & Krahenbuhl, K. (2023). Improving Social Belonging to Increase Success in an Online Doctorate Program. Impacting Education: Journal on Transforming Professional Practice, 8(1), 44–48. https://doi.org/10.5195/ie.2023.283

Slee, R. (2019) 'Belonging in an age of exclusion,' *International Journal of Inclusive Education*, 23(9), pp. 909–22. https://doi.org/10.1080/13603116.2019.1602366

Stentiford, L. & Koutsouris, G. (2022). 'Critically considering the "inclusive curriculum" in higher education', *British Journal of Sociology of Education*, 43(8), pp. 1250–72. https://doi.org/10.1080/01425692.2022.2122937. This article was published online in 2021.

Taylor, S. (2023) 'The changing landscape of doctoral education: A framework for analysis and introduction to the special issue', *Innovations in Education and Teaching International*, 60(5), pp. 606–22. https://doi.org/10.1080/14703297.2023.2237962

Trowler, P. (2022) 'Doctoral supervision: Sharpening the focus of the practice lens', *Higher Education Research & Development*, 41(5), pp. 1743–56. https://doi.org/10.1080/07294360.2021.1937955

Taylor, S. & Wisker, G. (2023) 'The changing landscape of doctoral education in the UK', *Innovations in Education and Teaching International*, 60(5), pp. 759–74. https://doi.org/10.1080/14703297.2023.2237943

10

Fostering Inclusion and Support in Doctoral Education

Susanna Calkins and Aubrey Penney

Introduction

What does it mean to foster inclusion and support in doctoral education? Why does it matter that we do? In many ways, graduate students are a particularly vulnerable group in higher education. They may be less connected – geographically, socially and culturally – to the families and communities that raised them. They may have entered academic environments that are more intense and competitive than what they experienced as undergraduates, and they may be highly dependent on a single supervisor or mentor to fund and guide their studies and professional development. They may be on their own financially, struggling to make ends meet. They may have others in their care, which can impact their ability to take on new opportunities, demonstrate initiative or to perform well in their studies. For graduate students of colour and for those holding marginalized identities, this vulnerability and precariousness may be even more exacerbated in their higher education contexts. This is particularly the case when it comes to doctoral programmes where students holding these diverse identities and backgrounds have historically been underrepresented (Jordan et al., 2022). Given the challenges which these students face, it is imperative that the programmes assist them in developing a sense of belonging to the programmes; to help them feel they have a right to be included and to be given equal respect and opportunities within the programme.

Thus, it is essential for educators to think deeply about what it means to foster inclusion and support in doctoral education, by exploring their own biases and identities and considering the impact on their graduate students. Fostering inclusive learning environments in classrooms, labs and clinical settings is crucial for student retention, persistence, motivation and sense of belonging in higher education and in the field.

This chapter will focus on three key components involved with fostering inclusion and support in doctoral education. First, we will explore what it means to create an inclusive and equitable learning environment in a graduate course. We will discuss how an instructor's identities, assumptions and biases, as well as approaches to teaching and learning, can impact their perceptions of students, which can ultimately intersect with and impact students' learning, motivation and sense of belonging. As they think about their syllabus and overall course design, readers will be encouraged to work through a syllabus assumptions activity and course equity map, identifying issues related to representative and inclusive course content, equitable assessment, and inclusive teaching methods and assessing course climate.

Second, the chapter will explore how instructors can facilitate inclusive learning environments outside the classroom, in such settings as the clinic, lab and studio, providing strategies to ensure that their graduate students are able to contribute to the research and practice in meaningful and constructive ways.

Lastly, the chapter will focus on how educators, departments and schools can provide access to resources to help students have what they need to succeed in graduate school. Such resources might include access to writing support, access to quantitative support (e.g. statistics support) and access to resources that support basic needs (access to health centres, grocery stores, recreation, childcare).

Instructor identities and inclusive teaching

Many educators teach as they were taught, or in ways that seem to conform to expectations of their field or discipline. As subject matter experts and scholars, they may have received very little training around teaching and pedagogy and may view teaching as a process of transmitting information to passively receptive students (Ashwin et al., 2026). Such attitudes may keep them from engaging with their students and helping them make meaning for themselves during class. Such perspectives may also cause educators to shy away from acknowledging students' prior knowledge and lived experiences, thereby confirming the assumption that only the teacher's subject knowledge matters. Additionally, many traditional classroom practices (e.g. lecture, timed in-person exams, 'cold calling', 'Socratic discussion') as well as 'active learning strategies' (small group work) can have a negative impact on students if they exclude diverse experiences critical to the identities of many students. These negative impacts particularly affect students from historically marginalized groups, eliciting a range of harmful feelings and risks to their learning such as stereotype threats, microaggressions, epistemic injustice and imposter feelings. These are frequently interrelated and raise critical issues linked to student academic performance; it is important for educators to understand and be aware of the identity-based threats to students' inclusion and learning.

Identity-based threats to student inclusion and learning

Stereotype threat: First identified by Claude Steele and Joshua Aronson in 1995, stereotype threat is 'being at risk of confirming, as self-characteristic, a negative stereotype about one's group' (p. 797). Stereotype threat evokes student concerns that their performance may confirm the stereotype with others and these negative feelings undermine performance. Initially discovered in research on Black student performance in academic testing environments in the United States, stereotype threat has been subsequently identified in a wide range of students who identify with social groups with prevailing negative stereotypes of performance in particular types of learning environment. Williams et al. (2021), for example, identified stereotype threat in female doctoral students studying sports management.

Micro-aggressions: In addition to the experience of stereotype threat, Williams et al. (2021) also found that many of the female doctoral students also experienced 'microaggressions' during their doctoral study, experiences which reinforced their experience of stereotype threat. In 2007, Derald Wing Sue defined microaggressions as 'the everyday verbal, nonverbal, and environmental slights, snubs, or insults, whether intentional or unintentional to target persons based solely upon their marginalized group membership' (Sue et al., 2010, p.3). As Sue explains, the experience of microaggressions is observed in most, if not all, marginal social sub-groups and negatively impacts student identities and performance. In the case described by Williams (2021), the findings concerned gender-based microaggressions from faculty and other students.

Epistemic injustice: A further identity-related experience that negatively impacts doctoral students is termed the 'epistemic injustice'. In a recent review of the literature, Gonzalez et al. (2024) described epistemic injustice as 'an injustice where knowers and knowledge claims are unduly dismissed due to an imbalance of power between knowledge claimant(s) and an audience that has authority to legitimate the knower/knowledge' (p. 423). There are different forms including having your experience or knowledge claim dismissed based on the group identity (class, race, gender and so on). Or being excluded by virtue of not having the vocabulary or experience of the knowledge claims being made by the prevailing group, and/or having the knowledge claims of one's own epistemic identity group wilfully dismissed.

Imposter feelings: While students experience epistemic injustice as an external threat to their work, a fourth negative experience related to identity is an internalized threat, it is generally referred to as the 'impostor syndrome'. Students experience this when they feel they do not merit being part of the programme, but rather stumbled into it through good fortune, networking, lowering standards, charm or oversight. The experience is often accompanied by 'over-estimation of the abilities of others' (Sverdlik et al., 2020, p. 742) and feelings of being a fraud, fear of failure and of being found out. This negative perception is worsened by the persistent concern that others will expose their lack of merit, to the detriment of their mental well-being and their ability to thrive and advance in their development (Feenstra et al., 2020).

Addressing the threats: Inclusive teaching

To address these problems requires faculty to not only develop a deeper awareness and understanding of these threats but also to strive to implement inclusive teaching principles that reduce these threats. Inclusive teaching refers collectively to those practices that help ensure that all students are welcomed and included in a classroom and have what they need to succeed in a course. One need will be a knowledge and understanding of these threats to their learning and sense of belonging in the programme. Sverlik et al. (2020) recommend that students be made aware of them early in their studies. When students feel a real sense of belonging to a community from the outset, they develop a better understanding of the academic standards and what they need to do to meet those standards. It helps them better situate themselves in the community, as well as contribute and be valued for their own experience and perspectives. This may include challenging prevailing assumptions – assumptions that they are often best placed to recognize. This, in turn, can support faculty to cultivate broader more inclusive teaching perspectives (see Research Brief 1).

An inclusive teacher will also consider how their own identities might influence their teaching philosophy as well as how they interact with their students, particularly those who hold different identities from their own (Addy et al., 2021). Faculty will want to reflect on their own intersecting social-cultural identities (Fuentes et al., 2021), examine their beliefs, attitudes, biases and assumptions, and consider how these may be impacting their approaches to teaching and their students' learning. They will also want to examine how they perceive and engage with their students, both individually and collectively. For example, Hannah, a professor of religious history, began to recognize that as a white woman she was interacting differently and more comfortably with certain graduate students who resembled her, both in terms of her racial and gender identities and her educational background, then with students of colour. She began to consciously consider how she was responding and reacting to her different students, and question what about her own thinking might have accounted for those differences. Similarly, James, a professor of psychology heavily influenced by Christian values, found that he was avoiding questions posed by students holding queer identities. He spent some time journaling and reflecting, and eventually confronted some of his deeply held biases and assumptions that were colouring his perspective. Lastly, Eun, a literature professor, recognized that she regularly tokenized Latinx students by having them explain texts and examples to their peers. She also recognized that she only asked students to read scholarly works holding dominant and mainstream views and perspectives. After this realization, she began to educate herself more by reading outside her own knowledge base and deepening her understanding of material she had taught for years. Taking proactive steps to examine personal inclinations and biases, as these educators did, allows professors to even the playing field for students before coursework begins. Reflection Activity 1 can help educators examine their beliefs, actions and behaviours before they teach.

Faculty can also think more deeply about creating course content that is more representative of a diversity of voices and perspectives and be attentive to what their students need. Viral, discussed in Case Study 1, recognized that the graduate school at his university was not sufficiently preparing students to develop their own awareness and understanding of how deeply rooted social and cultural issues impacted who gets to *do* science. He and his fellow doctoral students successfully advocated for a new course – a journal club that focused on issues of equity, diversity and inclusion in science, and which was required for all students. This was important for students to feel supported, and their voices heard.

RESEARCH BRIEFING 10.1: INCLUSIVE TEACHING

Inclusive teaching refers collectively to those practices that help ensure that all students are welcomed and included in a classroom and have what they need to succeed in a course.

Being an inclusive teacher begins with examining one's beliefs, attitudes, biases and assumptions, and critically reflecting on one's own intersecting socio-cultural identities (Fuentes et al., 2021). An inclusive teacher will also consider how their own identities might influence their teaching philosophy as well as how they interact with their students, particularly those who hold different identities from their own (Addy et al., 2021). Hogan & Sathy (2022) also recommend that faculty adopt an inclusive mindset, in which educators look at who is being included and who is being left out, recognize that diversity is an asset to be leveraged, and that inclusive teaching is an ongoing lifelong process.

Inclusive teaching also means reflecting on – even interrogating – the course syllabus, by scrutinizing each pedagogical and curricular choice. Educators might ask themselves why they privilege certain theorists, texts or approaches, or why they highlight the voices of some scholars while ignoring or dismissing others. Inclusive educators will consider whose voices are being represented and who is being left out or silenced. Fuentes et al. (2021) discuss what it means to cultivate a diversity, equity and inclusion mindset when developing a syllabus, and recommend that educators 'adopt a diversity-centered approach', so that diversity-related issues and topics weave through and underlie the entire curriculum, rather than remaining isolated to a single assignment or activity. Similarly, Hogan and Sathy emphasize the value of structuring a course around inclusion, and regularly collect feedback around what supporting inclusive practices, and what is not.

REFLECTIVE ACTIVITY 10.1: ASSUMPTIONS ACTIVITY AND COURSE EQUITY MAP

You may find it fruitful to use the Course Assumptions Activity and Course Equity Map to reflect critically on your own assumptions, biases and identities, and how those may impact your pedagogical and curricular choices as well as how you engage with your students. You may first ask yourself such questions as:

- Why do I teach the way that I do? Am I teaching the way I was taught?
- What do I assume about myself as an educator, and about my students as learners?
- Do my own salient social identities impact on how I engage with my students?
- Do I have different expectations or assumptions for different students? Why?

From here you may wish to use a Course Equity Map, interrogating each component of your course through an equity lens. Equity refers to the condition where every student has what they need to succeed, regardless of the different skills, abilities and privileges that they bring to the class. An Equity Map allows an educator to deconstruct a course, examining the pedagogical and curricular components in turn. These categories include learning objectives, assessment, content, class activities, syllabuses, teaching strategies and approaches, and policies.

Content: What theories/themes/content/big ideas does this course centre around? Who or what is being privileged and highlighted? Who or what is being marginalized, omitted or silenced?

Learning objectives: Is it clear what students are supposed to be able to know, do or value in this course? How are students expected to engage or interact with their peers? What kind of personal growth or improvement is expected of students?

Assessments and grading: Are your expectations around grading and performance clear/present? How are you gauging performance, growth and improvement? Could any of the grading or assessment policies impact on some students differently than others? Why/How?

General course policies: What policies have you identified as important? Why? Could any of your policies affect/impact some students differently than others? Why/How? What kind of resources and support are being made available to students? Do you share expectations around office hours, guidance, questions, help seeking?

CASE STUDY 10.1: VIRAL – A GRADUATE STUDENT'S ADVOCACY

Viral, a sixth-year neuroscience graduate student, was first inspired to pursue research through a summer programme that made an intentional effort to recruit minority students into STEM. From the inception of his scientific career, he has been deeply committed to diversifying science and its practitioners by addressing systemic issues that prevent access to research. 'It's hard to ignore these issues when you're exclusively hanging out with racial, ethnic and gender/sexual minorities in STEM. So, my scientific training in the lab occurred alongside my awareness and attention to who was not in the lab or did not feel represented or supported in the lab. To me, it's impossible to think about science in the abstract without thinking about who is invited to actually do science work and what work they're invited or encouraged to do.'

Then, in the aftermath of the 2020 murder of George Floyd and subsequent nation-wide conversations in the United States, Viral collaborated with fellow graduate students to find ways to transform their campus through these discussions. 'We would talk about these inequalities, discrimination and harassment in the workplace, the complexities of immigration status, and working to support so many different types of students. That diversity made us smarter and made our work and community more fulfilling … but there was no real structure on how to address these things as students. After that event there was this outpouring of people wanting to learn more but not knowing how, or where to start, or what to do … this was a need I could directly address from my own research. People are yearning for information on this conversation, so let's provide the resources and make the space for that to happen.'

Viral reached out to the school's Dean and the head of the curriculum committee on behalf of the student body, advocating to give these conversations a foundational place in students' education. 'Fortunately, [the dean] was willing to engage with us on this.' Over the course of the next two years, the students collaborated with the dean's office and curriculum committee in crafting syllabi and implementing two new courses focused on the history and philosophy of science and a journal club on diversity, equity and inclusion in the sciences. As he recalls, the school leadership 'took our concerns seriously and advocated for us. Some faculty were supportive'. At the same time, he noted that other faculty were 'very vocally dismissive and opposed and saw it as a waste of time and a distraction from the "real work." Ultimately, we convinced enough faculty to be able to continue, but I'd argue the process actually took a lot longer simply due to the intransigence of some faculty. So, did I feel heard and valued? By some but definitely not by others'.

The course now shapes how trainees understand and support each other better as members of the larger scientific community. 'This is about who's next to you at the bench, and the lives of your colleagues. It has huge, meaningful, tangible effects on work. People say that's politics, not science. But then you can't hire a great postdoc because of visas, or they can't start because they can't get into the country. These topics change your lab. It matters. And these are decisions that are made by governments and officials. We should value, as a democracy, people being informed about the issues of their lives. Now we have an opportunity for students to share and educate each other about these issues, which is a beautiful thing.'

Facilitating inclusive learning environments in clinical, lab and studio settings

For graduate students, working in a clinic, lab or studio may feel like the first step in meeting their future career goals. Not only are they learning new skills and involved in the construction of new knowledge and creative outputs, but they are also developing their autonomy, scholarly judgement, professionalism and body of work. As future professionals, it is critical that they be engaged in their own learning and process of discovery, with their ideas welcomed and carefully considered during lab, clinic and studio meetings. It is incumbent upon faculty to treat their students as future colleagues – even more so for students of historically marginalized identities, to counterbalance the systemic barriers and pernicious attitudes that can plague their experiences in such environments.

Creating a culture of mentoring

Faculty who work with graduate students may consider key aspects of mentoring and explore areas where they might more fully develop. Effective mentors are transparent (communicating expectations as well as boundaries); available (while being respectful of time and paying attention); timely in giving specific and constructive feedback; mindful of students' progress, achievements and milestones; encouraging (for both successes and failures); open and approachable; empathetic (considering students' holistic well-being as well as being conscious of stereotype threat and impostor feelings); aware of their own limitations, as well as being flexible and willing to learn. In a lab, clinical or studio setting, mentors will work with their students to develop shared expectations around:

- communications and meetings
- the student's role on different projects and their own project development
- the student's participation in group meetings
- manuscript development (including disciplinary norms around authorship)
- opportunities for feedback (how, when it is delivered)
- networking opportunities and professional meetings

- time away from campus (anticipated absence)
- completion of milestones (including post-programme)
- professional goals and skills – what does the student want to develop, and are their expectations a healthy balance of ambitious and achievable?

Normalizing important practices in the lab, clinic and studio, such as help-seeking and question-posing, can increase a student's sense of inclusion and belonging. Some faculty will also normalize risk-taking and innovation, as well as failure, in order to promote a culture where not only do mistakes and errors happen, but they can also lead to new innovations and ideas. In an architectural studio, maker-space or sound studio for example, students may be encouraged to push themselves out of their comfort zone, express their ideas respectfully and make sense of difficult or incongruous feedback. Recognizing that students will and should have different opinions and creative approaches from their own is essential as well. For Holly (see Case Study 2), creating an environment where students know they can make mistakes and take risks fosters a sense of belonging and community while creating new opportunities for growth.

CASE STUDY 10. 2: HOLLY'S INCLUSIVE LAB

For Holly, creating an inclusive laboratory environment is crucial for mentoring students and welcoming them into the larger scientific community. As a graduate student, she received excellent mentoring, which fostered her love for research and a desire to pursue the mysteries of the brain. Now, as an early career faculty member leading her own lab, she is determined to provide the same opportunities for her trainees. As she explains, 'We are an inclusive lab and prioritize taking [students] to mentor the next generation of scientists.'

Holly often provides advice and guidance to students from the perspective of a woman in science who has overcome hurdles and had to pivot and improvize to find success in her field. At the same time, she creates space for trainees to pursue their own ideas, providing them with the opportunity to try, fail and grow within the lab. She explicitly welcomes a diversity of perspectives in her lab and creates a space for conversations about health equity, recognizing that is one of the reasons students are drawn to her lab. 'We are focused on women's health throughout aging, and I think this attracts students who are interested in health equity and that creates a great environment.'

She is attentive to their financial needs, ensuring that her lab (through grant funding) pays for her trainees to attend conferences. 'To create a more inclusive environment, I work to send all students to conferences so that they can network.

Many times, [students from historically marginalized backgrounds] experience barriers to attending these expensive conferences because they have to pay costs up front and be reimbursed later. I try to make sure the lab pays everything up front and [the university] has allowed us this possibility with a travel card.'

Moreover, Holly ensures that her students have regular opportunities to share their progress and struggles with her, proactively creating these discussions rather than leaving the onus on her students. In addition to weekly lab meetings, she checks in regularly with her trainees on not just science, but also their mental state and life in general. 'Every Friday I also try to give everyone a shoutout on our [social media app] – give them a high five for something they accomplished that week, no matter how small. In terms of lab energy, every few months I send out an energy quiz to gauge how everyone is doing and if any students are at risk for burnout. This has worked well and sometimes students share and other times they keep to themselves, but either way they realize where they are and what they need to focus on. It's a check-in and reset.'

These conversations allow Holly to catch frustrations and difficulties in the lab early and create an environment of encouragement and collaboration that actively fights burnout and isolation. This dovetails neatly with her efforts to combat the hierarchical lab structure of the past and encourage students to pursue their own ideas with passion and confidence.

My lab is run with an open-door policy, and I give my students the freedom to ask their own questions and to challenge existing protocols in the lab. I want us to grow in new directions and for that we have to take risks.

RESEARCH BRIEFING 10.2: INCLUSIVE LAB ENVIRONMENTS

In recent years, researchers have begun to examine laboratory culture in higher education, as part of the larger call for creating diverse, equitable and inclusive learning environments that support the learning of all students. For example, as Miller & Roksa (2020) discovered in a study of sixty-seven biology PhD students, women do more service, including routine laboratory tasks, than men, and men of colour do more service than white men. Similarly, the hierarchical apprentice model still prevails in many clinical and lab settings, as does long-standing hierarchical thinking, which can quell student motivation, learning and ability to engage. As such, there has been a push to more fully examine those practices that include – and exclude – students in STEMM (science, technology, engineering, mathematics and medicine) laboratory settings, particularly those from historically underrepresented and/or underserved groups (Marshall et al., 2023).

Faculty from a range of US research institutions and medical schools identified key aspects for principal investigators (PIs) and educators to consider when creating an inclusive laboratory. Marshall et al. (2023) have identified the following:

(1) ensure that trainees understand instructions and feel comfortable asking clarifying questions
(2) celebrate large and small lab-related accomplishments through dinners, excursions and team-building activities outside of the lab
(3) foster a culture of cultural humility (ongoing reflection on assumptions, unconscious biases and stereotypes)
(4) create sub-leaders in the lab to foster leadership opportunities and to encourage collaboration, interdependence and innovation
(5) develop a culture of interdependence that fosters collaboration and communal behaviour
(6) form accountability groups with other labs to encourage mentoring, collaboration and intercultural communication
(7) offer regular training and professional development opportunities
(8) develop inclusive infrastructure within the lab through collaborations forced with historically underrepresented and underserved groups, and recruitment of underrepresented and/or underserved group trainees
(9) encourage personal growth of trainees (e.g. through 'life coaches')
(10) promote work–life balance and opportunities to volunteer at organizations that connect and contextualize their work
(11) demonstrate work–life balance among PIs through professional development opportunities
(12) support trainee mental health
(13) consider all trainee's ideas and provide constructive feedback (rather than reject outright)

Additionally, faculty may allow their graduate students opportunities to get out of the lab, clinic, studio and/or classroom, by encouraging them to engage in campus activities, particularly those that support their well-being and connection to the community. Again, Holly thought it was important to support students' professional development and networking opportunities at conferences to help socialize them into the greater scientific community.

Providing access to resources

Creating a supportive environment for doctoral students also means providing them with the academic, financial and social resources they need to succeed while in graduate school. As Research briefing 3 suggests, students may be struggling for many reasons but may feel ashamed to seek help or may simply not even be aware of who to ask for help or where to go.

Faculty can actively work to destigmatize these issues within their scholarly and creative communities. For example, they can proactively present information related to resources (e.g. food pantries, meal plan scholarships, thrift or second hand stores) that are available either at the university or in the community on their course syllabi or lab manuals. Gerald, a Sociology professor, worked with graduate students and faculty across the institution to create a student resource page, providing information on local food banks and counselling services for both students and their families. Faculty can bring in speakers or community members who have experienced need in different forms, to provide real-life and authentic insights to what needs exist and how such need can be met. Such initiatives can mitigate stigma and open the door to conversations for students who would otherwise feel compelled to conceal or minimize their struggles.

Given the enormous impact a lack of basic needs can have on academic performance, continued enrolment and mental and physical health, demonstrating care for student needs is perhaps the most efficient way to communicate a holistic interest in student well-being. It can also serve as a stepping stone towards larger conversations around community involvement and social support by connecting students with communities, both on campus and off, that provide social connections in addition to material support. For example, Lee, an Economics professor, extended office hours to accommodate students taking public transportation while caring for family members and working.

Faculty can also be proactive in destigmatizing student need for academic support, such as writing centres, statistics support and dissertation bootcamps. Enhanced writing support and regular writing workshops can increase writing competence and even writing engagement and enjoyment (Zimmer et al., 2022). Sharing all these resources with students to demonstrate support for every aspect of their growth, development and health is the first step towards creating a fully inclusive environment where every student can flourish.

RESEARCH BRIEFING 10.3: BASIC NEEDS AND RESOURCE ACCESS

Not only are US college students five times more likely to experience food insecurity than adults in the general population, but those experiencing food insecurity may also be at greater risk of emotional eating, leading to negative health outcomes (Frank et al., 2023). Struggles with food insecurity only worsened with the onset of the Covid-19 pandemic, and the level of food insecurity students experienced mirrored the dramatic worsening of food insecurity across the country, including the disproportionate effect on students with marginalized identities. Students experiencing food insecurity were more likely to withdraw from or drop courses, and even drop out of a programme entirely, when holding other factors constant (Mechler et al., 2024). Other studies looking specifically at academic performance showed a strong correlation, demonstrating that food insecurity increased the odds of being among the lower 10 per cent GPA and reduced the odds of being among the upper 10 per cent GPA (Leung et al., 2021). Moreover, as Coakley et al. (2022) found, both food and housing insecurity screenings are needed to identify and address student needs, as well as combat the prevalence and stigmatization of these problems within student populations.

Conclusion

Ultimately, fostering inclusion and support for graduate students requires thought, care, openness to new ideas and a willingness to change. Faculty must recognize that creating inclusive environments, where students have what they need to succeed, can be developed and sustained in small ways. Are we examining our biases and assumptions about ourselves as educators and researchers? Are we considering how we engage and interact with our students? Are we welcoming and respecting our students' ideas? Are we clearly communicating our expectations? Are we reflecting on our courses, considering who and what is privileged, ignored or dismissed? Are we checking in with our students, to make sure they are okay and have what they need to survive – socially, financially and academically? This is not about spoon-feeding students, which is not a faculty member's responsibility. But we need to ensure that our students are sufficiently supported so that they will persist in their degrees and in their careers.

References

Addy, T.M., Dube, D., Mitchell, K.A. & SoRelle, M. (2021) *What inclusive instructors do: Principles and practices for excellence in college teaching.* New York: Routledge, Taylor & Francis Group.

Ashwin, P., Blackie, M., Boud, D., Calkins, S., Coate, K., Hallett, F., Kandiko, K., Light, G., Luckett, K., MacLaren, I., McArthur, J., McCune, V., Mpamhanga, K., Schendel, R. & Tooher, M. (2026) *Reflective Teaching in Higher education.* 3rd ed. Bloomsbury Academic, e-book.

Ashwin, P., Boud, D., Calkins, S., Coate, K., Hallett, F., Light, G. ... & Tooher, M. (2020) *Reflective teaching in higher education.* London: Bloomsbury Academic.

Coakley, K.E., Cargas, S., Walsh-Dilley, M. & Mechler, H. (2022) 'Basic needs insecurities are associated with anxiety, depression, and poor health among university students in the state of New Mexico', *Journal of Community Health*, 47(3), pp. 454–63. https://doi.org/10.1007/s10900-022-01073-9

Feenstra, S., Begeny, C.T., Ryan, M.K., Stoker, J.I. & Jordan, J. (2020) 'Contextualizing the impostor "syndrome"', *Frontiers in Psychology*, 11, pp. 575024. https://doi.org/10.3389/fpsyg.2020.575024

Frank, M.L., Sprada, G.B., Hultstrand, K.V., West, C.E., Livingston, J.A. & Sato, A.F. (2023) 'Toward a deeper understanding of food insecurity among college students: Examining associations with emotional eating and biological sex', *Journal of American College Health*, 71(5), pp. 1463–71. https://doi.org/10.1080/07448481.2021.1936536

Fuentes, M.A., Zelaya, D.G. & Madsen, J.W. (2021) 'Rethinking the course syllabus: Considerations for promoting equity, diversity, and inclusion', *Teaching of Psychology*, 48(1), pp. 69–79.

Gonzalez, L.D., Pasque, P.A., Farris, K.D. & Hansen, J.M. (2024) 'Epistemic injustice and legitimacy in U.S. doctoral education: A systematic review of literature', *Review of Educational Research*, 94(3), pp. 423–64. https://doi.org/10.3102/00346543231187628

Jordan, D.R., Shortridge, A. & Darden, J.T. (2022) 'Exploring persistent racial and ethnic representation disparity in US geography doctoral programs: The disciplinary underrepresentation gap', *The Professional Geographer*, 74(2), pp. 193–220.

Leung, C.W., Farooqui, S., Wolfson, J.A. & Cohen, A.J. (2021) 'Understanding the cumulative burden of basic needs insecurities: Associations with health and academic achievement among college students', *American Journal of Health Promotion*, 35(2), pp. 275–8. https://doi.org/10.1177/0890117120946210

Marshall, A.G., Vue, Z., Beasley, H.K., Neikirk, K., Stephens, D., Wanjalla, C.N. ... & Hinton, A. (2023) 'Diversity, equity and inclusion in the laboratory: Strategies to enhance inclusive laboratory culture', *Molecular Cell*, 83(21), pp. 3766–72.

Mechler, H., Coakley, K., Walsh-Dilley, M. & Cargas, S. (2024) 'Examining the relationship between food insecurity and academic performance: Implications for diversity and equity in higher education', *Journal of College*

Student Retention: Research, Theory & Practice, 26(1), pp. 3–18. https://doi.org/10.1177/15210251211053863

Miller, C. & Roksa, J. (2020) 'Balancing research and service in academia: Gender, race, and laboratory tasks', *Gender & Society*, 34(1), pp. 131–52. https://doi.org/10.1177/0891243219867917

Nazmi, A., Martinez, S., Byrd, A., Robinson, D., Bianco, S., Maguire, J., Crutchfield, R.M., Condron, K. & Ritchie, L. (2018) 'A systematic review of food insecurity among US students in higher education', *Journal of Hunger & Environmental Nutrition*, 14, pp. 725–40. https://doi.org/10.1080/19320248.2018.1484316.

Saroyan, A. & Amundsen, C. (eds) (2023) *Rethinking teaching in higher education: From a course design workshop to a faculty development framework*. Taylor & Francis.

Sathy, V. & Hogan, K.A. (2022) *Inclusive teaching: Strategies for promoting equity in the college classroom*. West Virginia: West Virginia University Press.

Sue, D.W. (2010) *Microaggressions and marginality: Manifestation, dynamics, and impact*. Washington, DC: Wiley & Sons.

Sverdlik, A., Hall, N.C. & McAlpine, L. (2020) 'PhD imposter syndrome: Exploring antecedents, consequences, and implications for doctoral well-being', *International Journal of Doctoral Studies*, 15, pp. 737–58.

Williams, S.B., Taylor, E.A., Greenwell, T.C. & Burpo, B.M. (2021) 'Differences in sport management doctoral students' experiences with gender microaggressions and stereotype threat by gender', *Sport Management Education Journal*, 16(1), pp. 17–29.

Zimmer, W.K., Chang, C.N., Semma, B.M. & Fowler, D. (2022) 'Developing graduate writing habits and skills: Establishing writing sessions with STEM graduate students', *College Teaching*, 70(2), pp. 133–44. https://doi.org/10.1080/87567555.2021.1909524

11

Understanding and Nurturing Identity and Well-being

Baohua Yu and Peihua Li

Introduction

As mentioned throughout this book, the doctoral experience is a complex journey involving numerous challenges, obstacles and tensions. It also serves as a crucial socialization process that supports the professional development of doctoral students. Given the central role of identity in this process, it is essential to understand how doctoral students construct and experience their identities at various stages of the journey. This understanding is key to effectively supporting their academic success and future career prospects. Furthermore, recognizing how students' perceived identities shape their actions – and how these actions, in turn, influence their well-being across academic performance, professional growth and personal life – is particularly important.

This chapter explores the intersection of identity and well-being in the doctoral journey by examining cases and examples from doctoral students in Hong Kong (all names in these case studies are pseudonyms). These narratives offer valuable insights into how identity formation affects both the subjective and objective dimensions of well-being. Through a reflective analysis of these experiences, the chapter aims to contribute to the revitalization of doctoral education by critically evaluating existing policies and pedagogical practices. Central to this effort is the promotion of positive identity development, the provision of meaningful support for doctoral students' professional socialization, and the enhancement of their overall well-being during their studies.

Knowing doctoral students' identities

Doctoral education aims to cultivate and transform students into scholars, researchers and professionals through structured programmes that combine personalized mentorship, rigorous training and diverse academic activities (Balaban, 2020). Within this process, students are progressively socialized to acquire and transmit the knowledge, skills, norms, values and ideologies of their disciplines, facilitating their development as members of professional communities (Boden et al., 2011; Gardner, 2007; Gardner et al., 2014; Rhoads et al., 2017). This socialization also plays a crucial role in shaping doctoral students' academic identities.

Identity, defined as 'the way we make sense of ourselves and the image of ourselves that we present to others' (Day, 2011, p. 48), is a core aspect of the doctoral experience. It influences how students perceive their abilities, motivation and resilience, and it evolves throughout the often challenging and isolating journey of doctoral study. Doctoral student identity thus refers to how individuals perceive and represent themselves within academic contexts.

Recognizing and understanding doctoral students' identities are essential for informing programme design and institutional support. The following sections explore how identity is formed, experienced and transformed, its impact on academic life and how institutions can foster its positive development.

CASE STUDY 11.1 EMERSON: MY SELF-DEFINED IDENTITIES

Emerson from Germany is a PhD student in Hong Kong. He has a strong sense of his doctoral identity as a researcher and a scholar, although he recognizes his inexperience and immaturity in doing research.

> *... [I am] more scholar than researcher, even though also more researcher than teacher. Teacher comes always with this idea of knowing something better than somebody else, of course we all know something better than somebody else like this is how it works. We're all experts in our own right, but I like ... scholar, because it includes, like it has this connotation that you engage with knowledge. I realize this researcher. It did sound almost like it's very labor-like. When I do research, it's like an occupation by scholar. It is a lifestyle. ... [for the identity of scholar], I mean if there's a hierarchy, I'm very low in the hierarchy in there. Of course, there is an institutional aspect to the circle, and in this institutional hierarchy I'm very low, based on educational level, but then again, I think ideally, we all are committed to some kind of virtue here. Ideally this is something we share.*

According to Stets et al. (2020, p. 200), identity is 'a set of self-meanings derived from being a distinct person, role player, or member of a group or category'. Beyond markers such as age, gender and race, doctoral students define themselves within the academic context, shaped by their interactions in doctoral programmes and scholarly communities. Distinct from students at earlier educational levels, doctoral students focus primarily on research, knowledge production and academic contribution. They often attach high expectations and a strong sense of responsibility to their roles.

Typically, doctoral students identify as researchers and scholars, demonstrating a commitment to advancing knowledge and contributing to societal progress within their fields. Many also regard supervisors, faculty and peers as professional collaborators, reflecting their view of doctoral study as a shared research endeavour. Concurrently, some students emphasize their learner identity, highlighting the importance of acquiring independent research skills in preparation for academic careers. These overlapping and, at times, conflicting identities – particularly among early-stage doctoral students – shape their behaviours, experiences and achievements throughout the doctoral journey.

Doctoral student's identity formation and development throughout their academic journey

Social identity theory posits that an individual's sense of self is composed of multiple identities, each shaped through social interactions, the roles assumed within institutions and social structures, and the feedback received from others (Stets & Burke, 2000). Within this socialization process, doctoral students continuously construct, negotiate and develop their identities by seeking affirmation and validation in their academic environments. Numerous factors – including cultural background, faculty relationships, peer interactions, research engagement, a sense of belonging within the academic community and prior educational experiences – have been identified in the literature as influencing the formation and evolution of doctoral student identities (Douglas, 2022; Gruber et al., 2022; Hall & Burns, 2009; Kuo et al., 2021; McAlister et al., 2022; Murphy et al., 2023; Robertson & Nguyet Nguyen, 2021; Sweitzer, 2009).

Among these, mentorship, collegial peer relationships and the process of conducting independent research emerge as particularly significant in shaping how doctoral students perceive and position themselves within the academic landscape.

Although the pace of identity development varies among individuals, doctoral students consistently identify key milestones that signify their progression, such as enrolment in doctoral programmes, the formulation of research projects, the successful completion of topic defences, approval of PhD candidacy, initial academic presentations at conferences, the publication of their first academic articles and the successful defence of their doctoral dissertations. These milestones reflect the trajectory of doctoral students' academic careers, marking their transition from dependent to independent researchers.

CASE STUDY 11.2 DANIEL: THE TIME I FEEL LIKE A PhD STUDENT

Being a Year-2 PhD student, Daniel reflected on his initial identity in the first year of doctoral study. Though enrolling in doctoral programme, he did not view himself as a PhD student until the confirmation of his PhD candidature by the university.

> *I know [I have been a] Ph.D. student since I enrolled, and I got a sheet of paper, and it told me you have the offer today. Well then, I did not even feel like it as soon as I was here. I do not get excited about something until it really has happened. Sometimes I know good things will happen, but I do not get too excited until it has happened. And of course, being a year and having the title of being PhD student until my Candidature was confirmed, I have felt anxious about it. After a topic defense I feel better about myself. It feels like you are already safe, in limbo, because you were obviously preliminarily accepted. It is a weird feeling. I mean I did this, which was an important moment for me, that I had confirmation that you are accepted now. I can concentrate on my work and those are the moments where I feel like a PhD student when I can just do my work.*

As the highest level of academic study, doctoral education represents a rigorous and demanding journey that enables students to develop comprehensive research capabilities, ultimately qualifying them as experts, researchers and scholars in their respective fields. According to Burke's (2006) Identity Control Theory, an individual's internal identity is dynamic, continuously adjusted and reaffirmed through social interactions. In this context, doctoral students undergo a process of identity transformation, evolving from novice researchers to emerging researchers, and ultimately to experienced, independent scholars.

CASE STUDY 11.3 RYAN: IT GIVES ME THE OPPORTUNITY

Instead of a career mindset, Ryan displays his great passion for doing research and the aspiration for sustaining his research interest as a scholar in academia.

> *I am aware we do not think there are some people who do this for a career. It is like we all do it just as a career, but you know for some people they have a strong career mindset. I do not have that. … I will be a scholar. Ideally, I will also stay in academia. It does not need to be academia wherever I find a place that I can do research, and I can engage with the world around me in terms of research. I would love that, and I know I do not really care whether in academia or in a private economy. I mean I can even live alone in the mountains and write books, or how I see the world technically is not a preferred lifestyle, but you know this is what makes me happy. So of course, I would try to [stay in] academia because it seems like the first logical choice. … it gives me the opportunity to engage with thoughts [and] to share my thoughts. You cannot do this with every job. It is a creative occupation, I think.*

REFLECTIVE ACTIVITY 11.1: EXPLORING IDENTITY

Reflect on your role in guiding doctoral students' identity development. Consider how you have helped students shape their academic and professional identities. Think about the actions or behaviours you've taken that influence their self-perception as researchers, scholars and future professionals. Reflect on any challenges or shifts you have observed in students' identities throughout their journey.

Discuss common identity-related challenges doctoral students face, such as balancing the roles of student and researcher or experiencing imposter syndrome. Share how you have helped students navigate these challenges and explore how you can better support students in developing a positive and confident academic identity.

Note specific strategies you have used or could use to support students' identity development, such as encouraging student autonomy while providing mentorship, creating opportunities for students to present their research early in their programme, or offering constructive feedback that reinforces their role as a growing scholar. After reflecting individually, discuss how these strategies can be adapted to various student needs.

Finally, note one key takeaway or insight you gained from this activity about supporting students' identity development. Reflect on how these strategies can be implemented more consistently in your supervisory role.

Doctoral students' identities and their academic aspirations

The way in which doctoral students perceive their identities and roles has a significant impact on their behaviour and performance within the academic sphere, which is characterized by a combination of rigorous study, intensive research and unpredictable career progression (Leshem, 2020). Given their distinct identities, doctoral students adopt varying approaches to learning, research and academic engagement. Specifically, those who strongly identify as researchers or scholars tend to exhibit higher levels of confidence, proactivity and resilience when confronted with academic challenges, often resulting in notable academic performance and productivity.

Additionally, doctoral students' sense of identity can influence their sense of belonging and engagement within the academic community. For example, students who perceive themselves as novices may be more likely to isolate themselves from their peers and show reluctance to engage in scholarly activities, such as presenting at academic conferences, due to lower self-confidence. However, from the outset of their doctoral journey, many students – particularly those pursuing a PhD – are deeply passionate and committed to their research interests, with a clear aspiration to pursue careers as scholars and professors in their respective fields after graduation.

Nurturing identities and well-being in doctoral education

Challenges to well-being posed by doctoral students' identities

Research by Yeigh et al. (2022) highlights the significant role of identity in predicting well-being. As such, identity plays a pivotal role in shaping the academic experiences of doctoral students, with a strong connection to their overall well-being, encompassing both psychological well-being (Ryff, 1989) and subjective well-being (Diener, 1984). Understanding the influence of identity on doctoral students' well-being is crucial for enhancing their holistic health, as fostering a strong and stable sense of identity can contribute to improved overall well-being throughout their academic journey.

Psychological well-being is often discussed in terms of stress levels, relationships with others, sense of purpose in life, life ambitions, perception of personal growth and sense of belonging (Alharbi & Smith, 2018; Li et al., 2014; Ryan et al., 2022). Doctoral students with a strong sense of identity as learners, researchers or scholars tend to have greater clarity regarding their purpose in life, ambitions and personal growth. Once they determine their research area during their PhD studies, they establish clear academic and career goals. They understand what they are striving for, what preparations are necessary for success and what outcomes they aim to achieve.

In contrast, even among doctoral students with similar academic identities, variations may emerge in areas such as stress management, interpersonal relationships and sense of belonging. For instance, those who primarily identify as students or learners often report a lower sense of belonging within the academic community. As a result, tailored activities and support services, such as cultural cafés or group writing activities, can be provided in doctoral programmes to address such challenges.

Subjective well-being, on the other hand, encompasses emotional health, life satisfaction, positive effect and negative affect (Alharbi & Smith, 2018; Renshaw & Bolognino, 2016; Travia et al., 2021; Zhang & Renshaw, 2020; Zhao et al., 2021). When doctoral students experience fulfilment that aligns with their academic identities, they are more likely to express positive emotions and satisfaction. Despite the uncertainties inherent in PhD study, a strong and stable identity appears to support greater optimism and motivation. Consequently, supportive resources – such as financial aid and privileged access to research facilities – are crucial for reinforcing both doctoral students' identity development and their subjective well-being.

CASE STUDY 11.4 ADAM: STRESS IS MORE LIKE STEAM IN AN ENGINE

Adam admits the stress imposed on himself deriving from his PhD identity. However, he holds a positive attitude towards it and views it as a momentum for his progress.

> *... identity does not impose stress to people. I reject saying that not because I am happy. I mean I have stress. It is good stress, an energetic stress. I said it is more like steam in an engine. To be fair, people use the word 'stress' a little bit or too lightly having something to do with being pushed to do something. We call this stress, but real stress is a little more pathological, if it would increase your heart rate yourself and enter real stress. Most of us never had this feeling. So, it means that you have a positive attitude towards stress. At least the stress I feel every day like I said it is more like steam that pushes the engine. It is nothing high I really suffer from. If I would not have to stress, then I would not have any momentum to move forward. So, that is a part, but we mean here with stress. And if I would not have this imposed from my role, I would have an identity crisis that I should not know what I should do with my life. So, I am very thankful for having this.*

RESEARCH BRIEFING 11.1: THE EXAMPLE OF NEURODIVERSITY

Background

Increasing numbers of students with a disability are enrolling in universities in Australia, England and other countries (Kilpatrick et al., 2017; Pino & Mortari, 2014). Emerging research suggests that this trend is contributing to a rise in the number of students with a disability pursuing doctoral study (Sandland et al., 2023). This development should be welcomed as an indicator of progress towards widening access to higher education and enhancing representation of persons with a disability in society, in line with the vision of the United Nations (UN, 2016).

Universities, both formally and informally, are increasingly using the umbrella term neurodiverse or neurodivergent student(s) to collectively describe students with autism, dyslexia, dyspraxia, dyscalculia, ADHD and Tourette syndrome (Robertson & Ne'eman, 2008). In this chapter, identity is defined as 'a set of self-meanings derived from being a distinct person, role player, or member of a group or category' (Stets et al., 2020, p. 200).

Many universities in Australia, England and elsewhere have established formal and informal support structures – such as projects, clubs, hubs, groups and networks – aimed at supporting this population (La Trobe University, 2024; University of York, 2024). The well-being of neurodivergent/neurodiverse students is often, either explicitly or implicitly, included in the purpose of these initiatives. These structures can serve as convenient and supportive sources of social connection and information for new doctoral students with a disability. For instance, a supportive PhD supervisor may ask at an initial meeting, 'Have you contacted our university's neurodivergent/neurodiverse student learning community?' Research highlights the importance of such social components, as many students with a disability experience loneliness and isolation during their university studies (Child & Langford, 2011; White, 2024).

Neurodiversity and identity in doctoral education

Referring to a PhD student as neurodivergent or neurodiverse, and applying these terms to specific communities, raises complex practical and ethical questions when considering identity and well-being in doctoral education. The terms themselves carry assumptions and tensions. Sociologist Judy Singer and journalist Harvey Blume coined neurodiversity in the late 1990s, arguing that neurological variation is a natural and essential aspect of human diversity (Dwyer, 2022; Ellis et al., 2023). Since then, neurodiversity has often served as a positive, affirmative self-label that recognizes neurological difference – rather than deficit – among people with autism, dyslexia, dyspraxia, dyscalculia or ADHD, in contrast to the so-called neurotypical population (Armstrong & Armstrong, 2021).

However, not all students with a disability – especially those with autism, dyslexia or ADHD – choose to identify as neurodivergent or neurodiverse. Some prefer more specific terms such as dyslexic or autistic. Bury et al. (2023) found that among a cohort of Australian adults with autism (n = 123), only 5.6 per cent preferred the term neurodivergent person (p. 685), with Autistic, Person on the Autism Spectrum and Autistic Person rated as most preferred and least offensive (p. 677).

These findings point to the subtle overlaps between formal and informal identity categories. Hamilton and Petty (2023), for example, argue that neurodiversity is one dimension of difference within an increasingly diverse student population, which overlaps – but is not synonymous – with disability (p. 1).

Disclosure and formal recognition

Despite the acknowledgement of diversity, university systems often do not formally recognize such identity categories unless accompanied by a formal diagnosis. In Australia, England and many other countries, disability support services typically require official documentation from a psychologist or psychiatrist before offering study accommodations (ADCET, 2024). This process of disclosure is essential for triggering 'reasonable adjustments' under legislation such as Australia's Disability Discrimination Act (DDA, 1992). These adjustments may include modified deadlines for submitting doctoral proposals or accommodations for oral presentations (see 'Supporting Progress through the Doctoral Journey').

Notably, a lesser-known provision of the DDA (1992) states that its protections and requirements – including the duty to make reasonable adjustments – apply even when a person is suspected of having a disability, regardless of formal diagnosis (Disability Royal Commission, 2020). Doctoral students in Australia who suspect they may have a disability but have not yet begun formal assessment should take note of this when engaging with university support services.

Barriers to access and help-seeking behaviour

Barriers to accessing support are a significant concern. Research on undergraduate help-seeking behaviour reveals a critical issue: many adult students do not disclose their disability until after academic problems arise (Van Hees et al., 2015; White, 2024). This delay can result in negative impacts on well-being due to heightened anxiety, frustration and emotional distress (Evans, 2014; White, 2024). In many cases, students exit their doctoral studies early, with low social and organizational identification and negative academic experiences cited as key factors – particularly among students with autism (Cage & Howes, 2020, p. 1664).

A small-scale longitudinal study by Van Hees et al. (2015; n = 23) sheds light on the reluctance to disclose. The study found that while students disclosed their ASD status to disability offices to obtain accommodations, they often withheld this information from peers and academic staff due to fears of stigma, prejudice or rejection (p. 1681).

Positive impacts of tailored support

On a more hopeful note, research affirms the benefits of personalized support and the consistent application of reasonable adjustments in doctoral education (ADCET, 2024; Cage & Howes, 2020; Van Hees et al., 2015). When such practices are implemented from the outset, they can significantly enhance the overall well-being of neurodivergent students, fostering both a positive academic experience and a greater sense of belonging.

Supporting and strengthening doctoral students' professional identity

Doctoral students' identity is a central aspect of their academic journey, continuously developing within the social and academic communities to which they belong. At the same time, a doctoral student's present self is connected to their future self through the alignment of 'actions necessary to attain a future self and other salient aspects of the current self' (Oyserman & James, 2011, p. 135).

Accordingly, institutions and universities can play a critical role in strengthening students' professional identity by fostering an inclusive and supportive academic environment. This can be achieved by carefully designing doctoral programmes in terms of curricula, assessments, academic activities and faculty–student relationships.

For example, the Education Doctorate (EdD) is more practitioner-oriented than the PhD, aiming to prepare doctoral students to become professional practitioners who identify as educational leaders, educational researchers, and ultimately, researching professionals (RPs) (Buss, 2020, p. 1). In this chapter, we introduce a set of features, concepts and guiding principles for the (re)design of EdD programmes, which may serve as an inspiration for the development of various doctoral programmes.

Founded in 2007, the Carnegie Project on the Education Doctorate (CPED) is a consortium aimed at guiding its members in redesigning and strengthening EdD programmes, with the goal of fostering the development of advanced practitioners in education (CPED, 2025). EdD programmes are typically characterized by three key components: the development of practical research skills, the provision of experiential learning opportunities in real-world contexts, and the cultivation of a connection between acquired skills and future professional careers. Additionally, given the critical role that identity plays in empowering doctoral students to become academic professionals, it is essential to incorporate an identity-focused perspective into these three components when designing EdD programmes.

RESEARCH BRIEFING 11.2: THE CARNEGIE PROJECT ON THE EDUCATION DOCTORATE (CPED) IN THE UNITED STATES

Buss (2020, pp. 1–15) conducted a study on the Carnegie Project on the Education Doctorate (CPED) in the United States. The study presents Six Guiding Principles for Programme Design and Six Programme Design Concepts, which can be applied to reflect the practice of doctoral programmes.

The six CPED guiding principles are:

- Framing programmes around questions of equity, ethics and social justice;
- Preparing leaders to apply knowledge to make a positive difference in people's lives;
- Providing opportunities to develop collaboration and communication skills in diverse communities;
- Providing field-based opportunities to analyse problems of practice and develop solutions;
- Integrating both practical and research knowledge that links theory with systemic and systematic inquiry;
- Emphasizing the generation, transformation and use of professional knowledge and practice.

The six CPED programme design concepts are:

- Scholarly practitioner
- Signature pedagogies
- Inquiry as practice
- Laboratories of practice
- Dissertations in practice
- Problem of practice

For example, the development of practical research skills can be disciplinary specific. In the sciences, this may mean laboratory techniques, in the social sciences, interview techniques and, in the Arts and Humanities, research skill acquisition may relate to the ability to understand archive material.

The second component, the provision of experiential learning opportunities in real-world contexts, is similarly discipline specific but the principle behind such provision is fundamental to all research degree programmes; impact and knowledge exchange are necessary for a successful post-doctorate career.

This relates to the cultivation of a connection between acquired skills and future professional careers. In the past, a doctorate might lead to a career in academia; this is (largely) no longer the case. Whilst the focus of the Carnegie Project was the Education Doctorate, such approaches will help cultivate a strong and confident professional identity among doctoral students, thereby facilitating the development of a practitioner-scholar identity.

The integration of guiding principles and design concepts is vital in the development of doctoral programmes, as they help align the educational process with the programme's strategic objectives. Beyond the features of doctoral programmes, the concept of identity formation should be embedded in these guiding principles and design concepts to bridge the gap between

REFLECTIVE ACTIVITY 11.2: RETHINKING SUPPORT FOR DOCTORAL STUDENTS' IDENTITY IN PROGRAMME DESIGN

This activity is designed for use when engaging in the design or redesign of a doctoral programme. Drawing on the features, guiding principles and design concepts outlined in the Carnegie Project on the Education Doctorate (CPED), reflect on the doctoral programme you are planning:

- What type of doctoral programme are you designing? Is it a professional doctorate or a research doctorate?
- What are the key features of your doctoral programme?
- Regarding the facilitation of doctoral students' professional identity development, which design concepts will you emphasize in terms of training approaches and the overarching goals of the doctoral programme?
- What are the specific guiding principles you will adopt in your programme design to strengthen doctoral students' professional identity?

students' current identities and their future professional identities. While students' current identities are primarily shaped by their origins, their future professional identities are closely linked to their anticipated career paths. The incorporation of identity formation can be reflected throughout the educational process, ensuring that the guiding principles and design concepts are consistently applied at every stage of the programme.

Conclusion

This chapter has explored various aspects of doctoral students' identity development and its significant impact on their well-being. The relationship between their evolving identities and overall sense of well-being was crucial to both their academic and personal experiences. The identities doctoral students formed throughout their journey profoundly influenced their psychological, emotional and physical health. Therefore, supporting and strengthening these identities was essential for improving their well-being. Universities played a key role in fostering an environment that promoted the holistic development of doctoral students.

The progression of doctoral students' identities typically followed a trajectory, beginning with the role of student, evolving into that of learner, transitioning into researcher and ultimately maturing into scholar. As they navigated a demanding academic path, maintaining a strong and positive sense of identity helped students balance their academic responsibilities with personal well-being. Understanding how identity influenced doctoral students' well-being provided valuable insights for educators, counsellors and policymakers, enabling them to design and assess doctoral education programmes more effectively.

References

Alharbi, E.S. & Smith, A.P. (2018) 'Review of the literature on stress and wellbeing of international students in English-speaking countries', *International Education Studies*, 11(6), p. 22. https://doi.org/10.5539/ies.v11n6p22

Armstrong, D. & Armstrong, G. (2021) *Educational trends exposed: How to be a critical consumer*. London: Routledge.

Australian Disability Clearinghouse on Training and Education (ADCET) (2024) Sharing your disability information while studying. Australian Government Department of Education. https://www.adcet.edu.au/students-with-disability/disclosure#:~:text=Information%20about%20your%20disability%20cannot,is%20treated%20with%20strictest%20confidentiality

Balaban, C. (2020) 'Diversifying the missions and expectations of doctoral education: Are we losing the distinctive "added value" of the PhD?' In: Cardoso, S., Tavares, O., Sin, C., Carvalho, T. (eds) *Structural and institutional transformations in doctoral education. Issues in higher education*. Cham: Palgrave Macmillan, pp. 325–45. https://doi.org/10.1007/978-3-030-38046-5_11

Bastalich, W. (2017) 'Content and context in knowledge production: A critical review of doctoral supervision literature', *Studies in Higher Education*, 42(7), pp. 1145–57. doi:10.1080/03075079.2015.1079702

Boden, D., Borrego, M. & Newswander, L.K. (2011) 'Student socialization in interdisciplinary doctoral education', *Higher Education*, 6(6), pp. 741–55. https://doi.org/10.4324/9781003446187-10

Burke, P.J. (2006) 'Identity change', *Social Psychology Quarterly*, 69(1), pp. 81–96. https://doi.org/10.1177/019027250606900106

Bury, S.M., Jellett, R., Spoor, J.R. & Hedley, D. (2023) '"It defines who I am" or "It's something I have": What language do [autistic] Australian adults [on the autism spectrum] prefer?', *Journal of Autism and Developmental Disorders*, 53(2), pp. 677–87.

Buss, R.R. (2020) 'Exploring the development of students' identities as educational leaders and educational researchers in a professional practice doctoral program', *Studies in Higher Education*, 47(6), pp. 1–15. https://doi.org/10.1080/03075079.2020.1836484

Cage, E. & Howes, J. (2020) 'Dropping out and moving on: A qualitative study of autistic people's experiences of university', *Autism: The International Journal of Research and Practice*, 24(7), pp. 1664–75. https://doi.org/10.1177/1362361320918750

Child, J. & Langford, E. (2011) 'Exploring the learning experiences of nursing students with dyslexia', *Nursing Standard (through 2013)*, 25(40), p. 39.

CPED (Carnegie Project on the Education Doctorate) (n.d.) Carnegie Project on the Education Doctorate Framework. https://cdn.ymaws.com/www.cpedinitiative.org/resource/resmgr/CPED_Framework.pdf.

Day, C. (2011) 'Uncertain professional identities. Managing the emotional contexts of teaching'. In: Day, C. & Lee, J. (eds) *New understandings of teacher's work*. Dordrecht: Springer, pp. 45–54.

Diener, E. (1984) 'Subjective well-being', *Psychological Bulletin*, 95(3), p. 542.

Disability Discrimination Act (1992) (Cth).

Disability Royal Commission (2020) Public Hearing 7: Barriers experienced by students with disability in accessing and obtaining a safe, quality and inclusive school education and consequent life course impacts. https://disability.royalcommission.gov.au/public-hearings/public-hearing-7

Dong, A., Jong, M.S.Y. & King, R.B. (2020) 'How does prior knowledge influence learning engagement? The mediating roles of cognitive load and help-seeking', *Frontiers in Psychology*, 11, pp. 591203. doi:10.3389/fpsyg.2020.591203

Douglas, A.S. (2022) 'Dimensions of fit for doctoral candidates: Supporting an academic identity', *Research Papers in Education*, 37(6), pp. 954–74. https://doi.org/10.1080/02671522.2021.1905704

Dwyer, P. (2022) 'The neurodiversity approach(es): What are they and what do they mean for researchers?', *Human Development*, 66, pp. 73–92.

Ellis, P., Kirby, A. & Osborne, A. (2023) *Neurodiversity and education*. London: Sage.

Evans, W. (2014) 'If they can't tell the difference between duphalac and digoxin you've got patient safety issues: Nurse lecturers' constructions of students' dyslexic identities in nurse education', *Nurse Education Today*, 34(6), pp. e41–e46.

Foot, R., Crowe, A.R., Tollafield, K.A. & Allan, C.E. (2014) 'Exploring doctoral student identity development using a self-study approach', *Teaching & Learning Inquiry*, 2(1), pp. 103–18. doi:10.20343/teachlearninqu.2.1.103

Gardner, S.K. (2007) '"I heard it through the grapevine": Doctoral student socialization in chemistry and history', *Higher Education*, 54(5), pp. 723–40. https://doi.org/10.1007/s10734-006-9020-x

Gardner, S.K., Jansujwicz, J.S., Hutchins, K., Cline, B. & Levesque, V. (2014) 'Socialization to interdisciplinarity: Faculty and student perspectives', *Higher Education*, 67(3), pp. 255–71. https://doi.org/10.1007/s10734-013-9648-2

Gonida, E.N., Karabenick, S.A., Stamovlasis, D. & Metallidou, P. (2019) 'Help seeking as a self-regulated learning strategy and achievement goals: The case of academically talented adolescents', *High Ability Studies*, 30(1–2), pp. 147–66. doi:10.1080/13598139.2018.1535244

Gruber, M., Crispeels, T. & D'Este, P. (2022) 'Who am I? The influence of knowledge networks on PhD students' development of a research role identity'. In *Minerva* (Issue 0123456789). Springer Netherlands. https://doi.org/10.1007/s11024-023-09492-1

Hall, L.A. & Burns, L.D. (2009) 'Identity development and mentoring in doctoral education', *Harvard Educational Review*, 79(1), pp. 49–70. https://doi.org/10.17763/haer.79.1.wr25486891279345

Hamilton, L.G. & Petty, S. (2023) 'Compassionate pedagogy for neurodiversity in higher education: A conceptual analysis', *Frontiers in Psychology*, 14, p. 1093290.

Jeung, D.Y., Kim, C. & Chang, S.J. (2018) 'Emotional labor and burnout: A review of the literature', *Yonsei Medical Journal*, 59(2), pp. 187–93. doi:10.3349/ymj.2018.59.2.187

Kilpatrick, S., Johns, S., Barnes, R., Fischer, S., McLennan, D. & Magnussen, K. (2017) 'Exploring the retention and success of students with disability in Australian higher education', *International Journal of Inclusive Education*, 21(7), pp. 747–62. https://doi.org/10.1080/13603116.20

Kuo, P., Washington, A. & Woo, H. (2021) 'Professional identity development and multicultural identity among international counselor education doctoral students', *Journal of Multicultural Counseling and Development*, 49(2), pp. 116–28. https://doi.org/10.1002/jmcd.12210

La Trobe University (2024) 'Support for neurominority students'. Available at: https://www.latrobe.edu.au/students/support/wellbeing/resource-hub/Neurodiversity/study-and-accessibility

Laufer, M. & Gorup, M. (2019) 'The invisible others: Stories of international doctoral student dropout', *Higher Education*, 78, pp. 165–81. doi:10.1007/s10734-018-0337-5

Leshem, S. (2020) 'Identity formations of doctoral students on the route to achieving their doctorate', Issues in *Educational Research*, 30(1), pp. 169–86. https://search.informit.org/doi/10.3316/informit.085953915040529

Li, J., Wang, Y. & Xiao, F. (2014) 'East Asian international students and psychological well-being: A systematic review', *Journal of International Students*, 4(4), pp. 301–13. https://doi.org/10.32674/jis.v4i4.450

McAlister, A.M., Lilly, S. & Chiu, J.L. (2022) 'Exploring factors that impact physical science doctoral student role identities through a multiple case study approach', *Science Education*, 106(6), pp. 1501–34. https://doi.org/10.1002/sce.21754

Mermelshtine, R. (2017) 'Parent–child learning interactions: A review of the literature on scaffolding', *British Journal of Educational Psychology*, 87(2), pp. 241–54. doi:10.1111/bjep.12147

Murphy, P.K., Kim, T., Joy, E.E., Shein, B. & Allan, B.A. (2023) Social mobility through doctoral education: Exploring identity, classism, and belongingness', *Journal of Diversity in Higher Education*, 18(1), pp. 16–24. Advance online publication. https://doi.org/10.1037/dhe0000477

Oyserman, D. & James, L. (2011) 'Possible identities'. In: Schwartz, S., Luyckx, K. & Vignoles, V. (eds.) *Handbook of identity theory and research*. Springer-Verlag, pp. 117–45.

Pino, M. & Mortari, L. (2014) 'The inclusion of students with dyslexia in higher education: A systematic review using narrative synthesis', *Dyslexia*, 20(4), pp. 346–69.

Renshaw, T.L. & Bolognino, S.J. (2016) 'The college student subjective wellbeing questionnaire: A brief, multidimensional measure of undergraduate's covitality', *Journal of Happiness Studies*, 17(2), pp. 463–84. https://doi.org/10.1007/s10902-014-9606-4

Rhoads, R.A., Zheng, M. & Sun, X. (2017) 'The methodological socialization of social science doctoral students in China and the USA', *Higher Education*, 73(2), pp. 335–51. https://doi.org/10.1007/s10734-016-0023-y

Robertson, M.J. & Nguyet Nguyen, M. (2021) 'Robing up: Transactional identity development of Vietnamese PhD students', *Asia Pacific Journal of Education*, 41(2), pp. 312–22. https://doi.org/10.1080/02188791.2020.1772197

Robertson, S.M. & Ne'eman, A.D. (2008) 'Autistic acceptance, the college campus, and technology: Growth of neurodiversity in society and academia', *Disability Studies Quarterly*, 28(4). https://doi.org/10.18061/dsq.v28i4.146

Roelle, J., Glogger-Frey, I., Waldeyer, J. & Renkl, A. (2020) 'The self-regulation-view in writing-to-learn: Using journal writing to optimize cognitive load in self-regulated learning', *Educational Psychology Review*, 32(4), pp. 1089–126. doi:10.1007/s10648-020-09541-1

Rogoff, B. (1990) *Apprenticeship in thinking: Cognitive development in social context*. New York: Oxford University Press.

Rogoff, B. (2014) 'Learning by observing and pitching in to family and community endeavors: An orientation', *Human Development*, 57(2–3), pp. 69–81. doi:10.1159/000356757

Ryan, T., Baik, C. & Larcombe, W. (2022) 'How can universities better support the mental wellbeing of higher degree research students? A study of students' suggestions', *Higher Education Research and Development*, 41(3), pp. 867–81. https://doi.org/10.1080/07294360.2021.1874886

Ryff, C.D. (1989) 'Happiness is everything, or is it? Explorations on the meaning of psychological well-being', *Journal of Personality and Social Psychology*, 57(6), p. 1069.

Sandland, B., MacLeod, A. & Hall, N. (2023) 'Neurodiverse students within higher education: Initial thoughts from a collaborative project', *Good Autism Practice (GAP)*, 24(2), pp. 13–22.

Starke-Meyerring, D. (2011) 'The paradox of writing in doctoral education: Student experiences'. In: Thomson, P. & Walker, M. (eds) *Doctoral education: research-based strategies for doctoral students, supervisors and administrators*. London: Routledge, pp. 75–95.

Stets, J.E. & Burke, P.J. (2000) 'Identity theory and social identity theory', *Social Psychology Quarterly*, 63(3), pp. 224–37. https://doi.org/10.2307/2695870

Stets, J.E., Burke, P.J., Serpe, R.T. & Stryker, R. (2020) 'Getting identity theory (IT) right', *Advances in Group Processes*, 37, pp. 191–212. Emerald Publishing.

Sweitzer, V. (2009) 'Towards a theory of doctoral student professional identity development: A developmental networks approach', *Journal of Higher Education*, 80(1), pp. 1–33. https://doi.org/10.1353/jhe.0.0034

The Carnegie Project on the Education Doctorate (CPED) (2025), What is the Carnegie Project on the Education Doctorate (CPED)? April. https://www.cpedinitiative.org/

Travia, R.M., Larcus, J.G., Thibodeau, K.R., Hutchinson, Wall, A. & Brocato, N. (2021) Measuring Well-being in a college campus setting [White paper]. American College Health Association. https://www.acha.org/wp-content/uploads/2024/07/Measuring_Well-Being_In_A_College_Campus_Setting_White_Paper.pdf

United Nations (UN) (2016) Convention on the Rights of Persons with Disabilities (CRPD). General Comment No. 4. The Right to an Inclusive Education. United Nations, Office of the High Commissioner, Geneva. https://www.ohchr.org/en/documents/general-comments-and-recommendations/general-comment-no-4-article-24-right-inclusive

University of York (2024) 'Neurodiversity' Available at: https://www.york.ac.uk/students/support/neurodiversity/

Van Hees, V., Moyson, T. & Roeyers, H. (2015) 'Higher education experiences of students with Autism Spectrum Disorder: Challenges, benefits and support needs', *Journal of Autism and Developmental Disorders*, 45(6), pp. 1673–88. https://doi.org/10.1007/s10803-014-2324-2

Vasileiou, K., Barnett, J., Thorpe, S. & Young, T. (2018) 'Characterising and justifying sample size sufficiency in interview-based studies: Systematic analysis of qualitative health research over a 15-year period', *BMC Medical Research Methodology*, 18, pp. 148. doi:10.1186/s12874-018-0594-7

White, J.F. (2024) 'Neurodiversity & nursing: Reflection of a final year general nursing student', *Nurse Education Today*, 141, pp. 106318.

Wijaya, K.F. (2021) 'English education master students' self-regulated learning strategies in academic writing', *Journal of English Teaching*, 7(1), pp. 15–29. doi:10.33541/jet.v7i1.2313

Winget, M. & Persky, A.M. (2022) 'A practical review of mastery learning', *American Journal of Pharmaceutical Education*, 86(10), ajpe8906. doi:10.5688/ajpe8906

Yeigh, T., Willis, R., James, S., Lake, W., Lynch, D., Peddell, L., Knight, B., Lee, M. & Samojlowicz, D. (2022) 'Teacher of mathematics identity as a predictor of teacher wellbeing,' *Australian Educational Researcher*, 50, *0123456789*. https://doi.org/10.1007/s13384-022-00553-0

Zhang, D.C. & Renshaw, T.L. (2020) 'Personality and college student subjective wellbeing: A domain-specific approach', *Journal of Happiness Studies*, 21(3), pp. 997–1014. https://doi.org/10.1007/s10902-019-00116-8

Zhao, J.L., Chen, F. & Jia, X.M. (2021) 'The development and validation of the doctoral student identity scale', *Frontiers in Psychology*, 12 (December), pp. 1–11. https://doi.org/10.3389/fpsyg.2021.688948

PART FOUR

Achieving a Doctorate: The Role of the Supervisor

12

Giving Constructive Feedback on Research Progress and Outputs

Gregory Light

Introduction

Providing graduate students feedback on their work is at the core of doctoral education. It shapes the key educational relationship between supervisor and student. It consists of responses given to the student on a wide spectrum of intellectual, practical, social and interpersonal challenges regarding their performance and understanding (Wisniewski et al., 2020). Feedback also included the abilities the student develops to make the most of feedback, sometimes referred to as feedback literacy (Carless & Boud, 2018). The quality of the feedback and the feedback relationship is therefore critical to the student's progress and success.

Feedback to doctoral students may be formal or informal and may be given in a wide variety of written, verbal and audio-visual formats. It spans the full breadth of doctoral education, including advice on what to expect during the process, help navigating the emotional ups and downs, tips on how to teach a class of undergraduates and insights on which journals to send research papers.

This chapter will concentrate on the practical aspects of giving constructive feedback to the student on the outputs of their research. The focus will be on feedback as a critical form of assessment of student learning in the completion of a unique and substantive research output. While the emphasis will mainly concern written outputs/creations, it will also apply to outputs, such as videos, posters, algorithms, musical and artistic creations. These outputs emerge in all stages of the research process, from early research outlines, plans and designs, through drafts, reports and presentations, to journal papers and the final dissertation or thesis.

The nature and scope of feedback

Feedback as academic socialization

Feedback on student work at the doctoral level is a dialogue between supervisor, student and the shared community in which the feedback occurs. It is a fundamental part of the student's socialization into the academic community (Carless et al., 2023). The academic community, in turn, is characterized by its members' practice, primarily the discovery, creation and dissemination of knowledge. In this respect, constructive feedback goes beyond simply being useful and timely; it is also formative, helping students acquire feedback skills which can be used in the academic community more widely. Constructive supervision is, then, more than the quality of the dialogue and the learning and the knowledge development. It includes the person as a specialized practitioner and knowledge creator in the academic field.

Feedback between supervisor and doctoral student is not the only dialogue which students encounter during their doctoral education. There are many other feedback opportunities with fellow students, conference members, research associates, peer-reviewers and other members of the research community. But normally feedback from the supervisor will be the most important and impactful. As such, feedback is both an entryway and a pathway for the student. And the quality of feedback provided plays a major role in how welcoming or hostile the journey will be. It will be difficult and bumpy, as meaningful learning often is, but guided by constructive feedback, it should be attainable and transformative.

The feedback landscape

In a study of student perceptions of success, Blanchard et al. (2019) report the provision of tangible advice and feedback on the student's work was the best predictor of success. Nevertheless, poor feedback on doctoral student work is a widespread student experience across most fields of doctoral study. Student critiques of the feedback they receive on their research concerns everything from the quality and depth of the comments they receive to the timing and relevance of the responses from their supervisors. To be fair, the provision of feedback is not a straightforward process. It embraces many moving pieces: the student themself, including their temperament, preparedness, motivations, status (full-time, part-time, domestic, international), part of a team, sole researcher, their stage in the process and so on; the supervisor: sole supervisor, co-supervising, part of a team, multidisciplinary; and the many relationships: between student, supervisor, other supervisors and/or team members. The permutations are considerable.

In a recent review of research on supervisory feedback, Chugh et al. (2022) report five areas of feedback in which students may encounter serious problems. These areas describe what might be called a 'feedback landscape'.

Area One: Feedback content. The feedback needs to be clear, focused and specific. Vague and unclear feedback may be compounded if English is not the first language for either or both the student and the supervisor. The detail of the feedback can also be problematic. On the one hand, if feedback stays at the level of punctuation, grammar and word choice, the bigger issues or deeper questions may not be addressed. On the other hand, if the feedback is excessive, students may feel their ownership of the material has been reduced. This may have the effect of marginalizing the student's role and changing the direction of their work.

Area Two: Format and delivery of the feedback. For convenience, timeliness and legibility, students tend to prefer electronic feedback to handwritten and oral feedback in person or via Zoom to oral over phone or recorded (Gillis & Pellegrine, 2023). Timeliness is a widely reported problem and includes supervisors deliberately delaying feedback, and/or not being available to meet in person or online. Both undermine the trust essential to a good student-supervisor relationship as does the consistency and tone of the feedback. Inconsistent and conflicting feedback is difficult for students, especially from different supervisors. A harsh and/or needlessly cruel tone undermines confidence and motivation, while too 'nice' feedback often lacks needed critique and depth.

Area Three: The student. Part of receiving feedback is learning how to receive feedback. For a whole host of personal and cultural reasons some students may be fearful, defensive, arrogant and miss much that is positive in the feedback. Many students, especially at the outset of their doctoral training, are not proactive in seeking feedback. Others may be overly needy or demanding. In a large study of student views of receiving feedback, Molloy,

E. et al. (2019) describe a broad set of student feedback skills necessary for effective learning from feedback. In addition to understanding the purpose of feedback, they include a recognition that feedback is a reciprocal process which requires commitment and active engagement. This includes actively seeking information, making judgements on the information, reflecting on its impact on their work and managing their emotions throughout the feedback process.

Area Four: The supervisor. Like many students, the supervisor may be unprepared for their role. They may not have, or feel they do not have, the appropriate knowledge and expertise for the student's research project. Or they lack the supervision skills and experience to develop a working relationship with the student and to give meaningful feedback. This may be compounded by a demanding workload which doctoral supervision is squeezed into. Co-supervising may help to learn skills and to lighten the load, but often complicates the situation further (Pyhältö et al., 2023). Or they may not have considered how their own assumptions and identities intersect with those of their students. The feedback may be informed by implicit biases, which may influence how the supervisor communicates the feedback, and what feedback they decide to provide.

Area Five: Divergent expectations. It is rarely the case that supervisor and student expectations of each other and of the feedback process are aligned at the beginning, particularly if they are from different backgrounds (e.g. their countries of origin, the languages they speak and their educational backgrounds) and/or hold different salient social identities (e.g. race, ethnicity, gender, religion and class). Such disconnects may lead to periods of confusion and misunderstanding which should be addressed early on, and regularly revisited throughout the course of the supervisory relationship. The issues do not simply concern the roles played by the supervisor and student, but also how those roles, the subsequent feedback and the student response to the feedback will change over the course of the supervision – normally moving from a more dependent relationship at the beginning to a more independent relationship by the end. That will provide its own challenges as every set of mis-matched expectations are unique to that changing relationship.

The feedback landscape may feel like a minefield at times, but there are usually good, or at least explicable reasons behind the problems, as well as solutions based on good practice to address them. Most supervisors have good intentions but get lost in the landscape. In the following sections of this chapter, we will look at the best practices and research on feedback to provide some useful signposts and practical guidance.

The feedback agreement

Setting shared guidelines at the outset of the supervisory-supervisee relationship is critical to getting the experience of feedback off to a good start. Quality feedback does not emerge from a vacuum. All kinds of assumptions and expectations are present before the first words have been exchanged. Ideally, doctoral programmes will provide the supervisor and student a general idea of what to expect and a basic description of the role of the supervisor and the candidate. By definition, however, every relationship is different by virtue of the fact that every person is different, and their particular circumstances are unique. Only the participants in the feedback relationship can establish the guidelines for their relationship and the actual feedback and response (written or verbal) shared between them. Guidelines at this level have sometimes been referred to as a 'learning contract' between student and supervisor (Phillips & Pugh, 2005), but they are best thought of as an agreement as the latter term is generally less formal and open to change as the learning and the relationship proceed. Indeed, the changing nature of the exchange should be recognized in the agreement.

Critical elements

While the specific content of the feedback agreement should be negotiated, there are critical elements which need to be included. There must be agreement at the outset, for example, that the feedback be learner centred. It must permit the student to bring their own knowledge and experiences into the exchange. It should also enable them to be an active participant in the process and encourage them to be curious, reflective, critical and increasingly independent. It should focus on the improvement of their work and their ability to do the work. In this respect, there must be mutual understanding that the feedback requires meaningful action by the student: that is to say, sufficiently challenging while at the same time actually possible.

In addition, the agreement needs to identify the overall goals of the project, as well as the specific learning outcomes and research outputs to be achieved. Meaningful discussion (and negotiation) about these elements will help clarify the supervisor's and the student's expectations during what will be an evolving process. It will highlight what to include in the agreement such as the nature of the content (relevance and quality), as well as a schedule (formal or informal) for the timely submission of research outputs, and the timely response of supervisor's feedback. It will also look at the kind of roles the supervisor and student might expect.

A feedback agreement can never specify everything, certainly not at the outset, but it can specify times when it may need to be revisited. It ensures both participants are more or less on the same page. In this respect, creating a written agreement (however flexible and malleable) is time well spent. It can be a useful research document and a record of student development. In the rest of this section, we will look at roles and expectations. In the following sections we will unpack various practices of giving feedback.

Roles

The role which a PhD supervisor plays vis-à-vis the student is not fixed. It will, of course, be different for different students, but it should be fluid, changing over the course of the candidate's study, shifting in accordance with the challenges which arise in the feedback process. Common feedback challenges supervisors face include the overall focus of the feedback, the approach taken to giving feedback and the nature of the feedback given (Carless et al., 2023). The first concerns the degree to which the feedback focuses on the process or on the tangible outputs of the research. The second concerns intervening versus supporting the student to explore for themselves, and the third relates to the balance between critique and encouragement in the feedback.

The permutations of these factors characterize different roles which the supervisor and student might take during the supervision process. Activity 12.1 provides a reflective exercise on the roles a supervisor and candidate might play. While some of these roles seem somewhat eccentric, they can reveal the different relationships that might emerge during the supervisory process. The exercise might also stimulate a discussion about the beginning roles played (Expert-Novice, for example) versus those at the end (Colleague-Colleague). In this respect it provides a useful vocabulary if/when the feedback relationship goes wrong – especially when it comes to untangling misaligned expectations.

Identifying and sharing expectations

What are reasonable expectations? Research and good practice have identified helpful expectations for both supervisors and students to share from the outset as part of a feedback agreement. Broadly speaking, students expect their supervisors to be available, to read their work in advance of

REFLECTIVE ACTIVITY 12.1: ROLES BETWEEN SUPERVISOR AND STUDENT

Share the following list of roles with your doctoral student (feel free to add or subtract from the list). Discuss what these roles suggest to you in the supervision context, what they signify to you, what diverse types of doctoral relationships they indicate, and how they might play out over the supervision process.

Supervisor	Student
Director	Follower
Coach	Player
Teacher	Pupil
Expert	Novice
Guide	Explorer
Project Manager	Team worker

Supervisor	Student
Editor	Author
Senior Partner	Junior Partner
Colleague	Colleague
Friend	Friend
Mentor	Mentee
Counselor	Counseled

Source: Adapted from Light, Cox & Calkins (2009).

discussion, to give detailed and meaningful comments on their written work, to provide the feedback in a timely and accessible manner, to be friendly and encouraging, to know the area, to be sufficiently interested in their work to help them progress in the community, to provide opportunities to give and publish papers, and to support their job search. Supervisors generally expect their students to be available, to keep to a research schedule, to produce clearly written outputs, to follow their advice, to respond to their feedback, to be honest and excited about their research, and to work towards being an independent colleague. Research brief 12.1 provides a list of corresponding supervisor and PhD student expectations.

How these expectations play out, however, will depend on the stage of the process and the activity being undertaken. Expectations need to be recognized, communicated and regularly reviewed and negotiated. Supervisors, for example, must recognize what outputs a student can reasonably achieve within a certain time frame, and how quickly they can become fully self-directed researchers. Students, on the other hand, must be realistic about the time and resources their supervisor can devote to them, how much detailed feedback they can provide and how much they can realistically help them in their career. But it is reasonable to expect that each will seriously consider the other's expectations over the course of the supervision.

RESEARCH BRIEF 12.1: SUPERVISOR AND PhD STUDENT EXPECTATIONS

Supervisors expect their PhD students	Students expect their supervisors
• To be independent, even though aspects of the research process may require conformity	• To supervise them • To read their work in advance
• To respond to their feedback • To produce written work that is clear and comprehensible	• To give timely feedback • To give easily accessible feedback
• To have regular meetings	• To be available • To be friendly, open and supportive • To structure sessions to support easy exchange of ideas
• To be honest when reporting progress	• To have good knowledge of research area • To have sufficient interest in their research to put more information in the student's path
• To be excited about their research	• To be sufficiently involved in their success to help them get a good job at the end of it all!

Source: Adapted from Gillis & Pellegrini, 2023; Phillips & Pugh, 2005; Woolhouse, 2002.

CASE STUDY 12.1: MANAGING DIVERSE EXPECTATIONS

Kate, a new faculty member in English and fresh from her doctoral studies, has learned she must supervise three students. Although her own experiences being supervised have varied, she recalled often feeling unsupported and distanced from supervisors, and she did not want to replicate that experience with her own students. She wanted to offer her students guidance and support but also let them wrestle with the research process as well.

She decided to meet with each student to get to know them as individuals, but also to get a sense of their abilities and interests. With each student, she helped them set up an individual research plan, where she outlined her expectations about the final product, and let them explain the kind of support and supervision they thought would personally work for them. Two of the students, Margarite and Henry, preferred to meet monthly and send her drafts as they completed sections, while Ronan preferred to meet weekly and get more feedback as he developed his ideas.

Source: Light, G., Cox, R. & Calkins, S. (2009).

Giving feedback

While these student expectations are reasonable, they are not always easy to address, particularly when the student seems to be falling short of their side of the bargain. If the supervisor finds the student is unable or unwilling to keep to the agreement, a renegotiation of the goals and guidelines is an effective course of action. There are good reasons, personal and other, why a renegotiation is necessary, particularly when it is not clear the student has access to the resources they need.

Issues in giving feedback (practical guide of activities)

Giving feedback on student research outputs consists of responding to a range of very specific problems. Usually, it is insufficient for the supervisor to simply note problems; instead, a supervisor may need to help the student understand why it is a problem and what might be done about it. In the following section we look at key aspects of research output where problems will arise.

Nature of research: In the first instance problems often arise about what constitutes research in the field. Feedback is an opportunity to help students understand the nature of research or scholarship in their discipline. What constitutes a research output in the field? What makes a genuine contribution to the field? What formats must be mastered from a full thesis to journal papers to presentations? In what language(s) should the research be conducted and written? What are the theoretical, empirical and practical components of a research project?

Originality and creativity: Many PhD programmes specify that a PhD thesis must make an original contribution to the field. Students often have difficulty determining what such a contribution consists of, sometimes assuming at one extreme the creation of a grand new theory or at the other extreme something very limited (such as simply copying an experiment). Either may be sufficient depending on field, context and purpose, but originality and creativity in a thesis usually fall somewhere in between. Feedback on written research designs or plans provides an opportunity to raise these issues. Similarly, feedback should ensure the student develops a unique academic voice, in a way that does not marginalize them, but promotes their own sense of agency (Pretorius & Macauley, 2021).

Plagiarism and academic integrity: For many supervisors, plagiarism is obvious, but research has shown that students (even at the doctoral level) have different perceptions of what this includes (Tran et al., 2022). Many, for example, do not consider plagiarism dishonest. Some students regard repeating large sections of text and/or ideas in a paper or thesis without any critique or comments as appropriate, especially if they cite the authors. With the advent of artificial intelligence (AI) in academia, many students need guidance on how AI tools can be appropriately and ethically used in their works. Such conversations are critical to ensure that unintended violations of academic integrity do not occur. On a broader level, feedback should address the question of academic honesty and integrity, including between supervisor and student about their relationship and work. The supervisor will need to model these behaviours and be honest in the reasons for their feedback.

Critical thinking: To promote critical thinking, supervisor feedback should help the student see where the work lacks sufficient depth and why and what they need to do to address it. The supervisor might, for example, encourage students to reflect on their initial assumptions about the problem and the types of evidence they consider to be relevant. They may also challenge them to examine the concepts and logic of the problem. The feedback should urge them to explore diverse approaches, resources (knowledge, information, skills, instruments, people) and alternative explanations and solutions to addressing the problem.

Problem solving: During their doctoral education, PhD students will need to develop a wide range of problem-solving skills particular to research. They range from analysing and identifying the purpose of their research and the main research questions, to constructing a research plan, identifying methods for addressing the problems, analysing large amounts of data, drawing conclusions, presenting results and defending results. They also include the ability to communicate in the appropriate academic language. Feedback to the student will need to address the particular skills of constructing solutions in these areas of research: on the how as well as the what of the solution.

Taking action (enactment): Feedback should not assume students will respond. It should motivate students to respond. This process is referred to as feedback enactment. Does the PhD student actually do something to enhance their knowledge, skills and research outputs in response to the feedback? Indeed, Carter (2023) found in a survey of supervisors, that, in addition to the sheer amount of time and effort feedback required on basic sentence structure and format, just getting the student to produce something was often a challenge, and when they do produce an output, they frequently ignore previous feedback.

Carless et al. (2023) describe three supervisor approaches to giving feedback with respect to this problem: 'feedback as comments about student work; feedback as a responsive form of two-way communication; and feedback inputs encouraging enactment' (p. 538). Only the third approach directly engages with student enactment. Clear communication and transparency about the scope and nature of the enactment will help. And as Prieto (2020) notes, be constructive (i.e. do not point out problems without suggesting alternatives, new ways, next steps, etc.), mention that errors are part of the learning process and avoid making personal attributions (e.g. 'you are a bad writer').

Autonomy: The most important goal of feedback is autonomy. It is crucial for a student to become an independent researcher in the field. While feedback may initially focus more on helping the student manage problems and think through solutions, over time the supervisor must encourage them to find their own solutions and to engage with other members of the community in independent research activities. These include writing for refereed journals; making grant applications; coping with peer review; giving presentations; working in teams; and supervising their own students. Reflective exercise 12.2 offers a framework for addressing student problems and developing autonomy over time.

Feedback and co-supervision

Over the past decade, co-supervision of PhD students has become increasingly common (Pyhältö et al., 2023). This takes various forms, from one supervisor taking the overall lead with a second supervisor adding expertise in a particular area of research to two supervisors playing comparable roles, leading in their areas of expertise. In some cases, a doctoral student has a team of supervisors overseeing their doctoral research. While this can reduce the workload on individual supervisors and help newer supervisors develop their supervision skills, it can also be tricky negotiating the enlarged set of roles and expectations of the overall process.

The enlarged process can be particularly difficult for supervisees, especially when it comes to feedback. The main disadvantages reported include conflicting advice and disagreement on written feedback which can undermine confidence and stall progress. On the other hand, co-supervision can provide more frequent support and more targeted feedback. Even disagreement between supervisors can often provide a healthy debate, raising additional ideas, perspectives and options on their research (Pyhältö et al., 2023). When done properly, co-supervision can be of great educational benefit for PhD students. At the same time, for the co-supervisory team to be productive, negotiation of shared expectations must begin from the beginning (Olmos-López & Sunderland, 2017).

REFLECTIVE EXERCISE 12.2: RESPONDING TO STUDENT PROBLEMS

Think about a problem or a range of student problems on which you want to provide feedback. Keeping in mind where the student(s) is in their doctoral development, where on the spectrum of responses presented below might you best respond to the problem(s)? How might you do so? How would you phrase it?

Supervisor solution ↑		
	1	Take the problem from the student and solve it yourself.
	2	Listen to the student and offer advice or give the solution or tell the student where to find the solution.
	3	Question the student closely about the problem to make sure you (and the student) have completely understood the detail, then offer advice or give the solution.
	4	Offer advice on the basis of which the student should choose a solution for her or himself.
	5	List a number of possible solutions for the student and leave him/her to choose one.
	6	List a number of possible solutions and give the advantages and disadvantages of each as you see them.
	7	Get the student to list possible solutions as s/he sees them with their advantages and disadvantages. Sum up for the student in a way that clarifies the choice and the advantages and disadvantages.
	8	Get the student to list possible solutions and articulate the basis upon which s/he feels the choice should be made. Explore difficulties the student has in making the choice.
	9	Reflect back to the student what s/he seems to be saying, helping her/him to bring out implications and come to terms with the problem.
↓ **Student solution**	10	Sympathize, but do not address the problem.

Such shared expectations would exceed simply agreeing to timetables and areas of expertise but would also include a conversation around each co-supervisor's understanding of their roles, goals and expectations. It should include sharing frameworks for providing feedback as well as discussions of their style and overall approach. In this respect it is worth the team engaging in the reflective activities described above to formulate a feedback agreement among all supervisors and the student, and to regularly review that it is working for everyone.

Further forms of feedback

In addition to feedback on research outputs, there are other types of academic output which raise additional issues and require further skills and distinctive types of feedback. Feedback on peer-reviewed journals and academic conferences, for example, raises particular issues to consider. In the first instance, other academics and peers who do not know the candidate provide important feedback on the students' work and on their academic development. Moreover, there will be a summative element to the feedback, when the writing output is accepted or rejected for an academic publication or presentation.

These new outputs introduce new challenges for both supervisor and student about the nature of the peer-review process. The supervisor and the student will need to discuss journal submission, the peer-review process, the when, what and where to submit their work. The student may want to submit before the supervisor believes their work is ready or may be reluctant to submit their work even when their supervisor believes it to be ready. Supervisors are instrumental in helping students identify if their work is ready and aiding them in identifying appropriate journals. Feedback on the different criteria journals may have in format and structure, and what they consider acceptable forms of research, will be critical to the student's production of these forms of research output. The supervisor will need to provide advice on those cases where the feedback from peer reviewers conflicts with or directly contradicts with each other and with the supervisor's own feedback. Responding to diverging feedback is a critical skill the student will have to develop.

To help students develop these skills, Wilkins, S. et al. (2021) stress the importance of the supervisor co-publishing with the students when and where appropriate. Indeed, they suggest providing students opportunities to play a co-author role early in the doctoral process, however small it might be. This includes the benefits of student engagement with peers in doctoral groups sharing and providing feedback on writing and other research outputs (Cahusac de Caux & Pretorius, 2024). Participating in authentic feedback opportunities, co-authoring papers and co-presenting at academic conferences and meetings afford the PhD student exceptional opportunities to develop the skills of writing/producing these forms of research output. Providing feedback back to the supervisor and other peer authors enhances their own self-critique skills and builds confidence.

Some feedback, especially with respect to conference submissions (presentation, papers, panels, posters), requires skills the supervisor may feel under-prepared for themself, such as designing posters, PowerPoint slides, online presentations, oral and visual presentation skills. Indeed, the students may be more up to date on the technologies and skillset required. In many fields, the student may also be more skilled at employing recent discipline or field-dependent research technologies such as AI. Feedback exchanges integrating the supervisor's more advanced experience and understanding of the academic review process with the student's more advanced technological skill set can be invaluable in developing the professional dialogue at the centre of academic work.

More than likely, doctoral student engagement as an independent scholar through these peer-review research outputs will begin during later stages of the doctoral education process. The student will be more autonomous, and the supervision roles will have moved both participants towards being colleagues. This is often a useful goal to identify in the feedback agreement from the outset.

Conclusion

Providing feedback to students on their learning outputs, however described, is one of the most powerful methods of enhancing meaningful learning at all levels of higher education. At the doctoral level, where it defines the relationship between supervisor and doctoral students, it is paramount in supporting the completion of a unique and substantive research product. It is also part of a broader process of socialization in which the student becomes a full member of the academic community.

The chapter examined the main issues characterizing the feedback landscape which needs to be addressed in the feedback agreement. It also examined the practical aspects of giving effective feedback to doctoral students on their research outputs and progress. This highlighted the importance of establishing a feedback agreement, whether informal or formal, between the student and the supervisor (or supervisors). Such an agreement includes 'negotiating' the goals, the roles and the expectations on content, relevance, quality and the timely response to the research outputs submitted. It also includes the importance of the alignment of expectations and how these expectations will necessarily develop and change overtime.

Finally, the chapter looked at recent research to highlight key principles, approaches, strategies and techniques that supervisors can employ to enhance the feedback process. It offered a framework for giving feedback, emphasizing the importance of amending the feedback over the duration of the supervision. And it provided guidelines for supporting the doctoral student's autonomy as they move towards taking full control of their learning and research as an independent scholar and thinker.

References

Blanchard, C. & Haccoun, R.R. (2019) 'Investigating the impact of advisor support on the perceptions of graduate students', *Teaching in Higher Education*, 25(8), pp. 1010–27. https://doi.org/10.1080/13562517.2019.1632825

Cahusac de Caux, B. & Pretorius, L. (2024) 'Learning together through collaborative writing: The power of peer feedback and discussion in doctoral writing groups', *Studies in Educational Evaluation*, 83, p. 101379.

Carless, D. & Boud, D. (2018) 'The development of student feedback literacy: Enabling uptake of feedback', *Assessment & Evaluation in Higher Education*, 43(8), pp. 1315–25. https://doi.org/10.1080/02602938.2018.1463354

Carless, D., Jung, J. & Li, Y. (2023) 'Feedback as socialization in doctoral education: Towards the enactment of authentic feedback', *Studies in Higher Education*, 49(3), pp. 534–45. https://doi.org/10.1080/03075079.2023.2242888

Carter, S. (2023) 'Giving and receiving doctoral writing feedback: Advice for PhD supervisors on setting out clear expectations and strategies for delivering effective feedback to their doctoral students', *Times Higher Education*, 7 June. Available at: https://www.timeshighereducation.com/campus/giving-and-receiving-doctoral-writing-feedback (Accessed 28 May 2025).

Chugh, R., Macht, S. & Harreveld, B. (2022) 'Supervisory feedback to postgraduate research students: A literature review', *Assessment & Evaluation in Higher Education*, 47(5), pp. 683–97. https://doi.org/10.1080/02602938.2021.1955241

Gillis, S. & Pellegrini, C. (2023) 'What sort of feedback do PhDs want and need in the future?' *WONKHE*, 10 February. Available at: https://wonkhe.com/blogs/what-sort-of-feedback-do-phds-want-and-need-in-the-future/ (Accessed 28 May 2025).

Light, G., Cox, R. & Calkins, S. (2009) *Learning and teaching in higher education: The reflective professional*. Thousand Oaks, CA: Sage.

Molloy, E., Boud, D. & Henderson, M. (2019) 'Developing a learning-centred framework for feedback literacy', *Assessment & Evaluation in Higher Education*, 45(4), pp. 527–40. https://doi.org/10.1080/02602938.2019.1667955

Olmos-López, P. & Sunderland, J. (2017) 'Doctoral supervisors' and supervisees' responses to co-supervision', *Journal of Further and Higher Education*, 41(6), pp. 727–40. https://doi.org/10.1080/0309877X.2016.1177166

Phillips, E. & Pugh, D. (2005) *How to get a PhD: A handbook for students and their supervisors*. Buckingham: Open University Press.

Pretorius, L. & Macaulay, L. (2021) 'Notions of human capital and academic identity in the PhD: Narratives of the disempowered', *The Journal of Higher Education*, 92(4), pp. 623–47. https://doi.org/10.1080/00221546.2020.1854605

Prieto, L.P. (2020) 'Supervisor quickie: The post-it feedback method', *A Happy PhD*, 30 October. Available at: https://ahappyphd.com/supervisor-quickie-the-post-it-feedback-method/ (Accessed 28 May 2025).

Pyhältö, K., Tikkanen, L. & Anttila, H. (2023) 'The more the merrier? PhD supervisors' perspectives in engaging in co-supervision', *Innovations in Education and Teaching International*, pp. 1–12. https://doi.org/10.1080/14703297.2023.2258853

Tran, M.N., Hogg, L. & Marshall, S. (2022) 'Understanding postgraduate students' perceptions of plagiarism: A case study of Vietnamese and local students in New Zealand', *International Journal of Educational Integration*, 18(3). https://doi.org/10.1007/s40979-021-00098-2

Wilkins, S., Hazzam, J. & Lean, J. (2021) 'Doctoral publishing as professional development for an academic career in higher education', *The International Journal of Management Education*, 19(1), pp. 100459.

Wisniewski, B., Zierer, K. & Hattie, J. (2020) 'The power of feedback revisited: A meta-analysis of educational feedback research', *Frontiers in Psychology*, 10, p. 487662.

Woolhouse, M. (2002) 'Supervising dissertation projects: Expectations of supervisors and students', *Innovations in Education and Teaching International*, 39(2), pp. 137–44.

13

Supporting Progress through the Doctoral Journey

David Armstrong

Introduction

For most the doctoral journey is a process of personal growth (Foot et al., 2014). Advancing knowledge about a field of research typically entails new experiences and challenges as well as positives which novelty involves. The emotional energy entailed in personal growth is what psychologists refer to as 'emotional labour' and can be negative as well as positive in its psychological effects on an individual (Jeung et al., 2018). Emotionally exhausting doctoral study experiences can shift the balance from excitement to anxiety, leading over time, to demotivation and eventually burnout – a state of emotional exhaustion – raising the chances of an early exit and non-completion for a student (Ryan et al., 2022).

Staying motivated and emotionally positive in the doctoral journey are the bedrock for successful study: as essential as knowing how to complete a thorough literature review or knowing how to write an effective research question. This chapter focuses on what is likely to help a student remain motivated and emotionally positive in PhD, advising on helpful study habits which optimize progress, supporting student motivation and well-being.

As suggested earlier in this chapter, research-based knowledge about the learning process has benefits for teachers and students (Darling-Hammon et al., 2020). In this spirit the following, 'Stages in the learning process', is offered, below, adapted from Armstrong and Roy (2025):

REFLECTIVE ACTIVITY 13.1: THE LEARNING PROCESS AND WHAT IT MEANS FOR PHD STUDY

Here are two questions to first consider:

1. If you are supervising doctoral students, do you understand stages in the learning process?
2. Have you, as part of a supervision, ever discussed effective learning habits, strategies or practices with a student?

The answer to both questions might be 'no' and if this is the case then you are in good and extensive company. Many academics who supervise doctoral students were not exclusively or even mainly teachers in their career before becoming supervisors. Experienced, professional teachers furthermore are often not aware of stages in the learning process and what research indicates are steps in the learning process (Armstrong & Roy, 2025).

Reflection

To reflect on the roles of *attention* and *maintenance* in your learning please consider the following two questions.

Q.1 Consider the last time you met a friend or co-worker who was communicating some new information or experience for them, and your attention wandered. What happened to your learning? Did you effectively learn this new information or about their new experience?

Q.2 Consider a skill you learned in school (e.g. a new/additional language) and which you have not practised using since. Would you be now able to perform this skill at the same level as then?

RESEARCH BRIEFING 13.1: STAGES IN THE LEARNING PROCESS

Stages in the learning process

- **Attention/Acquisition** As highlighted in the above discussion, attention is an essential foundation for learning any new skill or acquiring new knowledge. 'Switching on' an attentional spotlight (focusing on the supervisor) and selecting what is relevant to attend to (what our supervisor is exactly saying about methodology) are part of this stage. Attention is known to be part of a wider suite of capabilities collectively called executive-function and which help humans organize priorities and decide goals (called goal-orientated behaviour) (Zwosta et al., 2015).

Application. All learning comes with rules and parameters ('the rules') set up by the context in which we learn and its purpose. This stage in the learning process involves performing the skill newly learned and applying it within the rules of the new learning. Application of this new knowledge is often tiring because, until we become fluent in applying new learning, we are using a large portion of our cognitive capacity. The term 'encoding' is used to describe the initial process of committing new learning to memory whilst attending to new learning.

Fluency. This refers to our capability to automatically, correctly apply new learning and without having to self-monitor or self-check. Like attention, fluency is itself a complex sub-process in learning, often, for example, involving the use fine motor skills (handwriting notes for instance in a PhD supervision meeting) as well as intellectual knowledge (Reber & Greifeneder, 2017).

Maintenance. We must regularly practise and frequently apply our new knowledge to maintain it for future use (reducing 'fading' in memory). Technically, practice is known as 'rehearsal' and involves regularly retrieving recent learning from memory to ensure that we can perform the same task or behaviour in future (Williams & Lombrozo, 2010).

Generalization. Once we can confidently, accurately retrieve new learning (concisely explaining new learning to a friend or peer with accuracy is a simple but effective test), we can generalize. Generalization refers to the ability to apply new learning beyond the original context we learned and in a different situation or different context (Ghirlanda & Enquist, 2003).

Mastery. Mastery refers to the social and/or professional recognition of competence in an area of knowledge and application in practice (Bloom, 1968; Lengetti et al., 2020). In this definition mastery is a social evaluation involving judgements about the depth of understanding (including any gaps in personal knowledge) shown by a learner as evidenced by the depth of learning they demonstrate in formal or informal assessments (McGaghie et al., 2014). Researchers have argued that a learner can deliberately aim for mastery by adopting a set of cognitive-behavioural strategies (Lengetti et al., 2014; Zimmerman, 2023). This approach to learning is known as 'mastery learning' and has some empirical support in research studies (Winget & Persky, 2022).

Table 13.1 illustrates how stages in the learning process apply to PhD study. The example given is premised on successful new learning about a methodology called 'action research' from the perspective of an anonymous PhD student. Flow-on effects of this successful learning are outlined.

Table 13.1 Stages in the learning process applied to PhD study

Stage	Example: Learning about action research methodology
Attention/ Acquisition	At the supervision meeting you (the student) listen carefully to your supervisor recommend that you use an action-research methodology for your study. The supervisor, very briefly, explains what an action-research methodology is and offers a reading. You take brief written notes after listening to this explanation, which detail the key points of the explanation given. Your effective attention means that you identify two points where the supervisor is not clear in explaining about action research and you add these queries to your notes. These notes act as helpful prompts for when the supervisor invites questions from you and addresses your queries. You add these answers to your note as clarification. The notes taken are a helpful start to learning about action research.
Application	You read the recommended reading and learn about the history of action-research, its methodological approach and constituent stages/parts. This learning is tiring but you start to see how action research might fit with your study design. You take initial written notes based on the reading (Key points, findings, recommendations) and compare these with your notes from the supervision.
Fluency	You feel sufficiently confident in understanding about action research to write a short 400-word outline about what action research is without having to double-check the reading given by your supervisor.
Maintenance	You are at a supervision meeting. You verbally outline the history and stages of action research methodology to your supervisor. This results in positive feedback from your supervisor. Now that you have maintained this information, your supervisor suggests applying this knowledge to your specific study. As guidance, your supervisor reminds you that action research is an iterative process and suggests that you consider this when applying it to your study.

Stage	Example: Learning about action research methodology
Generalization	You apply action research to your study in an 800-word written summary designed for the Methodology section of your study, you also explain how action research has been applied beyond the discipline it was originally used in, with the benefits and occasional problems of this extension.
Mastery	At the examination of your PhD the external examiner commends your explanation of why action research was a good fit for your study and applauds your 'deep knowledge' about the use of action research in a wide range of disciplines, with the benefits and occasional problems of this extension.

Problems affecting stages in the learning process and how to overcome them

Table 13.1 above emphasized an ideal wholly successful journey for a PhD student applied to learning about the methodological element of their study – action research. Circumstances could, however, have disrupted progress at any stage in the process. For example, the explanation given by the supervisor might have been rambling and unclear causing the PhD student to lose attention. Understanding stages in the learning process is useful here because a clear understanding of stages in the learning process helps you pinpoint where problems occur and focus your efforts to test out what works to solve or avoid problems altogether. The Vignette 'Jo' illustrates this in action.

Advice for Jo

Table 13.2 outlines the flow-on emotional impacts for Jo of problems in the learning process. As highlighted Jo's *emotional experience* of these impacts is an important component of the quality of *academic achievement* that Jo experiences as a PhD candidate. Research into the relationship between emotions and academic achievement supports the idea that this is a two-way relationship (Putwain et al., 2018). Negative emotions such as anxiety, experienced by Jo, are highlighted in research as having a detrimental impact on academic performance and subsequent academic achievement, leading to a cyclical, self-reinforcing, negative process that can ensnare some students like Jo (Mega et al., 2014; Putwin et al., 2018).

CASE STUDY 13.1: JO

Jo is studying within the School of Public Policy at an Australian University. Jo's research focus is on reform of Australian's flagship policy the National Disability Insurance Scheme (NDIS) and the role of stakeholders in the disability sector as partners in reform. Dr Aquib, PhD lead supervisor, regards Jo as a dedicated and capable doctoral student.

Jo is the first in family to attend university, let alone study for a PhD. Despite a calm, confident exterior, sometimes Jo feels unconfident and like an imposter as a PhD candidate. Jo has two young children, one of whom has a chronic health condition. Demands from study and carer responsibilities can sometimes make Jo feel anxious, overwhelmed and withdrawn.

Here are some of the problems which Jo experiences with study, mapped to stages in the learning process and set out in Table 13.2. For consistency, action-research methodology remains the focus.

Let's now consider how we might practically advise Jo, considering these insights about into the relationship between emotions and academic achievement. Please refer to Table 13.2 to help you understand advice discussed.

Reschedule the meeting – be proactive. Ideally Jo should be proactive and cancel the initial face-to-face supervision meeting with Dr Aquib. Given that Jo is exhausted from caring for a sick child this would be perfectly reasonable and would enable Jo to re-schedule the meeting for a time when Jo is ready to attend to learning. Changing the face-to-face meeting to an online one could be a related option. Depending on the software used, this could enable Jo to record Dr Aquib's explanation and re-listen multiple times when Jo is better able to attend to the meeting.

If rescheduling is not possible and the meeting must proceed in a face-to-face format here are two ideas for how Jo could aim for maximum attention at the supervision meeting.

1 **Call on prior knowledge – to help focus attention.** Prior knowledge (existing knowledge) is a powerful tool to aid engagement with new knowledge. Recent research highlights the cognitive routes through which prior knowledge assists learners when encountering new knowledge and can lead to improved performance (Dong et al., 2020). Following these findings from research, Jo could call on personal prior knowledge in two ways.

   i **Pre-reading**. Jo could establish some prior knowledge about action research by quickly reading about the topic prior to the meeting and as quick preparation for Dr Aquib's explanation of action research.

ii **Connect to prior personal or professional experience.** Jo could, with Dr Aquib's consent, relate and explore action research methodology to personal prior professional experience in the supervision. Jo could say: 'So Dr Aquib when I worked at organisation X, practitioners like me at that time noticed a persistent problem with practice Y – we might have used action research methodology in a project to collaboratively unpack this problem and work together to improve practice around practice Y, testing out, gathering data and refining this approach, based on the data, in cycles of improvement – is that a correct application?' Calling on Dr Aquib's assistance here is help-seeking. Dong et al. (2022) describe help-seeking as beneficial 'when students encounter problems that they cannot solve on their own, they can seek help from teachers and more knowledgeable peers who are able to scaffold them to find or develop solutions' (p. 11). As this definition highlights, help-seeking is also connected to the use of scaffolding in learning which is discussed next.

2 **Active questioning to promote scaffolding and attention.** Joe could use active questioning to help scaffold Dr Aquib's rambling, unclear, explanation. Scaffolding, in the context of learning, can be defined as 'the process by which an "expert" partner provides help to a "novice" partner, increasing or reducing the level of assistance according to the "novice" partner's performance' (Mermelshtine, 2017, p. 241). Scaffolding is further described by the idea of 'guided participation' (Rogoff, 1990) – led by an expert partner but with proactive 'Learning by observing and pitching in' behaviours from a student (Rogoff, 2014).

The practical advice given to Jo so far in the vignette has been focused on directly assisting Jo's attention in a supervision meeting. As emphasized by this vignette and detailed in Table 13.2, a failure of attention in the supervision meeting led to several flow-on problems and negative emotional experiences for Jo in working through the subsequent stages in the learning process. This problem occurs because attention is an essential foundation in the learning process. The reverse holds true, the benefits of effective, focused attention flow through into positives for subsequent stages in the learning process.

REFLECTIVE ACTIVITY 13.2: A SUPERVISION MEETING SCAFFOLD FOR JO

Given below are some points in a scaffold of prompts Jo might use in the supervision with examples of how each point might be verbalized.

Point	Jo asks	Jo writes
What (definition)	'Dr Aquib how can we briefly define action research?'	
Where/when	'What country did action research originate in and when Dr Aquib?'	
Who (researchers/ practitioners, theorists)	'Thanks for the reading – who are the leading researchers/practitioners, theorists in action research? Can you name any?'	
Why (purpose and application)	'Why was action research developed, how has it been applied?'	
Strengths	'What are the strengths of action research that you know of Dr Aquib?'	
Weaknesses/ limitation or downsides	'Are there any Weaknesses/limitation or downsides to action research that you know about?'	

Staying motivated, productive and positive in doctoral study

Research into the experience of doctoral study, as a whole population, indicates that it is 'a journey filled with many professional and personal challenges' and that 'for many, this journey will not end in success' (Laufer, 2019, p. 165). Attrition, better known as 'drop out' is a particular risk for students, like, Jo who first in family to attend university, with many such students reporting that they feel 'out of place' at university and suffering from 'imposter syndrome' (Holley & Gardner, 2012). It is outside the scope of this chapter to discuss what exact psychological strategies or supports might be given to Jo by professionals to help address Jo's negative feelings and thoughts about PhD study. Motivation to study is, however, strongly influenced by the psychological experiences we have as a student (Darling-Hammon et al., 2020) and feedback on doctoral writing by supervisors is a key driver of this experience.

Table 13.2 Jo

Stage	Example: Learning about action research methodology
Attention/ Acquisition	At the supervision meeting Jo listen carefully to Dr Aquib, who recommend that Jo uses an action-research methodology as part of the study. Dr Aquib, very briefly, explains what an action-research methodology is and offers a reading. **Problem**: During the meeting Jo's mind wanders, and attention is lost. Jo was awake at 3 am caring for the youngest child who was sick. The meeting ends and Jo has no clear idea of what action research consists of. Jo now must read the recommended reading, which uses highly academic language, 'cold' that is, without any prior knowledge. When Jo attempts the reading, Joe is already feeling overwhelmed and does not complete it.
Application	Due to a failure of attention, Jo makes huge efforts to understand what action research is and its history. To check understanding Jo turns to the internet which offers confusing information overload. Eventually, after much effort Jo has a little confidence in knowledge of the history and constituent stages/parts of action research. **Problem:** Worry around this understanding and the demands of extra time taken have taken an emotional toll.
Fluency	Jo works hard to write a short 400-word written outline defining action research and without having to check the reading given. Feedback from Dr Aquib is that Jo has missed several key features of action research. **Problem:** Jo is devastated emotionally and wonders about PhD study is the right personal option. This collapse in confidence leads to demotivation: Jo simply 'can't face' study for over a week.
Maintenance	At a supervision meeting Jo verbally outlines the history and stages of action research methodology to Dr Aquib. Before this meeting Jo was physically nauseous from anxiety and did not sleep the night before. Despite these challenges, Jo gives an accurate account of action-research, receiving positive feedback from Dr Aquib. **Problem:** Unfortunately, Jo is so anxious that this positive feedback and suggestions about where to go next, are unheard. Jo is in 'freeze' and is tearful afterwards.

Stage	Example: Learning about action research methodology
Generalization	Jo is exhausted but tentatively applies action research to the study planned and submits an 800-word draft on this topic. The writing is not confident but does explain how action research has been applied beyond the discipline it was originally used in. The benefits and occasional problems of this extension are missing because Jo was so tired and anxious after problems in the learning process. **Problem:** Dr Aquib asks Jo to redraft this submission, and this delays PhD planning, with knock on effects on the data-gathering and PhD completion schedule. As a result, the University research office require Jo to complete a lengthy delay form, which causes Jo much additional anxiety and frustration.
Mastery	At the examination of Jo's PhD, the external examiner, commends Jo's explanation of why action research was a good fit for the study and applauds your 'deep knowledge' about the use of action research in a wide range of disciplines, with the benefits and occasional problems of this extension. **Problem:** What the examiner does not know is the emotional price that Jo has had to pay for this content, or the many redrafts necessary to reach this standard, some of which could have been avoided has the learning process proceeded more smoothly.

Staying motivated in doctoral writing

Based on interviews with doctoral students about their experience of writing, Starke-Meyerring (2011) describes a cultural paradox affecting doctoral students, commenting 'what is normalized and appears universal to long-time members of a research culture is deeply culturally specific to that culture and therefore new to doctoral students' (p. 77). Mismatch between supervisor expectations and student expectations of written output is often a major cause of de-motivation amongst doctoral students, like Jo, because of the angst, dissatisfaction and sometimes even conflicts it drives.

Research with the field of self-regulated learning (SRL) can be applied to make a useful contribution to this discussion because SRL focuses on strategies typically used by successful learners in study and accommodates the psychological, for example, motivational, challenges of the PhD study process faced by Jo and many doctoral students. Overcoming challenges faced in the learning process and meeting personal learning goals in an adaptive, flexible, emotionally regulated, way is central to the purpose of theory and research referring to SRL. Zimmerman and Shunk (2012), two influential researchers in SRL, for example, define it in the following terms:

> Self-regulated learning and performance refers to the processes whereby learners personally activate and sustain cognitions, affects, and behaviours that are systematically oriented toward the attainment of personal goals. By setting personal goals, learners create self-oriented feedback loops through which they can monitor their effectiveness and adapt their functioning.
>
> (p. 1)

As the above definition by Zimmerman and Shunk (2012) highlights, research around SRL refers to learning in high-level psychological terms, involving behaviours and concepts relating to cognition or emotional regulation – not specifically the cultural practice of writing.

Progress on this translation has been made; however, by research into the application of SRL to assist academic writing in a higher-education context, with encouraging findings by several studies that have applied SRL to academic writing (Wijaya, 2021). The 'writing to learn' perspective has also emerged and is a promising bridge between SRL theory and writing practice, with growing empirical support within cognitive psychology (Nückles et al., 2020). On these grounds it is worthwhile to proceed and explore how aspects of theory on SRL might assist with advising Jo and benefit to the reader. To advance this goal, further detail is first necessary about SRL itself.

Zimmerman (2008) suggests that SRL has a forethought phase, a performance phase and self-reflection phase, with each phase consisting of the use of specific study strategies by a student, for example, 'goal setting' and also specific psychological strategies to regulate the emotional impact of the learning process – depicted in Figure 13.1.

What immediately follows applies the Forethought stages of self-regulated learning set out in Figure 13.1 to advise Jo in terms of written output about action research.

Forethought phase

- Task analysis
- Behaviour, action or strategy by Jo: Agree purpose, scope and practical aspects of task.

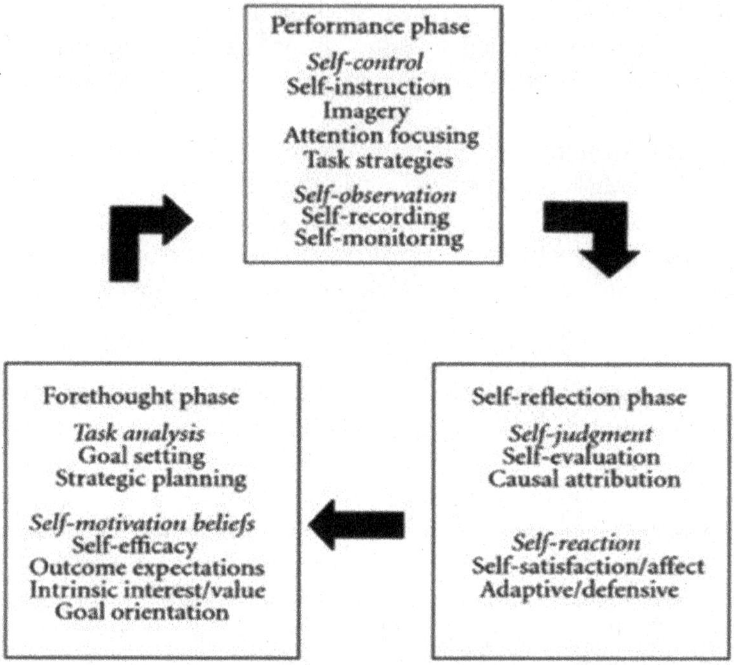

Figure 13.1 *Zimmerman (2002, 2008): stages of self-regulated learning.*

Jo agrees the purpose, scope and practical aspects of written outputs with supervisors (e.g. deadlines, for submission with supervisors, expected structural features such as the use of subheadings, citation style) before starting writing. Agreement can be reached verbally in a supervision meeting and noted down as a meeting outcome by the student (Jo) or received in written instructions e.g. by email. This behaviour is part of what is described as 'task analysis' by Zimmerman (2008) and in this application and enables a clear picture of what is required in the task as it clarifies expectation by supervisors. The closer the match created between student a student/Jo's understanding of tasks and between supervisor expectations, the higher chance there is that what is written by doctoral student meets what supervisors expect.

Without this clear, agreed, knowledge supervisor feedback is likely to highlight changes required to meet their expectations. The flow-on effects of this, often disheartening, feedback can be that the writer (Jo) falls into negative self-judgement, for example, 'I should have asked that question of Dr Aquib about the citation style expected', and consequently, negative causal attributions (perceived reasons for why this negative event has occurred), for example, 'I chose the wrong citation style because I am a bad student'.

Task analysis

- Behaviour, action or strategy by Jo: *Self-scaffold with meeting notes.*
  Joe could create structured meeting notes. This approach would reduce the cognitive demands of the writing process for Jo and aid the self-monitoring necessary to reassure Jo that progress is being made on this task. Here is how these notes might look:
- *Purpose:* a concise outline defining action research, which shows my understanding of its use as a methodology for improvement in practice. Can go in Methodology section of thesis.
- *Scope:* action research as applied as a methodology for improvement in practice.
- *Structure:* title – I choose, title chosen should fit with my take on the definition. No subheadings in definition. References section at end with subheading.
- *Deadline:* 27 May – submit by email attachment to Dr Aquib.
- *Word count*: 400 words
- *Citation style:* APA 7.

Collectively this clear list of prompts can act as a writing scaffold for a PhD student like Jo in the forethought phase and assist, going forward, into the performance phase (where writing occurs).

Task analysis

- Behaviour, action or strategy by Jo: *ask supervisors for an equivalent example of 'good' writing on action research – an exemplar written summary about action research.*
  Jo could ask Dr Aquib for an example of an example of 'good' writing which summarizes action research. This example provides a reassuring model for Jo's for follow in terms of structure, concepts used, how to phrase in-text citations, sentence-started phrasing and other practical elements of doctoral writing. There are some potential problems with this approach, however. Dr Aquib might not have such an exemplar however or it might not be exactly the right 'fit' for this task, for example, the exemplar is a 2,000-word summary, and will

therefore require some adaption by Jo, which could result in self-doubt or anxiety. Nückles et al. (2020) report findings from a study that applied the Freiburg Self-Regulated-Journal-Writing Approach evaluated by the authors, and which used exemplars (known as 'worked examples') in the genre of student subject-based journals (p. 1101). The authors highlight the benefits of using written exemplars for student self-regulated learning and motivation, in line with literature on this topic (Nückles et al., p. 1107).

Self-reflection and performative behaviours

Universities in Australia and elsewhere increasingly require doctoral students and supervisors to adhere to highly performative systems and procedures, typically defined on progress within a three-year timescale for a full-time doctoral student. Supervisors and students are also typically required to provide detailed written evaluations of progress towards timely completion and identify any problems which might negatively impact doctoral student performance, together with actions to address them. On this trend, Bastalich (2017) critically comments that 'the efficiency gaze has fixed on students and supervisors, or on their relationship, as the "problem" to be managed, in need of administrative regulation, skill improvement or perhaps emotional management' (p. 1145). The challenge here then, and now briefly discussed, is how to help Jo, and the reader better cope with the performative elements of study.

Self-evaluation and self-reflection are typically a key part of the candidate milestone and of the final PhD examination, whether by an oral defence (viva) or by submission of a written thesis. The self-reflection phase detailed in Figure 13.1 details the positives and negative emotions inherent in self-reflection, including a possible negative 'defensive' emotional response in the self-reaction element. This analysis suggests that self-reflection on learning is emotionally neutral, which is encouraging because this view infers that a learner, like Jo, can re-frame the self-reflection elements of PhD study and avoid becoming excessively self-critical on problems with study (e.g. difficulty taking effective written notes in meetings) or arising in the research process (e.g. difficulty recruiting participants for interviews). Acknowledging limitations in a study in the written PhD thesis can also often arouse a spiral of negative self-reflection for doctoral students.

CASE STUDY 13.2: LIMITATION SECTION IN A WRITTEN THESIS

Jo writes 'This thesis is limited. Time constrains meant that it was not possible to /consider/evaluate/explore X. Furthermore, difficulties in recruitment meant that the sample size (n = 14) was small and disappointingly smaller than anticipated. Problem with sample size reduces the generalisability of this thesis and its quality.'

Explanation. Due to negative self-evaluation, Jo has negatively evaluated the quality of the thesis overall rather than accepted that all research studies have limitations and responded appropriately. The defensive wording by Jo could provoke critical feedback from supervisors (likely to demotivate Jo even further). Here is how this section could be reframed.

Reframed limitation sections

> This thesis has several limitations which warrant caution when considering the findings. X, defined as '... ....' is a possible explanation for/theory pertinent to/Y detailed in Chapter 3. Future research (see recommendations) could explore this possibility. The sample size/number of participants (n = 14) was smaller than anticipated, despite careful efforts made by the researcher, detailed in Chapter 2 "Recruitment". Vasileiou et al. (2018), in their review of sample size adequacy in qualitative health research, conclude that transparency and assessment of data adequacy in terms of ability to answer research question set by a study, are paramount, rather than purely sample size itself (p. 1). The researcher has adhered to recommendations made by Vasileiou et al. (2018) on this topic, clearly stating the sample size in this thesis and highlighted in Chapter 5 how the quantity and quality of data gathered from participants sufficiently addressed the research questions.

Explanation. The above reframed statement recognizes that all research studies have potential limitations which do not reflect on the researcher's capacity or overall quality of a study. The text uses this acceptance to show reflection, learning and care in the process, thereby reducing the chance of demoralizing feedback from a supervisor or examiner. In this example Jo has avoided writing based on negative rumination and adopts a proactive response to inevitable, but small, limitations of what is, objectively, a high-quality thesis.

Conclusion

This chapter sets out key elements in the learning process and invites readers (doctoral supervisors) to consider how this knowledge applies to doctoral study, specifically problems often faced in study, including demotivation. To aid focus, we applied this knowledge to Jo, a vignette PhD student who is experiencing challenges with study and invited your reflection on how Jo might overcome 'bumps in the road' in the doctoral research process. One final point of reflection is that much of what has been suggested in this chapter places the onus on the student rather than on the supervisor(s). Supervisor(s) and the wider professionals who support PhD students at universities are equally responsible partners in ensuring that students, like Jo, stay motivated and emotionally positive. Offering advice to a student, proactively, about helpful study habits that optimize progress, supporting motivation and well-being, is a key tool to enable their success.

References

Armstrong, D. & David, R. (2025) *The inclusive teacher: A Practical Guide to Inclusion in Australian Classrooms*. London: Routledge. https://doi.org/10.4324/9781003669630

Bastalich, W. (2017) 'Content and context in knowledge production: A critical review of doctoral supervision literature', *Studies in Higher Education*, 42(7), pp. 1145–57. https://doi.org/10.1080/03075079.2015.1079702

Bloom, B. S. (1968) 'Learning for mastery. Instruction and curriculum', *Regional Education Laboratory for the Carolinas and Virginia, Topical Papers and Reprints*, Number 1. Evaluation comment, 1(2), n2.

Darling-Hammond, L., Flook, L., Cook-Harvey, C., Barron, B. & Osher, D. (2020) 'Implications for educational practice of the science of learning and development', *Applied Developmental Science*, 24(2), pp. 97–140.

Dong, A., Jong, M.S.Y. & King, R.B. (2020) 'How does prior knowledge influence learning engagement? The mediating roles of cognitive load and help-seeking', *Frontiers in Psychology*, 11, pp. 591203. https://doi.org/10.3389/fpsyg.2020.591203

Dong, H., Dai, J., Lipson, S.K. & Curry, L. (2022), 'Help-seeking for mental health services in Asian American college students: An exploratory qualitative study', *Journal of American College Health*, 70(8), pp. 2303–10. https://doi.org/10.1080/07448481.2020.1851234

Foot, R., Crowe, A.R., Tollafield, K.A. & Allan, C.E. (2014) 'Exploring doctoral student identity development using a self-study approach', *Teaching & Learning Inquiry: The ISSOTL Journal*, 2(1), pp. 103–18.

Ghirlanda, S. & Enquist, M. (2003) 'A century of generalization', *Animal Behaviour*, 66(1), pp. 15–36. https://doi.org/10.1006/anbe.2003.2174

Gonida, E.N., Karabenick, S.A., Stamovlasis, D., Metallidou, P. & Greece, T.C. (2019) 'Help seeking as a self-regulated learning strategy and achievement goals: The case of academically talented adolescents', *High Ability Studies*, 30(1–2), pp. 147–66.

Holley, K.A. & Gardner, S. (2012) 'Navigating the pipeline', *Journal of Diversity in Higher Education*, 5(2), pp. 112–21. doi:10.1037/a0026840.

Jeung, D.Y., Kim, C. & Chang, S.J. (2018) 'Emotional labor and burnout: A review of the literature', *Yonsei Medical Journal*, 59(2), p. 187.

Laufer, M. & Gorup, M. (2019) 'The invisible others: Stories of international doctoral student dropout', *Higher Education*, 78(1), pp. 165–81.

Lengetti, E., Kronk, R. & Cantrell, M.A. (2020) 'A theory analysis of Mastery Learning and Self-Regulation', *Nurse Education in Practice*, 49, pp. 1471–5953. https://doi.org/10.1016/j.nepr.2020.102911

McGaghie, W.C., Issenberg, S.B., Barsuk, J.H. & Wayne, D.B. (2014) 'A critical review of simulation-based mastery learning with translational outcomes', *Medical Education*, 48(4), pp. 375–85. https://doi.org/10.1111/medu.12391

Mega, C., Ronconi, L. & De Beni, R. (2014) 'What makes a good student? How emotions, self-regulated learning, and motivation contribute to academic achievement', *Journal of Educational Psychology*, 106(1), p. 121. http://dx.doi.org/10.1037/a0033546

Mermelshtine, R. (2017) 'Parent–child learning interactions: A review of the literature on scaffolding', *British Journal of Educational Psychology*, 87(2), pp. 241–54.

Nückles, M., Roelle, J., Glogger-Frey, I., Waldeyer, J. & Renkl, A. (2020) 'The self-regulation-view in writing-to-learn: Using journal writing to optimize cognitive load in self-regulated learning', *Educational Psychology Review*, 32(4), pp. 1089–126. https://doi.org/10.1007/s10648-020-09541-1

Putwain, D.W., Becker, S., Symes, W. & Pekrun, R. (2018) 'Reciprocal relations between students' academic enjoyment, boredom, and achievement over time', *Learning and Instruction*, 54, pp. 73–81. https://doi.org/10.1016/j.learninstruc.2017.08.004

Reber, R. & Greifeneder, R. (2017) 'Processing fluency in education: How metacognitive feelings shape learning, belief formation, and affect', *Educational Psychologist*, 52(2), pp. 84–103. https://doi.org/10.1080/00461520.2016.1258173

Roelle, J., Glogger-Frey, I., Waldeyer, J. & Renkl, A. (2020) 'The self-regulation-view in writing-to-learn: Using journal writing to optimize cognitive load in self-regulated learning', *Educational Psychology Review*, 32(4), pp. 1089–126.

Rogoff, B. (1990) *Apprenticeship in thinking: Cognitive development in social context*. New York: Oxford University Press.

Rogoff, B. (2014) 'Learning by observing and pitching in to family and community endeavors: An orientation', *Human Development*, 57(2–3), pp. 69–81. https://doi.org/10.1159/000356757

Ryan, T., Baik, C. & Larcombe, W. (2022) 'How can universities better support the mental wellbeing of higher degree research students? A study of students' suggestions', *Higher Education Research and Development*, 41(3), pp. 867–81. https://doi.org/10.1080/07294360.2021.1874886

Schunk, D.H., & Zimmerman, B.J. (2013). 'Self-regulation and learning'. In Reynolds, W.M., Miller, G.E. & IWeiner, I.B. (eds) *Handbook of psychology: Educational psychology*, 2nd ed. John Wiley & Sons, Inc., pp. 45–68.

Starke-Meyerring, D. (2011) 'The paradox of writing in doctoral education: Student experiences'. In: McAlpine, L. & Amundsen, C. (eds) *Doctoral education: Research-based strategies for doctoral students, supervisors and administrators*. Dordrecht: Springer Netherlands, pp. 75–95.

Vasileiou, K., Barnett, J., Thorpe, S. & Young, T. (2018) 'Characterising and justifying sample size sufficiency in interview-based studies: Systematic analysis of qualitative health research over a 15-year period', *BMC Medical Research Methodology*, 18, pp. 1–18.

Wijaya, K.F. (2021) 'English education master students' self-regulated learning strategies in academic writing', *Journal of English Teaching*, 7(1), pp. 15–29. https://doi.org/10.33541/jet.v7i1.2313

Williams, J.J. & Lombrozo, T. (2010) 'The role of explanation in discovery and generalization: Evidence from category learning', *Cognitive Science*, 34(5), pp. 776–806.

Winget, M. & Persky, A.M. (2022) 'A practical review of mastery learning', *American Journal of Pharmaceutical Education*, 86(10), p. 8906.

Zimmerman, B.J. (2008) 'Investigating self-regulation and motivation: Historical background, methodological developments, and future prospects', *American Educational Research Journal*, 45(1), pp. 166–83. https://doi.org/10.3102/0002831207312909

Zimmerman, B.J. (2023) 'Dimensions of academic self-regulation: A conceptual framework for education'. In: Schunk, D.H. & Zimmerman, B.J. (eds) *Self-regulation of learning and performance*. London: Routledge, pp. 3–21.

Zwosta, K., Ruge, H. & Wolfensteller, U. (2015) 'Neural mechanisms of goal-directed behavior: Outcome-based response selection is associated with increased functional coupling of the angular gyrus', *Frontiers in Human Neuroscience*, 9, p. 180. https://doi.org/10.3389/fnhum.2015.00180

14

Examining Doctoral Research

Fiona Hallett

Introduction

Doctoral examinations represent both a formal evaluation of students' scholarly contributions and a threshold for recognition as independent researchers. Despite its significance, the expectations associated with the doctoral examination often diverge considerably from the realities encountered by both candidates and examiners. Recent collections, such as those edited by Byram and Stoicheva (2022) and Kumar, Taylor and Sharmini (2023), offer valuable insights into the evolving nature of doctoral examinations, emphasizing the increasing recognition of diversity in their practices. Byram and Stoicheva (2022) provide a comparative analysis of doctoral examination standards, highlighting the differences in both the purpose and the implementation of these examinations across diverse contexts. Similarly, Kumar, Taylor and Sharmini (2023) examine the complexities involved in adapting doctoral examination processes to meet the shifting demands of academic and institutional priorities.

A notable area of divergence lies in the viva voce, or oral examination, which is an essential component of the doctoral process in certain regions. In the UK and New Zealand, for instance, the viva is a formal and integral part of the doctoral examination, typically involving two examiners – one internal to the institution and one external to the institution – and an independent chair. The primary objective of the viva is to assess the candidate's research through questioning and in-depth dialogue, facilitating the demonstration of the candidate's scholarly capabilities.

In contrast, some European countries adopt a more ceremonial approach to the viva. Here, the viva can function as a public event, one that primarily serves to confirm the recommendations made by the examiners prior to the examination. These events typically include presentations that aim to engage the broader academic community and mark the culmination of the candidate's doctoral journey.

Conversely, in countries such as South Africa and Australia, the viva is employed infrequently and often only in exceptional circumstances. When it is conducted, it is primarily to address specific concerns raised by the examiners or to seek clarification on particular aspects of the research. In these systems, written evaluations and alternative forms of assessment are prioritized over oral defences (Schulze & Lemmer, 2019).

Finally, in Australia, seminar-style defences, as described by Lovat et al. (2022), seek to foster a more collaborative and supportive environment, wherein candidates present their research in a manner that encourages constructive dialogue and feedback, rather than what may be perceived as adversarial questioning.

The purpose of this chapter is therefore threefold: to deconstruct the structure of the doctoral examination; to analyse the challenges inherent in the process, and to examine key areas of evaluation. By engaging in this analysis, the chapter seeks to provide an understanding of the mechanisms and frameworks through which the doctoral examination operates, exploring potentialities and obstacles that it may present to candidates and the criteria by which academic success is determined.

Deconstructing the structure of the doctoral examination

Written components: Style, format and purpose?

The inclusion of written components in doctoral examinations has traditionally served as a primary means of evaluating a candidate's scholarly abilities. However, this practice is increasingly being questioned as academic paradigms evolve to recognize a broader spectrum of intellectual contributions and scholarly outputs.

In disciplines such as the social sciences, the written thesis remains central, functioning as a key medium for engaging with theoretical frameworks, scholarly discourse and historical contexts. However, this model may not align as well with fields emphasizing practical application, creative production or empirical research, such as the arts, applied sciences and engineering. For these disciplines, the conventional dissertation may not fully capture the range of intellectual and practical contributions candidates offer.

As an example, in the creative arts, doctoral research often manifests in portfolios, performances or other non-textual forms of output that challenge the constraints of traditional academic writing. These alternative forms of expression can better reflect the transformative nature of the work when a written thesis might inadequately convey its full significance (Leavy, 2020). Arts-based research methods, in particular, challenge the dominance of the written word by promoting non-traditional approaches to knowledge dissemination and scholarly communication.

The PhD by Publication introduces an alternative model by focusing on a portfolio of published works – such as peer-reviewed journal articles or book chapters – rather than a single, unified thesis. While this format offers flexibility, O'Keefe (2022) critiques its potential to overemphasize metrics such as citation counts and publication volume at the expense of intellectual depth. Similarly, Frick (2019, p. 56) raises ethical concerns about this model, questioning whose interests are served by prioritizing publication and how issues such as authorship and author order are negotiated.

The roles of examiners and chairs: Objectivity, bias and academic politics

The roles of examiners and chairs in the doctoral examination process are fundamental to maintaining fairness, academic integrity and objectivity. While examiners are conventionally envisioned as impartial evaluators of intellectual merit, this ideal often diverges from the complexities of the viva process. Examiners, especially those affiliated with the candidate's institution or academic discipline, may unintentionally introduce personal biases, professional rivalries or ideological disagreements into their assessments. These factors can compromise the equity of the evaluation process, particularly given the examiner's dual responsibility as both evaluator of the thesis and gatekeeper to the academic profession (Teijlingen et al., 2022).

To address such risks, the appointment of a neutral chair or convenor has been proposed as a means of ensuring the impartiality of doctoral examinations (Kumar et al., 2020). This position, as outlined, is 'embedded with ideas of pastoral care for the candidates through four key strategies: 1) preparing candidates by setting expectations, 2) making the candidate feel at ease, 3) inviting a support person to attend and 4) building the candidate's confidence' (p. 1080). By fulfilling these responsibilities, the chair contributes to transforming the viva from a potentially adversarial evaluation into a constructive intellectual dialogue (Kumar et al., 2022), fostering both academic resilience and scholarly development.

Nevertheless, the role of the neutral chair is often inconsistently applied across institutions, which undermines its potential effectiveness. In some cases, the absence of clear, standardized guidelines governing the roles and responsibilities of examiners intensifies the challenges associated with academic politics in doctoral examinations (Tan, 2023). Without such guidelines, the focus of the viva can shift away from rigorous intellectual evaluation, making it more about navigating the interpersonal and political dynamics inherent in academia.

The oral defence: A test of knowledge or performance?

While the viva, or oral defence, is traditionally regarded as the final and ultimate evaluation of a doctoral candidate's intellectual capabilities, this view fails to fully acknowledge the extent to which the viva is not merely an intellectual assessment but also a performance. Houston et al. (2023) propose that the viva can be interpreted through a Habermasian framework as a 'dialogic occasion', wherein the interaction between the candidate and the examiners involves not only the exchange of knowledge but also the negotiation of power, identity and authority within the academic space.

This dialogic view brings to the fore the importance of mutual recognition and respect in the examination process, as it recognizes the viva as a performance influenced by various social dynamics that extend beyond the candidate's research output. In this context, Lantsoght (2022) advocates for reimagining the doctoral defence as an inclusive process that integrates both written and non-written forms of intellectual expression, recognizing that a candidate's scholarly contributions may not always be fully captured through written texts alone.

The viva, therefore, becomes a highly subjective and often unpredictable event, in which success is determined not solely by the quality of research but by factors such as verbal fluency, composure under pressure and the candidate's ability to think quickly on their feet. This introduces concerns about the viva functioning as a 'performance under scrutiny' rather than a purely objective intellectual evaluation. Wellington (2021) critiques this aspect of the viva, noting that interpersonal dynamics, the mood of the examiners and the specific context of the viva can disproportionately influence its outcome, rendering the process less predictable and more dependent on subjective factors. Similar debates around the online doctoral viva (Wisker et al., 2022) have emerged over recent years with setting, purpose and student/examiner engagement under debate.

For instance, Mushiwabe et al. (2021) contend that the emotional and intellectual pressures experienced by candidates during the viva contribute to what they term unclear, unfair and emotional labour, intensifying psychological burdens that may skew the evaluation of a candidate's academic work. These challenges are not merely peripheral but are deeply embedded within the viva process, posing a substantial threat to candidates' well-being and potentially undermining the objectivity of assessing their scholarly contributions. An intriguing question arises as to whether such psychological burdens might be mitigated or further amplified in an online context.

Ultimately, while the viva is ideally intended to serve as a rigorous intellectual assessment, the performance element – shaped by ambiguity, emotional stress and social dynamics – complicates its role as an objective measure of a candidate's academic prowess. Consequently, the viva becomes not only a test of knowledge but also a site where the candidate's ability to navigate complex, often arbitrary performance expectations may significantly impact the outcome.

The role of feedback in doctoral examinations

The role of the examiner in the doctoral viva is widely acknowledged as central not only to assessing the scholarly work of the candidate but also to providing meaningful feedback that fosters intellectual growth. Kumar and Stracke (2017, p. 219) contend that 'an examiner must also teach by giving the student feedback so they can develop and close the gap between their current and expected performance'. However, this ideal can be disrupted by the inherent power dynamics of the viva, wherein the aforementioned examiner biases and institutional allegiances can shape the questions posed to the candidate. As such, candidates may be tasked with defending their research not merely based on its intellectual merits, but in response to subjective perspectives, complicating the fairness and objectivity of the assessment process.

This issue is compounded by significant variability in the quality and depth of feedback provided by examiners. While some examiners offer thoughtful, detailed critiques that engage with the candidate's methodology, theoretical framework and scholarly contributions, others provide feedback that is vague or superficial, offering little in the way of constructive guidance. Chetcuti, Cacciottolo and Vella (2022) highlight this disparity, noting that it is often driven by individual examiner preferences, disciplinary norms or institutional culture, leading to a lack of consistency in evaluation standards. Consequently, the feedback may appear arbitrary, undermining its utility in promoting academic development.

RESEARCH BRIEFING 14.1: BEING A VALUED DOCTORAL EXAMINER

Kiley's (2009) work makes clear that doctoral examiners are often seen as a problem. Once appointed, they are in a position of considerable power, which some misuse – perhaps inadvertently. Kiley suggests that experienced supervisors 'see one of their roles in selecting examiners as protecting their doctoral students from the "bad and mad"' (p. 889). Confidential 'black lists' of bad examiners are not uncommon (p. 900). Against this difficult backdrop, it is worth asking ourselves: how can we be a doctoral examiner who is *valued* by doctoral candidates, their supervisors and their institutions?

Kiley's work suggests that we should reflect on several issues when considering acting as a doctoral examiner. Some of the most important issues are as follows:

- **Topic/methodology fit.** Examiners' expertise will vary when they consider different aspects of the thesis. For instance, they may be an expert on the topic of study but unfamiliar with the theoretical framework. Examiners should consider where their expertise is best placed in relation to evaluating the doctoral candidate's work, and where they may defer to other examiners. They should also refrain from making the student's work a focus for their wider discomforts or positions in the field. For instance, a doctoral candidate might have selected a methodology to which an examiner is hostile in principle. In such situations, it can be helpful to ask the student to reflect on their position within relevant methodological debates, but the examiner should not impose their own stance on the candidate's work.
- **Understanding of the system from which the dissertation is coming.** The criteria for doctoral dissertations and examination procedures vary widely: for example, between countries, institutions, disciplines and programmes. Such differences are becoming more visible over time, given the proliferation of interdisciplinary projects, different forms of doctorate and examinations with international participation (e.g. viva examinations using video conference). Examiners need to familiarize themselves with the context of the thesis and the relevant expectations. Doing so will often require *active* investigation of what is expected.
- **Our personal background and its implications.** Doctoral examiners often work very differently – depending, among

others things, on whether they are experienced or inexperienced, and on whether they come from within or outside academia. Kiley's work suggests that experienced supervisors who work within academia are typically the most valued by candidates and supervisors. This is because such examiners focus more directly on the work of the candidate and its value in relation to the qualification being sought and are less likely to be distracted by other issues. As one of Kiley's respondents says, experienced examiners have the 'confidence to say that something is good' (p. 897). Examiners should avoid focusing on issues that are not relevant to the qualification or – perhaps the worst-case scenario – using the doctoral examination as a vehicle for demonstrating their own intelligence.

- **Availability.** Doctoral examiners should appreciate the great importance of the examination to the candidate and their supervisors, and the high level of anxiety which can be associated with it. This work is a priority! Examiners should respond to communications promptly; give the maximum flexibility possible when indicating potential dates; provide reports within the stipulated deadlines; and, where asked to judge corrected or re-submitted work, respond promptly.

- **Personality.** Doctoral candidates and their supervisors *remember* examiners for a long period of time afterwards. Examiners whom supervisors wish to invite back in the future are usually those who acted in ways that were *fair*, even where high standards were being demanded; conveyed a sense of intellectual *curiosity* and emotional *generosity*; and who were *reliable* in fulfilling the commitments of their role.

If we have committed to act as a doctoral examiner, then we should strive to act as a *valued* examiner. If we do not believe that we can do so — whether in general, or because of our distaste for a particular piece of work — then we should consider whether it is wise to accept an appointment request in the first place.

While these challenges cannot be ignored, it is equally important to acknowledge the potential for the viva to be a highly productive space for intellectual engagement. Houston et al. (2023) argue that when structured around clear and transparent evaluative criteria, the viva can facilitate meaningful dialogue, allowing the candidate to receive immediate and actionable feedback. In such an ideal scenario, the viva could serve as an invaluable opportunity for candidates to refine their research, clarify uncertainties and contextualize their methodological choices. However, the potential for inconsistency in feedback quality and a lack of transparent evaluation standards means that this potential is not always realized.

When feedback is provided constructively, focusing on intellectual development, the viva offers a crucial moment for candidates to engage deeply with their research. Dally et al. (2020) argue that the viva provides 'the final opportunity for candidates to engage with examiner feedback and develop reflexive practices', stressing its dynamic and interactive nature. In its ideal form, the viva allows candidates to substantiate their methodological decisions, engage with critical questions and develop their reflexive practices through dialogue with examiners. Yet, when feedback is restricted to written comments or when the examination focuses more on personal dynamics or performance than on scholarly inquiry, the viva's role as an opportunity for intellectual engagement is diminished.

To maximize its potential, the viva must prioritize feedback as a central mechanism for scholarly growth. Stephenson, Jackson and Wilkes (2024) emphasize the importance of fostering a transparent and equitable process where feedback supports candidates in refining their research and advancing their academic capabilities. Similarly, Denicolo, Duke and Reeves (2020) advocate for reimagining the viva to focus on delivering constructive, developmental feedback that nurtures academic excellence. By addressing current shortcomings and ensuring that feedback is consistently clear, reflective and grounded in rigorous standards, the viva can better serve as both a robust evaluation and a transformative experience that empowers candidates to engage critically with their work and refine their scholarly contributions.

REFLECTIVE ACTIVITY 14.1: MAKING YOUR FEEDBACK RELEVANT AND ACTIONABLE

The most common outcome after a doctoral examination is to request that the student undertake more work (Share, 2016). In many cases, this may be a matter of requesting that the student add extra detail or clarification to aspects of their narrative. The student may sometimes be asked to undertake more empirical work and/or data analysis, with institutions usually having specific rules about how such requests are framed and the implications for the outcome of the examination.

Doctoral candidates and their supervisors find feedback useful when it is framed in ways that make clear the relevance of the comment and specify the action that is being expected. Consider the following request:

The candidate needs to re-consider the scope of their literature review.

The comment presents the doctoral candidate – and their supervisors, who will need to support the candidate's work of revision – with a vague request. Do the examiners reject the scope itself or merely wish to see it better justified? Are they expecting the student to re-write some specific section in their text, or amend text throughout a chapter or the whole document? To what extent does the candidate have permission to amend other aspects of their work if the new scope has knock-on consequences? And most fundamentally: Why do the examiners think that undertaking this work is important?

Examiners may write such comments because they assume that the context will make the meaning clear. For instance, the scope of the literature review may have been a topic of verbal discussion in a viva. Yet this assumption ignores that students may not remember their viva clearly, due to its length and the pressure of the situation.

Examiners should reflect on how their feedback is framed. In many instances, two or more examiners work together to produce their feedback, and so they should take an opportunity to reflect together, in a conversation, on the formulations they will use. When requiring extra work, they should strive to frame their comments *for each point* so that they meet the following criteria:

- Identify the *specific shortcoming* to be addressed;
- Specify why the point is *important* – in terms of the student's stated aims for their project, and/or the explicit criteria for the qualification provided by the institution;
- *Link* the comment explicitly to any relevant, prior aspects of the examination process (e.g. a specific question or conversation in a viva);
- Make clear the *extent* of the work that is being suggested (in pages of text, and/or in time taken);
- Make clear where certain actions are *required*, and where the student has more flexibility or choice.

For instance, the above comment might be expanded in various ways. One possible formulation is as follows:

> Fiona is required to address the shortcoming that the scope of her literature review is not explicitly justified or discussed. Such justification and discussion are important, because this scope heavily influences the tone of the contributions put forward at the end of the thesis. In the viva, Fiona discussed how the scope of her literature

review had changed several times throughout her PhD project, as she reflected on the academic audience she wished to address, and that this had resulted in an initial literature review being discarded. We require that this process of revising and reflecting on the scope of the literature review is documented, with the final scope of the literature review stated clearly. Addressing this comment will require adding around 2 pages of text near the start of the literature review chapter. Fiona is free to decide whether to incorporate this text into an existing section or introduce a new heading. Fiona may also wish to check that any formulations she puts forward in this new text are consistent with those used in the rest of the thesis and amend other formulations to ensure such consistency, if she finds this helpful for her work.

Key areas of examination in doctoral evaluation: Contribution to knowledge – originality versus practical relevance

The evaluation of a candidate's contribution to knowledge is a central yet highly complex aspect of the doctoral examination process. Doctoral research is expected to advance the field by providing new insights, whether through innovative theoretical frameworks, empirical findings or methodological developments. However, the concept of 'originality' remains contested and varies significantly across disciplines and research contexts. Anderson, Saunders and Alexander (2021) emphasize that originality may be defined differently depending on the field: in the natural sciences, it often involves empirical breakthroughs, while in the humanities, it might prioritize theoretical innovation or the reinterpretation of existing scholarship. These divergent disciplinary expectations create challenges for examiners, who must assess whether the candidate's work meets the standards of novelty and significance required for the award of a doctoral degree.

In addition, originality is not consistently defined or understood, even within specific disciplines. Examiners must carefully address these ambiguities, balancing adherence to disciplinary expectations with a critical assessment of the research's contribution to scholarly debates. The absence of a clear consensus on how originality should be interpreted or assessed further complicates the process, creating variability in judgements that may undermine the fairness of the evaluation (Tan, 2024).

In addition to originality, the increasing emphasis on practical relevance in doctoral research introduces an additional dimension to the evaluation process. Candidates are now often expected to demonstrate not only theoretical advancement but also the applicability of their findings to real-world challenges (Tzavara & O'Donnell, 2021). This dual expectation can create a tension between theoretical contribution and practical utility, which varies across disciplines. In fields such as engineering and the natural sciences, practical applications – whether in addressing societal challenges or developing new technologies – often form a central criterion of assessment. Conversely, in the humanities and social sciences, the focus may be placed more heavily on theoretical rigour and critical engagement, with practical relevance playing a secondary role.

This tension between originality and practical impact places additional demands on examiners, who must evaluate research that may excel in one area while appearing limited in another. Kumar, Taylor and Sharmini (2023) argue that the evolving priorities of academic institutions increasingly require examiners to consider broader societal and interdisciplinary implications of research. This shift has significant implications for the doctoral examination process, as it requires a broader framework for evaluating the intellectual and practical contributions of the candidate's work.

In a study examining international examiners across six European countries, two African countries, two South American countries and the Commonwealth of Australia, Nir and Bogler (2021) identified that various structural factors, cultural dynamics and personal connections significantly constrain the capacity of international examiners to effect meaningful changes in students' research. The authors argue that these constraints can restrict academic value and fail to fully engage with the potential for critical scholarly development across the international community.

Ultimately, the assessment of a doctoral candidate's contribution to knowledge requires a careful balance between competing priorities. Examiners are tasked with determining whether the research demonstrates sufficient originality while addressing the growing demand for practical impact. Ensuring fairness and consistency in this process calls for clear evaluative criteria, transparency and an appreciation of the diverse ways in which knowledge can be advanced.

Conclusion

The increasing variety of doctoral assessment formats calls for a reassessment of the traditional viva voce and its place in contemporary academic systems (Taylor, 2023). Historically, the viva has been the primary method for evaluating doctoral candidates, serving as a key indicator of scholarly competence and intellectual achievement. However, the rise of alternative assessment methods – such as seminar-style defences, online vivas and PhDs by publication – has raised questions about the ongoing relevance and suitability of the viva as the dominant model. While these new approaches offer potential benefits in terms of inclusivity, accessibility and transparency, they also present concerns regarding their ability to maintain the rigorous intellectual standards that have historically defined doctoral education.

Nonetheless, the movement towards alternative assessment models reflects broader academic trends, particularly the growing emphasis on interdisciplinarity, collaboration and public engagement. For example, seminar-style defences can foster a more inclusive intellectual exchange, encouraging candidates to position their research within a broader academic framework and engage with diverse perspectives. Similarly, the PhD by publication model seeks to align doctoral assessment with established academic publishing practices, promoting transparency and practical relevance.

A central concern in this shift is the potential loss of the critical depth and rigour that the traditional viva provides. The closed-door nature of the viva offers an intimate setting where examiners can engage in focused, probing questioning, exploring the intellectual merits and complexities of a candidate's research in great detail. This process often uncovers aspects of the research that may not emerge in more open or public formats. In contrast, the broader participation involved in seminar-style defences can lead to more generalized discussions, which may dilute the intensity of the examination. Furthermore, moving away from the one-on-one structure of the traditional viva raises concerns about diminishing opportunities for candidates to engage with the complexities of their work in real time, potentially limiting the depth of intellectual exchange and critical reflection that is crucial for academic growth.

As Denicolo, Duke and Reeves (2020, p. 5) highlight, while increasing transparency in doctoral assessment is a positive development, it should not come at the cost of intellectual rigour. The emergence of alternative formats brings to the fore a fundamental tension between the aims of democratizing and modernizing doctoral assessment, on one hand, and preserving the intellectual depth and critical focus that have been central to the viva, on the other. If these alternative formats are not carefully structured, there is a risk that the focus could shift from meaningful intellectual evaluation to procedural inclusivity, potentially compromising the depth of scrutiny required for doctoral research.

Nevertheless, the diversification of doctoral examination formats presents an important opportunity for reflection and innovation within the academic community. These alternative models should not be dismissed; rather, they provide a valuable impetus for reconsidering how doctoral assessments can better reflect the evolving needs and practices of academia while preserving the core values of scholarly excellence. The primary challenge lies in ensuring that these alternative formats are built on strong evaluative criteria, upholding high standards of intellectual rigour, fairness and depth. Effective implementation will demand clear institutional guidelines, examiner training and careful oversight to ensure that any new formats maintain the standards necessary for a fair and rigorous assessment.

At its core, the doctoral examination process must continue to promote intellectual growth, critical reflection and meaningful scholarly dialogue. While the traditional viva voce remains valuable as an in-depth evaluation of a candidate's intellectual contributions, its adaptation in response to broader shifts in academic practice is equally important. Striking a balance between innovation and rigour will require continuous engagement with both the strengths and limitations of emerging assessment models, ensuring that doctoral examinations remain intellectually rigorous, relevant and aligned with the evolving demands of academic scholarship. By navigating these complexities thoughtfully, doctoral examinations can continue to provide a strong foundation for the development of independent, innovative scholars capable of making meaningful contributions to their fields.

References

Anderson, T., Saunders, G. & Alexander, I. (2021) 'Alternative dissertation formats in education-based doctorates', *Higher Education Research & Development*, 41(3), pp. 593–612.

Byram, M. & Stoicheva, M. (eds) (2022) *The experience of examining the PhD: An international comparative study of processes and standards of doctoral examination.* 1st ed. London: Routledge. https://doi.org/10.4324/9781003248569

Chetcuti, D., Cacciottolo, J. & Vella, N. (2022) 'What do examiners look for in a PhD thesis? Explicit and implicit criteria used by examiners across disciplines', *Assessment & Evaluation in Higher Education*, 47(8), pp. 1358–73.

Dally, K., Holbrook, A., Lovat, T. & Budd, J. (2019) 'Examiner feedback and Australian doctoral examination processes', *Australian Universities Review*, 61(2).

Dally, K., Holbrook, A., Lovat, T. & Fairbairn, H. (2020) 'Supervisor perspectives on the "end-stage" of the doctoral examination process', *Higher Education Research & Development*, 41(2), pp. 315–29.

Denicolo, P., Duke, D. & Reeves, J. (2020) *Delivering inspiring doctoral assessment.* London: Sage.

Frick, L. (2019) 'PhD by publication – panacea or paralysis?' *Africa Education Review*, 16(5), pp. 47–59.

Houston, G., Lovat, T., Lunt, I., Holbrook, A. & Dally, K. (2023) 'The viva in doctoral examination: A Habermasian dialogic occasion'. In: Rayson, D. (ed.) *Education, religion, and ethics – a scholarly collection*. Cham: Springer, pp. 21–32.

Kiley, M. (2009) '"You don't want a smart Alec": Selecting examiners to assess doctoral dissertations', *Studies in Higher Education*, 34(8), pp. 889–903. https://doi.org/10.1080/03075070802713112

Kumar, V. & Stracke, E. (2017) 'Reframing doctoral examination as teaching', *Innovations in Education and Teaching International*, 55(2), pp. 1–9.

Kumar, V., Kaur, A. & Sanderson, L.J. (2022) 'PhD orals from the convenors' perspective: Implications for academics and candidates', *International Journal for Academic Development*, 29(1), pp. 62–74.

Kumar, V., Sanderson, L.J. & Kaur, A. (2020) 'Investigating the role of convenors in the PhD viva', *Assessment & Evaluation in Higher Education*, 46(7), pp. 1080–91.

Kumar, V., Taylor, S. & Sharmini, S. (eds) (2023) *Doctoral examination: Exploring practice across the globe*. London: Routledge.

Lantsoght, E.O.L. (2022) 'Doctoral defence formats', *Studies in Higher Education*, 48(2), pp. 343–55.

Leavy, P. (2020) *Method meets art: Arts-based research practice*. 3rd ed. New York: The Guilford Press.

Lovat, T., Dally, K., Holbrook, A. & Fairbairn, H. (2022) 'Oral defence as a feedback mechanism in doctoral development and examination', *Australian Educational Researcher*, 49(4), pp. 845–60.

Mushibwe, C.P., Musonda, N. & Kazonga, E. (2021) 'Candidates' evaluation of the process of the PhD oral examination: Is it achieving its intended purpose?' *International Journal of Educational Research and Review*, 2(6), pp. 61–71.

Nir, A. & Bogler, R. (2021) 'International examiners' participation of the viva: A ritual or an actual indicator of research quality?' *Quality Assurance in Education*, 29(2/3), pp. 183–97.

O'Keeffe, P. (2022) 'The PhD by publication as preparation for work in the "performative university"'. In: Chong, S.W. & Johnson, N. (eds) *Landscapes and narratives of PhD by publication*. Cham: Springer, 199–213.

Schulze, S. & Lemmer, E.M. (2019) 'The administration of the doctoral examination at South African higher education institutions', *South African Journal of Higher Education*, 33(2), pp. 180–94.

Share, M. (2016) 'The PhD viva: A space for academic development', *International Journal for Academic Development*, 21(3), pp. 178–93. https://doi.org/10.1080/1360144X.2015.1095759

Stephenson, Z., Jackson, A., & Wilkes, V. (2024) 'Student experiences of the "closed-door" PhD and doctorate level viva voce: A systematic review of the literature', *Assessment & Evaluation in Higher Education*, 49(5), pp. 601–15. https://doi.org/10.1080/02602938.2023.2282941. This article was published online in 2023.

Tan, W.C. (2023) 'Doctoral examiners' narratives of learning to examine in the PhD viva: A call for support', *Higher Education*, 86, pp. 527–39.

Tan, W.C. (2024) 'Empowering examiners to develop doctoral assessment literacy: A situated learning perspective', *Frontiers in Education*. Available at: https://www.frontiersin.org/journals/education/articles/10.3389/feduc.2024.1345661/full

Taylor, S. (2023) 'The changing landscape of doctoral education: A framework for analysis and introduction to the special issue', *Innovations in Education and Teaching International*, 60(5), pp. 606–22.

Teijlingen, E. van, Simkhada, B., Regmi, P., Simkhada, P., Hundley, V. & Poudel, K.C. (2022) 'Reflections on variations in PhD viva regulations: "And the options are …"', *Journal of Education and Research*, 12(2), pp. 61–74.

Tzavara, D. & O'Donnell, V. (2021) External Examining the Professional Doctorate as Distinct from the Traditional PhD: Differentiating and Developing Policy and Practice. 10.1108/S2055-364120210000038007

Wellington, J. (2021) *Examining doctoral work: Exploring principles, criteria and processes*. London: Routledge.

Wisker, G., et al. (2022) 'Across time and space: Examiner and candidate experiences of online doctoral vivas', *Innovations in Education and Teaching International*, 59(2), pp. 131–41.

Conclusion: The Importance of Reflection and Self-evaluation in Doctoral Supervision

Reflective practice is important to effective doctoral supervision, offering a meaningful mechanism for supervisors to critically examine and refine their methods. It enables supervisors to develop deeper self-awareness and responsiveness, fostering more meaningful and supportive relationships with doctoral candidates. Through ongoing reflection, supervisors can adapt to the demands of academic research and teaching, enhancing the overall quality of the doctoral journey.

Yet, for reflection to be genuinely transformative, it must be purposeful and critically engaged. Superficial or routine reflection, especially when disconnected from concrete action, can lead to stagnation. Rather than challenging assumptions or improving practice, such reflection may inadvertently reinforce entrenched habits and perspectives. This highlights the need for critical intent; supervisors must reflect not only on their practices but also on the underlying assumptions and broader contexts influencing those practices.

Beyond this, reflective practice should not be viewed solely as an individual responsibility. Overemphasizing personal introspection risks neglecting the structural and institutional dimensions that shape supervision, such as departmental culture, workload and policy frameworks. These factors significantly impact a supervisor's capacity to provide effective guidance and support.

For reflective practice to yield meaningful change, it must be embedded within a culture of dialogue, collegial feedback and institutional support. Supervisors benefit from opportunities to share experiences, engage in peer learning and receive constructive feedback. When reflection is linked with action and supported by institutional mechanisms, it contributes to the development of evidence-informed, responsive supervisory practices. In this way, reflective practice becomes a collective, dynamic process, one that supports the continuous improvement of doctoral education and aligns with the complex realities of contemporary academia.

The reflective supervisor: A conceptual framing

At the core of reflective practice lies the recognition that effective doctoral supervision does not exist in a vacuum. Rather, it must be situated within broader intellectual, ethical, institutional and pedagogical frameworks. The reflective supervisor is one who actively interrogates the meanings, assumptions and consequences of their everyday supervisory interactions, while also situating their role within the wider academic and socio-cultural context. Reflection, in this framing, is not a discrete or episodic act but a continuous, iterative process of self-examination, adaptation and growth.

Importantly, reflective practice should not be misconstrued as a passive or purely retrospective activity. It is instead a dynamic and anticipatory mode of engagement that equips supervisors to navigate complexity, anticipate challenges, explore alternative approaches and evolve in their roles as mentors, educators and academic leaders. Crucially, this reflective engagement must be outward-facing as well as introspective, recognizing that supervision is shaped by, and in turn shapes, the institutional structures, disciplinary norms and social forces that govern academic life. In this sense, reflective practice becomes a vehicle for transformative change, allowing supervisors not only to refine their own practices but also to contribute to more inclusive, equitable and ethically grounded supervisory cultures.

The theoretical grounding of this approach can be traced to foundational thinkers in education and critical pedagogy. Donald Schön's notion of 'reflective practice' foregrounds the importance of making tacit knowledge explicit, arguing that professionals develop deeper expertise through cycles of reflection-in-action and reflection-on-action. In the context of doctoral supervision, this means critically examining the subtle, often implicit dimensions of mentoring, communication and academic modelling that shape the candidate's experience. Schön's framework supports a vision of the supervisor as a practitioner-scholar who learns through doing, while also subjecting their practice to ongoing critical scrutiny.

Complementing Schön's work, Paulo Freire's emancipatory pedagogy introduces a more explicitly political and ethical dimension to reflection. Freire emphasizes dialogue, critical consciousness and the dismantling of hierarchical relationships in educational contexts. Applied to supervision, this perspective encourages supervisors to engage in dialogic, reciprocal relationships with candidates that challenge traditional power asymmetries and affirm the agency, voice and intellectual autonomy of the doctoral researcher. From this vantage point, reflection becomes not only a tool for personal and professional development, but also a means of enacting supervisory practices that are critically engaged, socially just and transformative.

Additionally, reflective supervision necessitates an acute awareness of positionality – the ways in which supervisors' own identities, backgrounds and professional trajectories inform their approach to mentoring. Supervisors bring to the supervisory space their own social locations, including dimensions such as race, gender, class, nationality and academic culture. These factors inevitably shape perceptions of authority, communication styles and implicit expectations, and can influence how feedback is given and received, how support is offered and how challenges are interpreted. By engaging in sustained reflection on their own positionality, supervisors become more attuned to the diverse realities of their candidates and more capable of cultivating supervisory relationships that are empathetic, inclusive and attuned to the power differentials inherent in academic life.

Self-evaluation as a companion practice

While reflective practice offers essential philosophical and emotional grounding for effective doctoral supervision, self-evaluation functions as its critical, structured counterpart, allowing supervisors to systematically assess and interrogate the efficacy of their practices.

Self-evaluation, by its very nature, provides a more explicit, objective process for supervisors to identify gaps between their intentions and their practices, ultimately facilitating more informed, intentional improvements.

However, it is important to recognize that self-evaluation, like any evaluative tool, is not without limitations. The evaluative process can be hindered by personal biases, unexamined assumptions and institutional constraints that may limit the scope of one's self-assessment. As such, self-evaluation must be understood as a process that is continually subject to scrutiny and revision, requiring a level of reflexivity on the part of the supervisor that goes beyond surface-level assessments.

The methods through which self-evaluation is conducted also carry inherent challenges. Common tools for self-assessment, such as reflective journals, peer feedback, candidate evaluations and institutional performance reviews, are valuable in their own right, yet they are not infallible. Reflective journals, for instance, allow supervisors to capture their thoughts on specific challenges and experiences; however, the subjective nature of journal entries means that they may not always provide an accurate or comprehensive picture of the supervisor's practices. Reflective journals may, for example, reflect a selective memory or a tendency to focus on particular incidents rather than a more holistic evaluation of supervisory interactions. As such, while reflective journals can be helpful in tracing personal development over time, they must be balanced with more structured forms of feedback and critical engagement with external perspectives.

Peer feedback, often regarded as a crucial component of self-evaluation, offers its own set of challenges. While peer reviews provide opportunities for collaborative reflection and the exchange of best practices, they can also become sites of conformity, where supervisors may hesitate to provide candid feedback for fear of damaging professional relationships or challenging established norms. Peer feedback can also reinforce existing power dynamics within academic departments, which may discourage honest critiques, especially when senior supervisors are involved. Indeed, peer reviews are not immune to the same biases that affect individual reflection. The capacity for peer feedback to contribute meaningfully to the self-evaluative process thus hinges on the willingness of academic communities to foster open, critical dialogues that are not only collegial but also truly reflective of diverse supervisory experiences.

Similarly, candidate evaluations offer important insights into the effectiveness of a supervisor's practice but are not without their limitations. Doctoral candidates, particularly those at earlier stages of their studies, may not possess the maturity or critical perspective needed to offer a fully informed evaluation of their supervisor's role. Their evaluations may be influenced by factors such as personal rapport or fear of repercussions, especially when there is an inherent power imbalance between the supervisor and the candidate.

Institutional performance reviews provide an external evaluative framework but are often subject to the limitations of administrative metrics and the standardization of assessment criteria. These reviews, while valuable for ensuring alignment with institutional goals, may lack the nuance necessary for fully capturing the complexities of doctoral supervision. Furthermore, institutional assessments are sometimes conducted with a top-down approach that neglects the intricacies of supervisor-candidate relationships, thereby offering a limited perspective on the quality of supervision.

Self-evaluation also critically engages with the alignment between supervisors' professed values and their actual practices. Supervisors must interrogate whether they are genuinely embodying the ethical and pedagogical principles they advocate for, particularly when it comes to values such as open communication, inclusivity and academic integrity. A supervisor who claims to prioritize inclusivity, for example, must critically assess whether their actions reflect a genuine commitment to fostering a diverse, supportive environment for all candidates, or whether their practices inadvertently perpetuate exclusionary structures.

Additionally, self-evaluation functions as a mechanism for accountability. By regularly engaging in self-assessment, supervisors are more likely to take responsibility for their professional development, remaining proactive rather than reactive in addressing challenges that arise in the supervisory relationship. In contrast to more ad hoc or reactive forms of feedback, self-evaluation should encourage supervisors to adopt a more intentional approach to their practice. This structured, ongoing process leads to more thoughtful and strategic improvements in supervision, as supervisors become more aware of the impact of their actions on candidates' academic, intellectual and emotional development.

Reflection and power dynamics in supervision

Doctoral supervision is fundamentally a relational process shaped by complex power dynamics between the supervisor and the candidate. Supervisors hold significant authority over a candidate's academic development, including decisions about research direction, evaluation of progress and access to professional opportunities. Given this inherent imbalance, it becomes essential for supervisors to engage in critical self-reflection on how power is enacted and experienced within the supervisory relationship. Such self-reflection requires an awareness of one's own positionality, how factors such as gender, race, socioeconomic status and professional identity influence interactions with candidates and impact the supervisory process as a whole.

Power in doctoral supervision manifests in both explicit and subtle ways, affecting the candidate's academic trajectory. For instance, supervisors may inadvertently shape a candidate's research focus through the nature of their feedback or guidance, encouraging certain topics or methodologies while limiting others. When supervisors dominate conversations, neglect active listening or prioritize their own academic agendas over the candidate's interests, the balance of power becomes skewed. This risks reducing the supervisory relationship to a one-sided dynamic, undermining the candidate's autonomy and intellectual agency. Critical self-reflection helps supervisors recognize these imbalances and adjust their approach to foster relationships based on mutual respect, collaboration and shared decision-making.

Beyond the immediate supervisor-candidate relationship, self-reflection must also consider the broader academic power structures that influence both parties. Institutional hierarchies, gatekeeping mechanisms and pressures linked to publication, funding and career progression create additional challenges for doctoral candidates. Supervisors who engage in critical self-reflection acknowledge these structural dynamics and the ways in which they impact candidates' experiences. For example, the demand to publish in high-impact journals or secure research funding can impose significant stress on candidates, potentially distorting their research priorities or impeding progress. By maintaining a critical self-reflective stance, supervisors can navigate these pressures more effectively, cultivating an environment where candidates feel supported rather than constrained by institutional demands.

It is important to emphasize that reflecting on power dynamics does not imply that supervisors should relinquish their responsibilities or reject necessary hierarchies. Instead, it calls for transparent and ethical navigation of those hierarchies, clarifying expectations, negotiating roles and empowering candidates to have meaningful input in decisions about their work. Critical self-reflection also invites openness to feedback regarding the supervisory process itself, promoting honest dialogue about how the relationship functions and fostering adaptability in supervisory practices.

Power is an integral, though complex, element of doctoral supervision. When supervisors critically engage with their own authority and remain receptive to feedback, they contribute to a supervisory culture characterized by respect, intellectual partnership and shared accountability. Such critical self-reflection not only strengthens individual supervisory relationships but also supports the development of a more inclusive and ethical academic environment. Through ongoing critical self-reflection on power, both interpersonal and institutional, supervisors can ensure that the doctoral journey is empowering, autonomous and conducive to scholarly growth.

Reflective tools and frameworks in doctoral education: Integrating pedagogical principles with criticality

Doctoral education demands that supervisors possess not only subject expertise but also a deep understanding of the pedagogical, ethical and relational aspects of supervision. Reflection within this context must go beyond informal or routine thinking; it requires a deliberate, structured and engaged process with supervisory practices. Such reflection is vital for supervisors aiming to enhance their effectiveness, support doctoral candidates' growth and challenge the underlying assumptions and power relations present in doctoral education.

Various reflective tools and frameworks have been developed to support supervisors in this work. These include case studies, vignettes, research briefings and structured activities designed to encourage self-evaluation and analysis. The value of these tools depends on how well they are linked with core pedagogical principles that underpin doctoral education. These principles prompt supervisors to question not just the methods of supervision but also the reasons behind their choices and the broader academic context in which they operate.

This book explores ten fundamental pedagogical principles and illustrates how integrating reflective tools with these principles encourages supervisors to engage in deep reflection and transform their supervisory practice.

Principle 1: Preparing students for academic and professional life beyond discipline

Doctoral education should prepare candidates for a variety of professional roles, not only academic careers. Through the use of case studies presenting real-world challenges, supervisors are invited to reflect on whether their supervisory approaches support candidates' readiness for diverse career paths.

Such engagement requires supervisors to consider if they are addressing systemic, cultural and political factors influencing professional life beyond academia. This reflection challenges supervisors to ensure that their practices are relevant and inclusive, supporting candidates to navigate complex career landscapes rather than simply preparing them for scholarly positions.

Principle 2: Reflecting on the production and legitimization of knowledge

While doctoral supervision involves specialized knowledge, supervisors must also examine how this knowledge is created, validated and shared. Research briefings and engagement with scholarly debates serve as tools to connect supervisors with ongoing discussions about the power relations embedded in knowledge production.

Reflection here means assessing whether traditional supervisory models reinforce academic hierarchies that limit doctoral candidates' intellectual freedom. Supervisors are encouraged to consider whether their practices promote genuine intellectual growth or simply maintain existing power structures. This awareness supports adopting supervision methods that empower candidates as active contributors to knowledge.

Principle 3: Valuing students' prior experiences with awareness

Candidates arrive with varied academic and professional backgrounds that can greatly enrich their research and learning processes. Peer dialogue and reflective activities help supervisors engage with these experiences more fully.

At the same time, supervisors must assess how their own assumptions influence their recognition of what constitutes valuable experience. They should consider whether they are truly listening to their students or imposing narrow, possibly biased, criteria. Reflecting on structural barriers that affect candidates' ability to express their experiences promotes a more equitable and inclusive supervisory relationship.

Principle 4: Scaffolding learning while navigating power relations

Providing scaffolding is essential for supporting doctoral candidates as they develop independence. Vignettes and scenario-based reflections enable supervisors to examine how their support functions in practice.

Supervisors must reflect on whether their scaffolding encourages autonomy or unintentionally fosters dependence and reinforces hierarchical dynamics. They need to consider how their guidance can strike a balance between support and empowerment, ensuring candidates gain confidence and intellectual agency.

Principle 5: Ensuring assessment aligns fairly with learning objectives

Assessment plays a key role in doctoral education, but it must be examined for its fairness, transparency and inclusivity. Case studies and reflective briefings assist supervisors in evaluating whether their assessment strategies truly capture candidates' abilities and developmental progress.

Supervisors should question whether traditional assessments, such as written theses or journal publications, favour certain types of knowledge or communication, which may disadvantage candidates from diverse backgrounds. Reflecting on alternative assessment approaches can help create a more equitable evaluation system that recognizes varied strengths.

Principle 6: Promoting active learner engagement amidst power imbalances

Active engagement is critical in doctoral education, yet supervisors must consider the power relations that influence how candidates participate in their learning. Tools like self-assessment exercises and peer feedback encourage supervisors to evaluate how effectively they are fostering student ownership of the research process.

Reflection here involves questioning whether supervisory practices promote genuine student agency or inadvertently sustain passive roles for candidates. Supervisors should aim to create an environment where doctoral students actively shape their research directions rather than simply following supervisors' agendas.

Principle 7: Balancing individual and social learning processes

Doctoral education requires both individual focus and collaborative learning opportunities. Case studies and peer discussions can highlight how supervisors balance these aspects in their practice.

Supervisors need to reflect on whether the structure of doctoral education promotes individualism at the expense of collective academic and social learning. They should consider if their practices encourage collaboration, peer support and knowledge sharing, or if institutional cultures and supervisory styles inadvertently foster competition and isolation.

Principle 8: Acknowledging and integrating informal learning

Informal learning – such as networking, mentorship and social interactions – is a vital part of doctoral education. Supervisors must assess how these opportunities are made accessible to all candidates.

Reflection should focus on whether informal learning environments favour those already connected to academic communities or with particular social capital. By examining these dynamics, supervisors can identify ways to structure informal learning opportunities that are inclusive and beneficial for all students.

Principle 9: Supporting supervisors' own learning and development

Effective doctoral education depends not only on candidates' learning but also on supervisors' ongoing professional development. Supervisors must reflect on whether their institutions provide adequate support for their growth.

This principle invites supervisors to consider institutional policies, resources and training opportunities. Reflecting on these factors helps supervisors identify gaps and advocate for improvements that enhance their ability to support doctoral candidates effectively.

Principle 10: Aligning institutional policies with reflective and supportive supervision

Institutional policy frameworks should prioritize doctoral candidates' learning and encourage reflective supervisory practices. Supervisors are encouraged to evaluate whether their institutions foster an environment that supports continuous professional development and meaningful reflection.

They must reflect on how policies facilitate or constrain their ability to engage in self-reflection and provide quality supervision. This reflection enables supervisors to navigate institutional structures more effectively and promote systemic improvements.

Conclusion

This book highlights the significance of reflective engagement within doctoral education as a means for supervisors to examine and enhance their approach to the demands of doctoral supervision. Such engagement extends well beyond mere self-examination of immediate supervisory techniques; it involves a comprehensive and analytical interrogation of the assumptions, power relations and institutional frameworks that collectively shape the doctoral journey. By framing reflective engagement in this expansive context, supervisors are encouraged to scrutinize not only their individual roles but also the broader structural and cultural forces that influence doctoral education in its entirety.

Engaging in this form of reflection compels supervisors to evaluate how their pedagogical strategies correspond with, or diverge from, the demands of contemporary doctoral training. This process fosters an appreciation of supervision as a dynamic and relational endeavour situated within wider academic and social milieus. It invites supervisors to go beyond routine or procedural reflections and to confront fundamental ethical considerations, questions of inclusivity and the complex distribution of power within supervisory relationships. In doing so, reflective engagement acts as a catalyst for the development of more equitable and student-centred supervisory practices, practices that genuinely recognize and respond to the diverse pathways and needs of doctoral candidates.

In addition, reflective engagement necessitates active attention to the institutional policies, cultures and hierarchies that shape supervisory practices. Supervisors are thus prompted to examine how organizational structures, allocation of resources and prevailing academic conventions influence the conditions of doctoral study and mentorship. This wider perspective equips supervisors to identify institutional barriers that may impede effective supervision and encourages advocacy for systemic reforms that promote supportive, transparent and inclusive doctoral environments. Through this lens, supervisors are positioned not only as educators but also as transformative agents within their academic communities.

At the heart of this process lies the acknowledgement that doctoral supervision is inherently shaped by asymmetrical power relations. Reflective engagement enhances awareness of how such dynamics emerge and are negotiated within supervisory interactions. By contemplating their own positionality alongside the relational complexities at play, supervisors can foster more collaborative, dialogic relationships with their candidates. This movement from hierarchical to participatory supervision models empowers doctoral students as active agents in both their intellectual development and professional trajectories.

Additionally, ongoing reflective engagement encourages supervisors to continuously assess the coherence between their supervisory goals, assessment methods and the diverse developmental needs of their candidates. This sustained appraisal supports the adoption of adaptable and inclusive assessment practices that recognize a broad spectrum of scholarly contributions and modes of knowledge production. Supervisors attuned to this reflective process are better positioned to cultivate environments where candidates flourish intellectually while retaining a strong sense of agency and authenticity.

Ultimately, reflective engagement within doctoral education is essential for fostering supervisory practices that are effective, ethical and responsive to the continuing transformations within higher education. It signifies a commitment to continuous professional growth and self-awareness that benefits both supervisors and doctoral candidates. By embedding reflective engagement at the heart of doctoral supervision, this book aspires to contribute to the advancement of supervisory roles that not only facilitate academic success but also uphold the values of integrity, inclusivity and social responsibility fundamental to the doctoral community.

References

Freire, P. (1970) *Pedagogy of the oppressed.* New York: Herder and Herder.

Schön, D.A. (1983) *The reflective practitioner: How professionals think in action.* New York: Basic Books.

Index